MW00424732

Synthese Library

Studies in Epistemology, Logic, Methodology, and Philosophy of Science

Volume 425

The aim of *Synthese Library* is to provide a forum for the best current work in the methodology and philosophy of science and in epistemology. A wide variety of different approaches have traditionally been represented in the Library, and every effort is made to maintain this variety, not for its own sake, but because we believe that there are many fruitful and illuminating approaches to the philosophy of science and related disciplines.

Special attention is paid to methodological studies which illustrate the interplay of empirical and philosophical viewpoints and to contributions to the formal (logical, set-theoretical, mathematical, information-theoretical, decision-theoretical, etc.) methodology of empirical sciences. Likewise, the applications of logical methods to epistemology as well as philosophically and methodologically relevant studies in logic are strongly encouraged. The emphasis on logic will be tempered by interest in the psychological, historical, and sociological aspects of science.

Besides monographs *Synthese Library* publishes thematically unified anthologies and edited volumes with a well-defined topical focus inside the aim and scope of the book series. The contributions in the volumes are expected to be focused and structurally organized in accordance with the central theme(s), and should be tied together by an extensive editorial introduction or set of introductions if the volume is divided into parts. An extensive bibliography and index are mandatory.

More information about this series at http://www.springer.com/series/6607

Alyssa Luboff

Facing Relativism

 Springer

Alyssa Luboff
Portland, Oregon, USA

Synthese Library
ISBN 978-3-030-43339-0   ISBN 978-3-030-43341-3   (eBook)
https://doi.org/10.1007/978-3-030-43341-3

This Springer imprint is published by the registered company Springer Nature Switzerland AG.
The registered company address is: Gewerbestrasse 11, 6330 Cham, Switzerland

For my three children, who braved 6 years of graduate school with me.

Preface

How can we teach open-mindedness? This is the golden question of an age where liberal education and values are under attack. How can we teach students as well as general citizens to value points of view other than their own? How can all of us learn to embrace diversity without feeling our own identity threatened? How can we acknowledge a plurality of conflicting viewpoints, and their legitimacy, without undermining the primacy of our own? And how can we do so without getting lost in a sea of meaninglessness? How can we stand for what we believe in and against what offends our deepest moral sense?

My hope is that this book will help to answer such questions. Relativism is the extreme conclusion of a liberal outlook, which not only recognizes diversity but finds value and legitimacy in the array of human experience and expression. In explaining what makes relativism a reasonable and attractive view, I hope also to shed light on the factors that make us open-minded, liberal thinkers. Relativism depends on a certain kind of analogical exercise; we must be able to see how others are different than and like us at the same time. Most importantly, relativism depends on the empathetic experience of difference. Instead of simply projecting our understanding onto others, we must learn to put ourselves in their viewpoint and then to turn and take a look back at ourselves from this new angle.

This book, while respecting the rigorous standards of argument set forth by analytic philosophy, is a work of a different sort. It is a work of experiential philosophy, taking our lived, first-person experience as an inextricable component of what we believe and why we believe it. It is also a work of contemplative philosophy, asking us to suspend judgment and to work through deep discomfort in order to gain better understanding of ourselves and of the world around us. I know very few philosophers who consider fieldwork to be an essential part of their research. However, for those of us who believe that the subject of our reflections should be our actions and that the purpose of our reflections should be to act well, there can be nothing more natural or coherent. And so, at some point in our careers – or perhaps at every step along the way – we are forced to explain why the most coherent path forces us to incorporate the intricacies and nuances of messy, everyday experience. And yet, we can do this with as much clarity and precision as our developing skills allow.

The experience of deep engagement with another way of life brings to light what no amount of abstract reasoning alone could ascertain. It not only teaches us that alternate points of view exist but reveals the grounds of their legitimacy. Through the lived negotiation of values and beliefs, we learn to recognize both the value of other viewpoints and a space for criticism. This opens up a complex landscape, where our values and beliefs coexist in a sea of alternatives, without straightforward universality or absolute justification. Through the conflicts that inevitably ensue, we learn to negotiate difference using our own capacity for reasoning and our deepest inner sense, despite their lack of total authority. We learn when and how much to stand steady in our values and beliefs, as well as when and how much to allow them to change. In other words, we move from the childish world of absolute right and wrong to the maturity of complex relationships.

It has now been nearly a quarter of a century since I first traveled to Ecuador. Much of the pristine rainforest I saw – once in grave danger – is now gone. Most of the native youth have moved to the city, where they speak Spanish and text on cellphones. In my last years of finishing this project, I saw my own country hurl itself far down the path of becoming a Trumpian dystopia. I would celebrate the timeliness of this book, if only I did not regret so deeply my own inability to change the course of events. When I began my research, I wanted to understand how Western materialism influenced the philosophy that I studied and practiced. If we take the fundamental questions of philosophy to be variants of the questions "Who am I?" and "How should I live?", how are these questions themselves shaped by the context of our own culture and times? How is the very asking of these questions – let alone their answers – shaped by our way of life?

Admittedly, these questions interested me for more than academic reasons. Reaching adulthood in the 1990s, I felt the effects of late capitalism and Western materialism very keenly. The way of life in which I grew up seemed empty. I didn't have the experience or conceptual resources to articulate what was missing, but I needed to figure it out. After 2 years teaching at a university in the Andes and a year of graduate school at the University of Chicago, I set out for the remotest region of the remotest place I knew how to reach. In fact, it had taken me a year just to figure out how to get there. According to my guidebooks, the only way to visit the Ecuadorian Chocó was through an international conservation and sustainable development project called Proyecto SUBIR. One day at the bus station in Riobamba, I met the friend of a friend who happened to be part of the project. I sent his boss my CV with a letter explaining to her that I was willing to do any work in the region without pay, although I could not afford to lose any money. She sent me with a $12/ month stipend to teach English for ecotourism in the Afro-Ecuadorian and native Chachi communities at the confluence of the rivers San Miguel and Cayapas. It felt very selfish to show up in the rainforest and say, "Teach me what it is like to be you," so I swore that, in exchange for whatever the people shared with me, I would share with them anything I had or knew that could be of use.

At the time, I had no idea how great the burden of my side of that bargain would turn out to be. Although the Chocó was the most different and distant region that I knew to reach, it was also a hotspot for globalization. I found myself watching the forest and all the abundant ways of life it once sustained disappear before my eyes. In many ways, it was like reading a playbook backwards; I could not save the people from suffering the same fate as so many native peoples before them. In other ways, it was like reading too far into the future; I could not fully convince the people of the value of what they were losing before it was gone. I ended up marrying a native of the Chachi tribe, with whom I have three children. Together, our families created a local nonprofit organization dedicated to community-generated solutions for conservation and sustainable development. The work always felt like throwing a bucket of water on a tall building consumed by fire. I could not expect our efforts to make a big difference, yet I could not help but try.

After 10 years of moving back and forth between Ecuador and the United States, I returned to graduate school in philosophy at the University of Chicago. On the one hand, the spread of the Colombian guerrilla from the north and the influx of Mestizo opportunists from neighboring Ecuadorian provinces made the region too dangerous for us to continue living or working there. I had truly shared everything I could with the people, and there was nothing left that I could do. On the other hand, I realized that I did finally have an answer to my quest. "Who am I?" and "How should I live?" – I could detect the influence of Western materialism not only in the answers but in the questions themselves. I could recognize not only the values and beliefs of other ways of life but the ground on which they stood. I could see another way of life before judging it, and I could look back at my own through different eyes. I could understand how, despite the colonial and material power that a country like the United States holds over others, to respect another way of life without pulling it into our own totalizing narrative of progress. I could recognize different solutions to the human experiment through different strategies – all necessarily with their point of view, yet none with a privileged point of view, despite the fact that each of us must call one our own. I could also begin to sense how we might become creative about shaping our own way of life and the choices that we make to define it.

I believe this last point is perhaps the greatest good that comes from the journey of facing relativism. At the beginning of our journey, we may fear, or perhaps even romanticize, difference. By the end, we earn the ability to see another way of life as much as possible on its own terms and to look critically back at our own. Our open-mindedness and the level playing field that it creates help us not only to see others but to see ourselves. They teach us respect not only for other ways of life but for our own. The alternative ways of life that come to light open up a free space for self-creation and new direction. Once we see that there are multiple solutions to the human puzzle, we realize that we have a choice – and a responsibility – for how we live. The fundamental questions begin no longer with "Who am I?" but with "Who do we want to be?" and "What should we make of our world?"

Portland, OR, USA   Alyssa Luboff

Acknowledgments

I thank, first of all, the people of Ecuador who helped me to understand the material in this book, especially my family, friends, co-workers, and other acquaintances in Loma Linda and San Miguel, as well as in all of the other communities who collaborated with Fundación Kumanii, and in Riobamba. I am forever grateful to my three children, A. Dyusapachi, C. Mishimbu, and M. Naraa, for teaching me through their own experiences and insights about interculturality and systemic injustice. I acknowledge the joy and wonder we experienced in Ecuador, as well as the violence and heartbreak. As proud as I am of this work, I wish I could take back the empty promise of graduate school and the academic job market – the constant stress, the lack of support, and the poverty that filled too much of their childhood. I thank their father, Rainel Chapiro, for signing up for this journey with me, for better and for worse. For every measure that we have all learned and grown together, may we find strength and blessing not only for ourselves but for our communities.

I thank my mentors and advisors in graduate school, including Michael Forster, Candace Vogler, Anubav Vasudevan, Martha Nussbaum, Michael Kremer, and Arnold Davidson. I am especially grateful to Richard Shweder for his willingness as an anthropologist to embrace my project and for always making time in his busy schedule to advise me. I am grateful to my parents, Barbara and Gary Luboff, for trying their very best to support my unique path, and to my friends, family, and other advisors for their warm encouragement, including Jeanette Miura, Beth Seacord, Ed Shorey, Miriam Eskenasy, Valerie Wallace, Brad Bassler, Laurie DeDecker, Yonah and Russell Klem, Sonia Dumont, Mark Mayerson, Bonnie Schulkin, Paula Ammerman, Kerry Prior, and Melodee Smith. I am grateful to Scott Bear Don't Walk, Bob Storrer, Donnie Dowd, and my classmates at Healing in America for encouraging me to connect my work with the experiences and insights of the native people of my own country. I thank Otávio Bueno, Editor of the Synthese Library book series, for his warm support of my work over the years. And last, but not at all least, I thank Rick Furtak for the decades of philosophical friendship, for curating my journals while I was off in the rainforest, and for always believing in the value of my work.

Contents

About the Author

Alyssa Luboff is an independent philosopher living in Portland, Oregon. She earned her B.A. in philosophy with honors from Yale University, and her Ph.D. in philosophy from the University of Chicago. She has taught at Grand Valley State University (Michigan), Portland State University (Oregon), and ESPOCH University (Riobamba, Ecuador). Her research brings together philosophical and anthropological reflection, drawing especially on her experiences living and working in the Ecuadorian Chocó rainforest. She believes that cross-cultural investigation is not only imperative in our rapidly shifting times, but that it may hold the key to solving our most pressing global problems.

Chapter 1
Deep Engagement

1.1 Introduction

1.1.1 Relativism and Cultural Diversity at First Glance

There are so many questions surrounding what we mean by relativism, and whether it can be a view which holds together, that it is hard to know what might be more misleading at the beginning of this work – to attempt to define relativism, or to refrain from so doing. I will say, as a matter of orientation, that I take relativism to make more or less the following claim: that there are multiple, perhaps infinite, ways of articulating, ordering, manipulating, and valuing the world; and that outside such a given system, outside, that is, a particular way of life, there are no standards for evaluating or weighing these articulations, orderings, manipulations, and valuations against each other. We may also think of relativism as in certain respects defining itself in opposition to absolutism. For the relativist, between two different ways of life there can be no impartial or highest arbiter of what is right, what is true, what is good, what is real, and so on.

My goal in this book is to develop a clear and full picture of relativism, and to show in the process that relativism is an appealing, coherent, and fruitful view for our times. The idea, and even the label, "relativism," is much abused by its numerous opponents, as well as, in a different way, by its more lackadaisical proponents. For this reason, I will spend a great deal of time in subsequent chapters exploring relativism and showing how it survives some very common objections. But for those who may already be won over, or just plain worn out, by these objections, I would like to begin by addressing a question that is even more basic than the project of defining and defending a particular version of relativism: What motivates relativism? Why should we even consider the view in the first place?[1]

---

[1] "And what *kind* of relativism do you mean?" I can already hear my most eager readers asking. After all, we can put any number of modifiers before the word "relativism": "moral," "cognitive,"

© Springer Nature Switzerland AG 2020
A. Luboff, *Facing Relativism*, Synthese Library 425,
https://doi.org/10.1007/978-3-030-43341-3_1

1

Since relativism makes such an important claim about different ways of life, it seems that a natural place to begin to look for an answer would be our own data on human cultures. In the historical and anthropological record, from the accounts of Herodotus to those of conquistadors, explorers, field anthropologists, and contemporary writers of culture, we find abundant examples of human practices and beliefs that appear strikingly different from our own. At a certain level, such data seems to support relativism. After all, how could there be only one set of right standards if different cultures at different points in space and time have solved the puzzle of life in such different ways? How could there be a final or highest arbiter of what is right, what is true, what is good, what is real, etc., if we seem to find among different peoples such a wide range of norms and conclusions both about how the world is and how it should be? Yet, it turns out that no description of foreign cultures, not even of the most peculiar and striking details – Inuit parricide, Kwakiutl cannibalism, Zande witchcraft substance – necessitates relativism. As we will see more clearly in the discussion below, even the wildest practices and beliefs are compatible, at least at a descriptive level, with absolutism. In order to account for them, all that we have to explain is how it can be that we ourselves are more or less right about the world, while other cultures, in as much as they differ from us, are wrong. It is, after all, one thing to suspect another culture of employing very different standards from our own, and yet an entirely separate matter to go so far as to grant those standards an authority and legitimacy equal to our own. So, we can easily account for variations in people's ideas of what is right and true over space and time without going so far as to make things like rightness and truth themselves vary over space and time. Why, then, resort to a view as extreme as relativism?

If the difficulty raised by the historical and anthropological record is merely how to account for the descriptions of diverse ways of life, then it gives us no reason to prefer relativism to absolutism. And if the former cannot garner any clear support from the social sciences, then we might even think that it should be given up altogether. After all, relativism is known as both a radical and difficult to formulate view, so if we do not need it to solve any special problem, then why do we need it at all?[2] On the other hand, if the difficulty raised by the historical and anthropological record is how to account for some other aspect of cultural diversity, beyond the raw data, the mere fact of it, which does not fit neatly into absolutism, or which pushes us towards relativism, then we may decide that relativism is well motivated

---

"linguistic," "cultural," etc. My brief description of relativism in the opening paragraph takes our blatantly normative claims ("is good," "is right"), as well as our descriptive (yet, I will argue, subtly and importantly normative) claims ("is true," "is real") to be relative to a way of life. This is a very broad definition that nearly encompasses all of the narrower branches of relativism. If we were forced to choose one of the pre-existing labels, "cultural relativism" would probably fit best. However, there are important differences between a culture and a way of life. There are also certain controversies surrounding the concept of "culture" which need not get in our way here. Let us say cautiously, then, that a culture is an important example of a way of life, and that cultural relativism is an important case of the kind of relativism that I have in mind.

[2] This is, in fact, a common anti-relativist argument. See, for example, John W. Cook, *Morality and Cultural Differences* (New York: Oxford University Press, 1999), 204.

after all. But before we can consider whether there is such an aspect and what it might be like, we will need to have a better, though still rather general, idea of how the non-relativist or absolutist[3] accommodates cultural diversity.

1.1.2   Cultural Diversity Without Relativism

Perhaps the simplest way to respond to cultural diversity without resorting to relativism is just to assert the absolute nature of our own standards: what is right for us is Right, what is true for us is True, what is good for us is Good, what is real for us is Real, and all other ways of life are mistaken. This attitude is quite common among conquistadors and missionaries, the originals of the past as much as the new variants we find today. The way it deals with the examples briefly mentioned above is rather straightforward. Even if we ourselves are not prepared to journey off to foreign lands, there is something about this crude absolutism which almost instinctively wells up inside us at first contact with examples of cultural difference. We believe that when the Inuit kill the elderly by sealing them in small houses of ice, they offend a responsibility for compassion and care which binds all human beings in all places and times. They should learn, we insist, not to kill, but to care for their seniors more like we do. In a similar way, we find Kwakiutl cannibalism morally abhorrent. They should not, we reclaim, have a society whose members ceremoniously eat foreign captives and slaves. We believe our own ways of handling human themes such as identity, otherness, power, and taboo to be absolutely more effective and humane. And for us, Zande witchcraft substance is not real. If only the Azande had Western Science, we are certain, they would understand how the world really works and see that their propositions concerning the actions of witchcraft are in all respects false.

While there is something undeniably intuitive about this direct and ethnocentric form of absolutism, there is also something very limiting. Cultural diversity, far from establishing relativism, becomes little more than a record of deviant trivia, of how strangely wrong other peoples can be about the nature of the world and how best to act in it. The approach is so globally deprecating that it leaves little of interest to say about other ways of life, except, perhaps, as the missionaries or

---

[3] Some have argued that absolutism/relativism is a false dichotomy and that the relativist cannot argue for her position by arguing against absolutism. As far as I can tell, the point of dissolving this dichotomy is to offer pragmatism as a third, middle-of-the-road solution. Whether pragmatism stands on its own or is forced to join camp with either absolutism or relativism depends on how narrowly we construe the alternatives. In the discussion below, I treat pragmatism as a variation of absolutism because, despite its emphasis on contextuality and fallibility, it offers success as a non-relative means of weighing the beliefs, theories, and practices of one way of life against another. In other words, success for the pragmatist takes on the role of an external and universal standard. Anyone who is bothered by my classification should just read "non-relativism" wherever "absolutism" includes or refers to pragmatism. I don't believe that it changes the force or structure of my argument.

government officials might urge, that we must convert the 'savages' to our 'civilized' way of life as soon as possible.

This limitation may help us understand why, in the early days of modern anthropology, a more sophisticated variation of absolutism became popular, which affirms the superiority of Western practices and beliefs, but leaves a much wider space for discussing the details of cultural diversity.[4] Evolutionism abides that what is right, true, good, real, etc. in the world is absolute and unchanging, but adds, importantly, that our understanding of such absolutes progresses with experience over time. What this distinction is supposed to help us discern is that our own (Western liberal) society is simply more evolved than others. We have by now developed a very good grasp of how things really are, while other peoples, enmeshed in other ways of life, are like earlier versions of ourselves. They embrace different truths than us not because concepts such as truth themselves are relative, but because they are less enlightened than us and have yet to understand the world as well as we do. So, we know absolutely that parricide and cannibalism are wrong, witchcraft substance is unreal, and Zande propositions describing its efficacious action in the world are false. The problem is that the Inuit, the Kwakiutl, the Azande, etc. have not yet learned enough about the world to see that this is so. The variation we find among different peoples' ideas of what is right, true, good, real, etc. reveals differences in the respective degrees of evolution in their societies, not the relative character of concepts such as rightness, truth, goodness, reality, etc. themselves.

Evolutionism makes other ways of life not globally and uniformly wrong, but deficient in critical ways. They are like building blocks toward the one right picture, pieces of an incompletely expressed truth. While this gives us more to say about cultural diversity than crude absolutism does, there are aspects of evolutionism that may not be as appealing to our contemporary sensibilities as they were to the early anthropologists. Nowadays, political correctness, if nothing else, tends to make us uncomfortable with the portrayal of the 'savage' foreigner as some childlike, pre-Western version of ourselves. And we are not always as comfortable with absolutes as an idealized ascent to the one right way of understanding life presumes.

Yet, surprisingly enough, evolutionism continues to be for us a rather common view. It simply takes a more pragmatic guise.[5] According to this variation, we do not have guaranteed or immediate access to absolutes because our grasp of what is right, true, good, real, etc. in the world is always fallible and expressed within a way of life. In this much, it agrees with relativism. However, it importantly continues, the great success of Western Science, Capitalism, and Democracy shows that our own sense of what is right, true, good, real, etc. must come closest to grasping the way the world really is in itself. This success is supposed to be indisputably

---

[4] See, for example, Edward Burnett Tylor, *Anthropology: An Introduction to the Study of Man and Civilization* (London: Macmillan, 1881), 448.

[5] See, for example, Karl Popper, "Facts, Standards, and Truth: A further Criticism of Relativism" in *Moral Relativism: A Reader*, eds. Paul K. Moser and Thomas L. Carson (New York, NY: Oxford University Press, 2001), 32–52; and Hilary Putnam, *Ethics without Ontology* (Cambridge, Mass.: Harvard University Press, 2004), 121–29.

manifest in our vast achievements – robots, airplanes, accurate weather modeling, low mortality rates, free citizens, open markets, the protection of human rights... After all, how could we not be right, or at least very close to right, about how the world is and should be, if we are so numerous, prosperous, and healthy, and so much of the physical and political world lies under our dominion? Sure, other peoples may have created vast empires in the past, but did they navigate spacecraft or teach all of their citizens to read? We have reached clear markers of success that transcend any particular way of life. In fact, our trend of rapidly increasing success shows that, despite being enmeshed in our own way of life, we are coming closer and closer to an absolute understanding of the world. Our standards are so well developed by now that they are the next best things to absolute standards. So, we can use them to extract what is, for all intents and purposes, a non-relativistic analysis of the practices and beliefs of other ways of life. Given our deep understanding of what is humane and just, we know that cannibalism and parricide are wrong not only in the context of our own way of life, but wrong simpliciter. Our science is so good that we are certain that Zande propositions asserting the efficacious action of witchcraft substance must be false not only in the context of our way of life, but according to the way the world is in itself. In short, the diversity we find across cultures in judgments about what is true, good, real, etc. does not indicate that truth, goodness, reality, etc. themselves are ultimately relative to a way of life, but that other peoples have not yet been as successful as us in grasping them.

We have now seen three broad strategies for asserting absolutism in the face of cultural diversity. These all work by construing our own standards as absolute, or nearly absolute, and alternative standards as in some way importantly deficient. Another possible anti-relativist response is simply to deny that cultural diversity runs very deep. According to the universalist view, there is ultimately only one set of absolute standards for determining what is true, good, real, etc., but these same standards will yield different results in different cultural contexts. So, for example, parricide is negligent and inhumane in conventional U.S. society because we have sufficient resources for taking care of the elderly, and such care is an act of reciprocity to the parents and guardians who once took care of us. The Inuit, on the other hand, are a nomadic people who must subsist with very limited resources in an extreme environment. Among them, parricide is respectful and humane because the healthy and the young cannot hunt and survive if they must stay back and take care of the elderly once they become weak and immobile. Parricide is an act of care from the elderly parents to their healthy children, which the latter will one day repay not back to their parents, but forward to their own children, when they, too, are no longer able to keep up with the group.[6] What appear on the surface to be different judgments (parricide is wrong, parricide is right) are actually applications of the same principles (respect for life, love of family, reciprocity, etc.) in different contexts.

---

[6] This is a popular example in the literature on relativism, which I believe dates back to Edward Westermarck, *Ethical Relativity* (New York: Harcourt, Brace and company, 1932), 184. Cook gives this universalist treatment to the example in Cook, *Morality and Cultural Differences*, 102–3; 165.

An interesting aspect of universalism is that it is in some respects more charitable than other forms of absolutism. It does not require that all foreign practices and beliefs which diverge from our own be wrong or false. Inasmuch as we find them to agree with underlying universal principles, we can acknowledge them as true and correct in their own context. Universalism, however, is importantly also a source of cultural critique: inasmuch as we find foreign practices and beliefs to violate universal principles, we can rebuke them as absolutely false and incorrect.[7] Curiously enough, universalists almost always take our own (contemporary Western) principles as guides to what the universal principles must be.[8] And somehow their proper construal within a particular cultural context almost always fits the limits of a liberal sensibility and imagination. So, while parricide turns out to be right in a particular cultural context, cannibalism, or else female circumcision, turns out to be absolutely wrong.

Crude absolutism, (classic) evolutionism, pragmatic evolutionism, and universalism represent four important strategies for accommodating cultural diversity without relativism. They give us an idea of the range of possible anti-relativist responses without, of course, exhausting all of the alternatives. I will return to them throughout this chapter, and throughout this book, because of the useful contrast they draw with relativism.[9] Yet I would be remiss at this point if I did not mention that others have given in response to cultural diversity not only many alternatives to relativism, but also many reasons for avoiding the view altogether. On the surface, quite a few of these reasons have to do with the objections that I will address in subsequent chapters, for instance: Relativism has an inescapable air of paradox. It cannot be formulated in a way that is not inconsistent or incoherent. It corrupts the very notions of rightness and truth, leaving us no way to possess our own moral convictions and beliefs. It forces us into an unmovable posture of tolerance, rendering us incapable of cultural critique, within our own way of life or beyond.[10]

Many treat these objections as if they were so forceful as to leave no room even to consider relativism. Yet, both relativism and its critique date back to ancient times. While certain aspects of the response that I will give to these objections may be novel, I can hardly claim to be solving a great riddle for the first time. It is hard not to think that there are deeper reasons for avoiding relativism, which in the arguments about paradox and inconsistency remain concealed, at times even to those themselves who craft them.[11] To embrace relativism is to place our own claims to

---

[7] This, in fact, is touted by the universalists as an advantage over relativism, which they mistakenly believe to be incapable of defending its own practices and beliefs. I will address this further in Chap. 6.

[8] While universalism can be more charitable than pragmatic evolutionism, the two views are not incompatible. In fact, the universalist may use the success argument to explain how we know that our own principles are not merely right in a particular context, but universally.

[9] See especially Chap. 6 for more discussion of universalism, Chaps. 3 and 4 for the "success" argument found in pragmatic evolutionism, and Chap. 2 for absolutism in general.

[10] I address all of these objections in Chap. 2. See also Chap. 6 for further discussion of tolerance.

[11] Cf Michael N. Forster, "On the very Idea of Denying the Existence of Radically Different Conceptual Schemes," *Inquiry* 41, no. 2 (06, 1998), 133–185.

understand the world and to operate well within it on a par with those of other ways of life. It is, if not to give up, at least to share our position of power and authority with those who are different from us in significant ways.[12] It is, in short, to relativize our own legitimacy. And, perhaps, at first, it can only be welcomed as a solution to cultural diversity by those who never expected human knowledge to be a matter of absolutes; and by those who, inspired by a sense of justice,[13] or a sense of what is missing in our own way of life,[14] are eager to empower the people whose different ways of life would otherwise only be found deficient.

1.1.3   The Turn Toward Relativism

Table 1.1 provides a summary of the different ways we have seen to accommodate the cultural diversity of practices and beliefs. Considering the number of alternatives to relativism, and of reasons for opposing it, we may find it surprising that, not long after the birth of modern anthropology, indeed, at its most formative stage, cultural thinkers took a significant, methodological turn towards relativism. We can see this in varying degrees among anthropologists of the time. For instance, Evans-Pritchard, with his neutral descriptions of Zande witchcraft, refused to adopt the deprecating stance of absolutism, which would have made the Azande's beliefs merely childish and silly. Instead, he found in them great coherence, organization and detail.[15] Malinowski, in developing the practice and theory of participant observation, opened up the fabric of Trobriander life. He showed that Trobriander sexual life, which conflicted deeply with Victorian mores, was organized by its own, very developed standards of good and bad behavior. His descriptions of the Kula Ring brought to life a system that escaped Western categories of trade and giving, but was nonetheless rich in detail and highly successful at imbuing several distinct cultures with meaning and order.[16] In a similar vein, Boas argued that Native American baskets must be interpreted in the context of the weavers' own culture, not as part of some universal, pan-human evolutionary scheme. His historicism stressed that not

---

[12] Cf Jack W. Meiland, "On the Paradox of Cognitive Relativism," *Metaphilosophy* 11, no. 2 (04, 1980), 115–126.

[13] In some ways, I take this to be a point made by Jesse Prinz, in his book Jesse J. Prinz, *The Emotional Construction of Morals* (Oxford; New York: Oxford University Press, 2007). However, the relativist must be clear that even this sense of justice is not absolute, but relative to a particular way of life. For further discussion of this point, see Chaps. 2 and 6 of this book.

[14] Cf Meiland, *On the Paradox of Cognitive Relativism*, 115–126

[15] Edward Evans Evans-Pritchard, *Witchcraft, Oracles and Magic among the Azande* (Oxford: The Clarendon Press, 1937).

[16] Bronislaw Malinowski, *Argonauts of the Western Pacific; an Account of Native Enterprise and Adventure in the Archipelagoes of Melanesian New Guinea* (New York: Dutton, 1922); Bronislaw Malinowski, *The Sexual Life of Savages in North-Western Melanesia: An Ethnographic Account of Courtship, Marriage, and Family Life among the Natives of the Trobriand Islands, British New Guinea* (London: Routledge, 1932).

Table 1.1 A range of possible responses to cultural diversity

Response to Cultural Diversity	Are divergent practices and beliefs wrong/ incorrect?	Are ways of life with divergent practices and beliefs inferior/ underdeveloped?	Is there an absolute sense in which practices and beliefs can be wrong/ incorrect?	Do different ways of life stand "higher" or "lower" than others on some absolute scale?
Crude Absolutism	Yes.	Yes. They are inferior.	Yes. Our own standards determine rightness and correctness absolutely.	Yes. Our way of life is superior to others with divergent practices/beliefs.
(Classic) Evolutionsim	Mostly. They are either wrong/ incorrect or incomplete.	Yes. They are less evolved than our own.	Yes. Our own standards have evolved to the point that they are absolute arbiters of rightness and correctness.	Yes. Our way of life is more developed than others with divergent practices/beliefs.
Pragmatic Evolutionism	Mostly. They are either wrong/ incorrect or incomplete.	Yes. They are less evolved than our own.	No. All of our standards for evaluating rightness and correctness are tied to the context of a particular way of life. However, we can tell by the success of our own standards that they are quite close to being absolute arbiters of rightness and correctness for all ways of life.	Yes. Our way of life is more successful and, therefore, more developed than others with divergent practices/beliefs.

(continued)

Table 1.1 (continued)

Universalism	Sometimes. Further cultural investigation will reveal either 1) that they are variants of universals that we all share, and so are not truly in conflict with our own practices/ beliefs; or 2) that they are in conflict with universals to which we all subscribe, and so are absolutely wrong/incorrect.	Universalism in itself does not take a stand on this question. If further cultural investigation reveals that divergent practices and beliefs are in conflict with shared universals, then this could or could not be due to inferiority/lack of development.	Yes. Universals provide such a shared standard.	Perhaps. Our way of life may be higher than other ways of life with divergent practices/belief if further cultural investigation reveals that these are truly in conflict with universal standards. Our way of life may also be more cognizant of universals and may adhere to them more closely than other ways of life.
Relativism	Only in a very specific sense. Divergent practices and beliefs can only be wrong/ incorrect relative to the standards of a particular way of life.	Not usually and never generally. A relativist could only claim that divergent practices and beliefs are wrong/incorrect relative to the norms of a particular way of life.	No. There are no standards of evaluation that transcend the limits of a way of life.	No. There is no non-relative standard for comparing ways of life. Any comparison between ways of life, or their individual practices and beliefs, must be relativized to the concepts, beliefs, practices, and other structures of a particular way of life.

only the objects, but also the beliefs and practices of a people, were most fully understood in relation to their own culture and to the particular history they had lived.[17]

---

[17] Franz Boas, "The Occurrence of Similar Inventions in Areas Widely Apart," *Science* 9, no. 224 (1887b), 485–486; Franz Boas, "Museums of Ethnology and their Classification," *Science* 9, no. 228 (1887a), 587–589.; Franz Boas, "Response to John W. Powell," 9, no. 229 (1887c), 612–614.; Franz Boas, "On Alternating Sounds," *American Anthropologist* 2, no. 1 (1889), 47–51; Franz Boas, *Race, Language, and Culture* (Chicago: University of Chicago Press, 1940), 647; Franz Boas, *The Mind of Primitive Man* (New York: The Macmillan company, 1922).

While relativism in later guises would be accused of derailing the progress of science, these anthropologists were actually driven by a desire to be more scientific and objective. Their goal was to provide a picture of the culture as it was in itself, with the least amount of distortion possible. They believed they had the truest picture of a culture when they subjected it as little as possible to their own concepts and values. Yet, since this was only an ideal, and of course one could not remove himself from his own culture entirely, they went to great lengths to acknowledge their own influences, what they were, and where they occurred. For them, these different aspects of methodological relativism – contextualism over absolutism, historicity in place of timelessness, particularity instead of universality – were of a piece with empiricism and the push to develop a mature science of culture.

Anthropology's turn toward methodological relativism may be very exciting to the philosophical relativist, because it is a practical application of her theoretical view. However, the two forms of relativism are quite distinct. Methodological relativism is merely a research technique for understanding a foreign way of life. Philosophical relativism, on the other hand, is a view about the fabric of a way of life – how it holds together, how it relates to life itself. There is nothing about adherence to the one form of relativism that requires adherence to the other. We can, as methodological relativists, seek to understand another culture in its own context, paying close attention to its history and the particularities of its existence, but then turn around and explain non-relativistically the different practices and beliefs that we thus uncover.[18] We may insist, for example, that they fit the same underlying universal principles as our own practices and beliefs, or that, in as much as they differ deeply from our own, they are simply deficient or less evolved.

In fact, the same devotion to the absolute progress of science may lead us both to adopt methodological relativism and to reject philosophical relativism. For example, in the name of science, we may strive to describe Zande witchcraft in a neutral tone, attributing as much coherence to native beliefs as possible. We may believe that this produces the most penetrating analysis possible. And yet, again in the name of science, we may hold that Zande propositions asserting the efficacious action of witchcraft in the world are absolutely false. After all, they seem to conflict with our best, scientific understanding of how the world works.[19]

I mentioned earlier that we could understand cultural diversity as motivating relativism only if there were some aspect, beyond the raw data, the mere fact of it which did not fit neatly into absolutism, or which pushed us towards relativism. As we have seen, methodological relativism *per se* does not force us to adopt

---

[18] We may imagine, as well, the case of the investigator who is a philosophical relativist and a methodological absolutist. Perhaps she believes herself so constrained to her own way of life that understanding another culture in its own context is not fruitful, or even possible. I do not believe such a constraint is a necessary consequence of relativism.

[19] This, it turns out, is more or less Evans-Pritchard's stance in *Witchcraft, Magic and Oracles among the Azande*. For more on how the relativist handles this apparent conflict, see Chaps. 3, 4, and 5 of this book.

(philosophical) relativism.[20] However, what I would like to argue in the remaining sections of this chapter is that there are certain aspects of the kind of deep, intercultural experience which the methodological relativist is bound to have that do make the philosophical view much more compelling. Their force does not come so much from the data that the methodological relativist uncovers as from the relation to it that she occupies, the way in which it is interwoven in her experience, the kind of interpretive charity and empathy to it that she extends. The great diversity of ways of life that we find in the historical and anthropological record may first raise our minds to the possibility of relativism, but it is the deep engagement with another way of life which makes what might otherwise seem an extreme and unattractive view at once fruitful, coherent, and well-placed.

1.2 Deep Engagement

1.2.1 A Few Caveats

In pointing to certain features of deep intercultural engagement, I hope to show how they complicate the absolutist views, on the one hand, and motivate relativism, on the other. Explaining what an experience is like, and the effect that it has on its subject, is necessarily an exercise that is a bit too removed. Though that distance itself has its own merits, the result is something like watching a cooking show, or reading a theatre review. It is instructive, helpful, yet not quite the same thing as smelling the sizzling food, or shivering in the suspense of the dramatic spectacle.

For me, the question of how we should live has always been deeply tied to the questions of who we are, what the world is, and the relation we bear to it. So, it was natural to look for answers as much in philosophical texts as in the experience of living around the world. At the age of 16, I devised a plan to inhabit places increasingly different from the Los Angeles suburb where I was born and raised. What started as a summer in Spain ended as a lifetime intertwined with the Chachi and traditional Afro-Ecuadorian people of San Miguel, a small, populated area of the Chocó rainforest.

My thought that relativism is an appealing, coherent, and fruitful view is the result of years of thinking through our experiences and trying to answer, or at least to situate, these questions. I have struggled just as long to find an adequate way to articulate and defend this thought. I brought Westerners to visit the Chocó so they could exchange experiences with the people there. I wrote narratives of my own life in Ecuador, as well as pieces of straight philosophical argument. I hope that my

---

[20] Unless explicitly stated, the reader should assume that by "relativism" I mean the philosophical relativism described at the beginning of this section, not the methodological relativism employed by anthropologists.

discussion here finds some middle ground between experience and reflection, between context and argument.

Although I will be using examples from anthropological fieldwork and from my own experience, I do not mean to imply that these are the only forms of deep engagement. In some cases, the encounter with another way of life may occur through literature, through historical investigation, or even primarily through the imagination. It does not require a journey to far-off lands, as romantic as that prospect sounds. We might find enough contrast with our own way of life by simply engaging a different generation, sub-group, or sub-class within our own society.

While I do not claim that deep engagement is an exclusive experience, I do mean that the argument for relativism depends on it in a special way. Those who are not open to it will simply deny the existence of the features below or the importance of the reasons that they bring to light. I will return to this point at the end of my exposition of deep engagement, in Sect. 1.3, and it is a theme that will accompany us throughout the book. To argue for relativism is to argue not that it is true for all people, at all places and in all times, but that it may be in some important way true for us. For now, we are only looking to see what might motivate us, given its challenges and the available alternatives, to consider relativism in the first place. We will see in the following chapters how well it answers those challenges. But at no point should we expect relativism to give what it posits that no theory can give, that is, a knockdown argument for the absolute truth of its claims.

Finally, I would like to caution the reader that, while I have tried to mark out the features of deep engagement that lead to relativism, my exposition is obviously somewhat artificial. A single experience could have many of these features, as well as other relevant ones that I fail to mention. The various features may also interact with each other in different ways. And although I have explained them in a particular order, I surely do not mean to imply that they follow a definite sequence or will be found in exactly this way.

1.2.2   Attributive Symmetry

From the outside, the practices and beliefs of another way of life may seem ill-reasoned, unenlightened, even foolish. The more deeply we become involved in that way of life, however, the more we come to see them as well-reasoned, coherent, even natural. This is not merely a matter of becoming habituated to another way of life, but of seeing it as an integrated whole. It is in this context that we come to attribute to other ways of life orderly, coherent patterns of thinking and acting which from the outside seem entirely lacking. This positive finding is what I call, "attributive symmetry." The symmetry is by no means mathematical or direct, but it arises along a common axis of human experience. Across it, we find patches of rough functional analogs that help us to recognize meaning, structure, and reason in the other way of life.[21]

Although Evans-Pritchard did not believe that witchcraft was an actual force acting in the world, he came to see that Zande thought about witchcraft was, for the most part, well regimented and organized – what would count, by most standards, as "rational."[22] His records of questions put to the poison oracle, with their lattice of conditions and cross-tests, look nearly like truth tables.[23] The Zande rules he explains for gathering, preparing, and administering the poison are as complex and involved as many a science experiment. And, perhaps what is most surprising, he reports, quite matter-of-factly, that he found the poison oracle a perfectly adequate system for running his own household.[24] In other words, he came to recognize a certain efficacy and structure in Zande beliefs about witchcraft, even though, by his own lights, they must be false.

Malinowski, similarly, came to understand Trobriander sexual behavior, which was scandalous by Victorian standards, as adhering to a strict code of good and bad behavior. While it was expected that young children would play games imitating sexual acts and that young adults would engage in a period of sexual experimentation before entering a more permanent, monogamous relationship, it was scandalous for a boy to live with his parents past puberty, or for a couple to share a meal together out of wedlock. Within the context of their own way of life, it seems as though we can describe Trobriander actions as something like "moral."[25]

At every level, a participant observer like Malinowski finds practices and beliefs that are in conflict with his own, but still hang admirably together within the context of another way of life. Some examples may be particularly dramatic. We see that Kwakiutl cannibalism is not a rash, retaliatory act, but a rite performed by members of an elite sect only after long training and preparation.[26] We see that the Inuit engage in parricide only to be able to support the young and the healthy in their harsh, nomadic lifestyle. In my own experience, however, it is the constant barrage of smaller, more mundane instances that is the most striking.

At every turn, I come to see that what I thought was obviously right, clearly negligent, or simply unintelligent, is, in the context of another way of life, just as obviously wrong, as clearly responsible, as simply well-reasoned. An action as innocuous and reflexive as washing my hands after going to the bathroom gets turned around, and suddenly I see that to the Chachi it is disgusting, even impolite. In the beginning, I am quite happy going from the outhouse to the kitchen, where I scoop up a

---

[21] Some might also argue that this is the axis where we find the beginnings of empathy and compassion.

[22] Evans-Pritchard, *Witchcraft, Oracles and Magic among the Azande*.

[23] Ibid., 300–309.

[24] Ibid., 270.

[25] Malinowski, *The Sexual Life of Savages in North-Western Melanesia: An Ethnographic Account of Courtship, Marriage, and Family Life among the Natives of the Trobriand Islands, British New Guinea*, especially 62, 438–440, 538.

[26] Ruth Benedict, *Patterns of Culture* (Boston: Houghton Mifflin, 1934), 173–222.

bit of soap and pour water over my hands. It is the strange look on the grandmother's face, amused, yet a bit disapproving, which causes me to look further. As I learn more about Chachi life, I realize how careful and deliberate their every movement is. I begin to see spaces and distinctions that were hitherto invisible. I come to understand that for the Chachi, my whole bathroom routine is pathetic and a bit comical: first, the way I clumsily tromp across the bamboo bridge to the outhouse, bouncing and sometimes breaking the poles; then, how I can't figure out how to create privacy by placing the short board over the doorway and squatting modestly; and finally, when I make my way back to the kitchen, how with great zeal, I scoop up a bunch of precious store-bought soap and pour half a bucket of water over my hands. I don't even think about the person who collected that water and carried it up the riverbank. I don't notice the chickens under the hut that I am wetting as I pour out the water. I don't realize that the bucket belongs to someone in particular. More importantly, I can't see that, for the Chachi, the entire premise of my hand washing is embarrassing and absurd: I would only be washing my hands if they were truly dirty, but only a child does not know how to urinate and defecate without soiling her hands. I should not be smiling as I wash with big, open gestures; I should be hiding myself, ashamed of my uncleanliness!

At first, when I see that the Chachi do not speak often to their children, that they rarely offer the patient explanation that my culture recognizes as a sign of good parenting, I assume that they lack the insight that we have in child development. When a canoe floats by with the children silently facing their parents, I think of all the learning opportunities lost. The adults should be pointing out the beauty of the little waterfall on the riverbank, telling the children the names of the birds flying overhead, explaining the work that each person they pass is performing – whether washing clothes, snorkeling for shellfish, or floating timber downriver to sell in town. In the same way, when I see a four year-old sitting at the edge of a raised hut pick up a machete and start tapping at a piece of wood, I wonder at his parents' negligence. Why aren't they concerned that he'll chop off his hand or fall 10 feet down to the ground? But as I learn how skilled the Chachi are at observation, how much communication passes between them in movement and gesture without words, how quickly they understand an object with their hands, I see these acts in a new context. I realize that the children in the canoe are already observing and learning to become good observers. They absorb information by closely following their parents, watching in quiet attention, and then trying. The 4 year-old has explored and knows his space too well to fall off the side of the hut. The parents are aware and quite pleased with his play. He holds the machete well and models carving techniques that he will soon use to build toys and, someday, important tools.

At first, when I bring home to my Chachi family a large sack of rice, I am dismayed that they want to eat it all right away. They want sweet rice for snack, rice with the evening meal, and again at the morning meal the next day. I am worried about what we will do when it is all gone. In the same way, when they find a tree in the forest full of fruit and carry home large basketfuls, I am concerned to see them sit on the floor and gorge themselves, popping one piece after another into their mouths. I think that they lack the skill, so important in my culture, of saving for the future; their actions strike me as severely shortsighted. But as my own produce rots and I constantly fight the rats and cockroaches ransacking my stockpile of dry goods, I realize that their actions, in the context of living in a tropical rainforest, are quite sensible. Their environment rewards those who seize the moment, not those who put things away.

This process of turning around, of coming to see practices and beliefs as well-reasoned, and well-grounded, is the essence of methodological relativism. Like all of the features of deep engagement that we will discuss, attributive symmetry does not in itself require that we adopt a more radical philosophical relativism. Practices and beliefs may become more coherent and reasonable in context, but this does not force us to acknowledge that they are accurate or right. Yet, attributive symmetry is a first step in coming to see that each way of life has its own shape, its own set of possible human conditions and responses that it brings into play. At the same time, attributive symmetry begins to complicate the non-relativist alternatives for explaining cultural diversity. In particular, crude absolutism starts to look like an unattractive, unreasonable position. Once we see that another way of life follows its own rigid standards of reasoning and conduct, it is hard to dismiss its practices and beliefs as simply mistaken or unenlightened. It begins to look as though other lives are not savage, irrational, or immoral, but organized quite differently than our own.

1.2.3   Reflective Symmetry

Attributive symmetry is a positive finding in the foreign way of life. We recognize in others logical thought and moral behavior, even though their practices and beliefs are at odds with our own. Reflective symmetry, on the other hand, is a negative finding, a reflection of anthropological inquiry back onto ourselves. We begin to see the context, limits, and constraints of our own practices and beliefs. Reflective symmetry happens along the same axis of common human experience as attributive symmetry. In the latter, we recognize rough analog patches of our own human experience as we look more deeply at the practices and beliefs of another way of life. In the former, we recognize the people of that other way of life looking back at us.

An important aspect of reflective symmetry is the discovery that the developmental judgments also go the other way around. We find not only our sense of disapproval, but our tendency to see others as inferior or less developed, mirrored in the foreign way of life. To the people with whom we are deeply engaged, we are also a kind of savage. My difference with the Chachi is not simply that hand washing is cleanly and polite for me, but disgusting and impolite for them. I tend to make a further judgment that they lack an important piece of knowledge, namely, they do not understand the germ theory of disease, so they cannot see why hand washing is important. If I were of an evolutionist bent, I might claim that they have simply failed to arrive yet at our level of scientific development. But for the Chachi, my bathroom ritual *also* reveals a lack of an important piece of knowledge: I don't have the proper care and dominion over my body of an adult. I am unaware of how I move, where I step, how I squat, how I sit. When I break a hole in the neighbor's floor with my step, when I am the only one at the end of a trek whose boots are full of water and pants are covered in mud, when I cannot sit in the canoe without wetting my bottom or unknowingly splaying my crotch before the other passengers, the Chachi recognize the same piece of missing knowledge: I carry myself like a child unaware of herself and her surroundings.

We should note that these developmental judgments extend far beyond the physical. For the Chachi, it is not just the way I move my body that is immature. They are struck, for instance, by the way that I want to talk my plans and ideas through with them. While it is quite normal and unremarkable in my culture to collect information, to ask questions, to give explanations, and to expect them in return, this habit of expressing everything discursively strikes the Chachi as excessive and infantile. If I am observant and attuned to my surroundings, I should see the answers without asking many questions. If I intuit well, I should know to act without spelling out every thought. There is no reason for so much explicit cogitation. Clearly, I have not learned, like the children sitting silently in the canoe, to observe well, to understand without relying heavily on words, to anticipate, interpret, and follow the movements of all around me.

This ability for quiet understanding that I lack is as much a cognitive as a social achievement. It is how the Chachi understand not only what is around them and how things work, but what people mean. They read the signs, movements, and parts in the world around them and know to speak through the same medium. A slight glance at the person passing by in a canoe is a greeting. The smallest gesture at a meal means, "pass the salt." This mode of communication fills the rainforest, from the floor to the canopy, from the distant sounds to the wafting smells, with meaning for the Chachi. They see other forms of life unfolding, drama, amusement, food, medicine, tools, clothes, instruments, adornments, where I catch only a muddy floor and a sea of green. And somehow with this power of seeing they can also pick up any machine from my world that I show them for the first time and immediately know how it works. For the Chachi, not only do I lack fluency in Cha'palaa, their spoken language, but I seem almost not to grasp any observational language at all. I have poor corporeal control, severe linguistic dependency, and a very underdeveloped observational capacity.

Of course, when the Chachi judge that I am disgusting, impolite, inobservant, or maladroit, this is a sort of first-blush reaction to my way of life. They, too, can and often do contextualize my actions to see them as more coherent and reasonable. They see the gadgets that I bring with me to the rainforest and adduce, through their own process of attributive symmetry, that I must not need to be as aware of my surroundings as they are because I have technology to help me. They know from their interactions with development projects, loggers, and government agencies the power that comes with my language, my citizenship, and my dollars. So, they figure that, despite my physical, social, and observational deficiencies, I must dominate some other aspects of human life. With greater exposure to my way of life, they might come to appreciate that each person, each entity, each piece of information is considered so separately that highly discursive communication becomes essential to

managing and integrating it all. Though these would not be their terms for expressing it, the Chachi, too, can be charitable in their interpretation of another way of life,
and the backwardness of our behavior does at least become more reasonable in
context.

Through reflective symmetry, we become the subjects of the natives' anthropological investigation, and we begin to see our own way of life from a different angle.
While attributive symmetry allows us to see perhaps as much reasonableness in
their way of life as our own, reflective symmetry stops us from looking for complete
coherence in either one. It limits attributive symmetry, or at least produces a sort of
negative attribution. We find ourselves acknowledging inconsistency on both sides
of the divide, in the foreign way of life as well as our own. In other words, they are
about as coherent, and as irrational, as us.

Many foreign practices and beliefs that first appear strange and objectionable
become reasonable to us through the contextualization process that is part of attributive symmetry. Yet there are others that resist this effort and remain confounding.
Evans-Pritchard, for example, remarks that it is strange the Azande should be so
concerned with uncovering who among them is a witch. Given that witchcraft is an
inherited quality, that the Azande are connected through close kinship ties, and that
there are known witches in every line, it would follow that all of them are witches.
Somehow, when presented with this reasoning, the Azande are not swayed; they are
just as intent as ever to uncover who is truly a witch.[27] There is something foundational about this incoherence. Witchcraft lies at the core of Zande life, yet they cannot explain its logic completely. And neither can Evans-Pritchard. At a certain point,
he must, like them, shrug his shoulders.

We need not assume that Zande thought follows exactly the same rules and patterns as our own.[28] We may also question whether a society or way of life is an entity
that lends itself to the absence of contradiction, or to the sort of formal coherence
that Western logic conventionally envisages.[29] But what reflective symmetry teaches
us with its inverted gaze, is that some of our own practices and beliefs share this
same inexplicable quality. We come to realize that from the outside not only do we
seem inferior and savage, but inconsistent. Malinowski discusses a particularly
embarrassing discrepancy for the Trobriander between their stated conventions and
actual practices. When confronted with their firm maxim that no man would willingly copulate with an unattractive woman, on the one hand, and the evidence that
an old, decrepit woman is responsible for infecting several young men with gonor-
rhea, on the other, the natives refuse to acknowledge any inconsistency. But what is
most instructive about their denial is the way that Malinowski himself simply shrugs

[27] Evans-Pritchard, *Witchcraft, Oracles and Magic among the Azande*, 28.

[28] Cf Lucien Lévy-Bruhl, *La Mentalité Primitive* (Paris: Librairie Félix Alcan, 1922).

[29] Cf Ernest Gellner, "Concepts and Society," in *Rationality*, ed. Bryan R. Wilson (Oxford:
Blackwell, 1970), 18–49; Graham Priest, *In Contradiction: A Study of the Transconsistent* (Oxford:
Clarendon Press, 2006).

it off. He remarks, simply, *"Tout comme chez nous."*[30] With these words, he is asking the reader to see that our own behaviors lack the same consistency. It is one of the few phrases in his tome written in French. Malinowski knows that his English readers will comprehend the phrase, but that it will strike us somewhat from the outside. This is exactly what happens through reflective symmetry. We understand our own idiosyncrasy, our own perverseness, not so much through anything explicit that the Trobriander or the Chachi tell us, as through the feeling of having ourselves, our way of life under their anthropological gaze.

Typically, the deeply engaged person is the one who initiated the anthropological inquiry in the first place, but through reflective symmetry, she finds the same tools, the same pattern of analysis turned back on herself and on her own way of life. In thinking about the associative and intuitive patterns of reasoning that are so important to the Chachi, I see, for instance, how important causal reasoning is to our way of life. We assume that causal explanation is the best, and, in some cases, the only, form of explanation. We take science as our highest example of good (causal) explanation. And yet in physics, arguably our highest and most theoretical science, both causality and a related concept, temporal order, break down. While this is a concern for philosophers of science, it is not one that unravels our way of life. Walk us through the argument that causal explanation cannot be as paramount as we take it to be, and we shrug our shoulders. We still care, we still fixate on it in the same way as the Azande do with witchcraft. It captures something central and foundational in our way of life that we can neither give up nor entirely explain.

Our nation is founded on another instance of inconsistency. We take ourselves to be the greatest democracy, the light and champion of freedom to the rest of the world. We abhor genocide, slavery, and the subjugation of peoples anywhere. And yet the United States could not exist where and how it is if we had not decimated the Native Americans and stolen their land, let alone enslaved so many Africans. For some reason, this does not disturb us as much as an outsider might think it should. We lightly brush off the inconsistency in the idea of a great, free nation predicated on atrocious privations of liberty.

Of course, there is no need, for us, or for the natives, to be uncritical of one's own way of life. It is precisely the possibility of one's own inconsistency that the inverted gaze of reflective symmetry helps to open up. Moreover, the idea of relativism itself seems to press liberal society at such a point of inconsistency. We are pluralists; we recognize a multiplicity of traditions, types of people, and perspectives. We are also committed to equality; we believe that all people are guaranteed the same rights and should be afforded the same opportunities. Yet we want to say that our own tradition and our own perspective are somehow better. If liberalism itself must come out on top, doesn't this trivialize pluralism and warp equality? Why aren't we more troubled by this inconsistency? Why can't we grant that other traditions, other ways of life, stand on the same level of ground as our own?

---

[30] Malinowski, *The Sexual Life of Savages in North-Western Melanesia: An Ethnographic Account of Courtship, Marriage, and Family Life among the Natives of the Trobriand Islands, British New Guinea,* 294–5.

These are larger questions, to be addressed in time. But what we can see now is that, as reflective symmetry suggests to us our own deficiencies and inconsistencies, it throws a wrench in the evolutionist views. It becomes quite difficult to claim that other groups are more primitive, somewhere farther back in the process of coming to understand the world more or less as we do, once we realize that they, in turn, see us as lacking, as less developed than them. Of course, we could write off these contrary judgments as deluded, or diminish their importance by claiming that the other way of life relies on inferior standards, false premises, or mistaken notions. But to the person who is deeply engaged in that way of life, these judgments do not miss their target; they refer to something, and whatever it is demands an adequate characterization. She appreciates the complex tasks that the Chachi master by intuition and quiet observation. She feels her own inadequacy when she is the only one who is covered in mud at the end of the trail, or who punches a whole in the floor as they walk across the hut. She is full aware of the inadequacies and inconsistencies in her own way of life. And all this suggests to her another possibility: that one way of life is not superior to or more evolved than another, but that each has its measure of reason and inconsistency, of morality and inhumanity, drawn in a different way. Not only our claims about what is right or good or evolved, but the standards by which we arrive at them, the very terms with which we evaluate the world, are relative to a way of life.

1.2.4 Complexity of Context

The more deeply we become engaged in another way of life, the more we see not discrete practices and beliefs, or emotions and tastes, but an intricate web in which they are all tethered together. In my first months living with the Chachi, there are a few times when, out of great frustration, I am reduced to tears. At these times, I am shocked that they leave me alone, that my suffering does not immediately inspire any offers of consolation or aid. They seem to lack what is for us a fundamental virtue, sympathy. We would even stop to ask a stranger who is in tears what is the matter. We generally accept that if a difficulty has brought an adult to such a public display, it must be of considerable gravity, and it is therefore our duty to help. But if I cry anywhere within the Chachi's keen field of awareness, they seem angry, repulsed – the greater my emotional distress, the greater their fury and disgust. They are moved to the verge of asking me to leave their community. They say that I have lied to them about who I am; I could not be the educated person that I claim to be. Their responses do not make sense to me. When I think that I have cried quietly in my house alone, two children come with steamed leaves for me to inhale because, they explain, their parents fear I have a bad cold. After I have been upset for some time, an adult approaches me, looking very embarrassed and awkward, not to console, but to explain how urgent it is that I get ahold of my emotions.

As I become more familiar with Chachi life, I gain a fuller context in which to situate their reactions to my crying. The Chachi traditionally live in large, multigenerational family groups, with an average of perhaps 15 people living in 1000 square feet. Their huts are raised about 15 feet off of the ground, have a high, thatched palm leaf roof and, typically, no exterior or interior walls. Even the palm wood floorboards have small, regular gaps between them. This is an excellent way to manage the heat, humidity, and pests in the rainforest. The breeze easily passes through, keeping the hut cool and dry. The smoke from the cooking fire penetrates the entire dwelling, keeping away mosquitoes and bats. The openness leaves very few dark corners for spiders and cockroaches to hide. The simple design means that dirt, pests, even a young child's urine, can all be easily rinsed or swept away. But this style of living also means that the Chachi can always see each other's movements both inside and outside their homes. They are such fine observers, and their daily space is so open and shared, that they are always aware of each other. The mother swinging her baby in a hammock by the cooking fire, her husband outside clearing the bush with a machete, the couple in the river heading to cut plantain in their canoe, the girl on the far bank washing clothes, her mother pounding plantain cakes in the tall hut behind her, the rest of the neighbor's family gathered at the morning meal, all know of each other's actions.

Because they have so little physical seclusion, the Chachi define space as well as its use primarily by social means, with minimal physical markers. The dining room is created not by a table and chairs, but by the cook placing her pot on the floor. She takes the eating ware down from the hanging baskets, pulls out her grinding stone, and the family gathers around. The bedroom, similarly, is created not by walls and a door, but by an evening ritual. The person in charge of that space will take a broom and sweep the floorboards, pull down a sleeping mat, and hang the mosquito net. There is now a private space in which to change clothes, to sleep, to quietly make love.

Through a process of attributive symmetry, I come to see that, in the same way, the Chachi use a sort of Stoic control over their emotions to create a private realm in what would otherwise be an all-public world. They have no closed doors. In fact, doors are so uncommon to them that they have just one word, "juukapa," which we might translate as something like "opening," to refer to what are for us both "door" and "window." The personal, private realm cannot be for the Chachi, as it is often literally for us, a "world behind closed doors." Instead, it must be a realm behind their skin, so to speak, only felt, rarely expressed. In the course of their everyday life, they do not show strong emotions. They seem unperturbed, moved neither to great anger nor to great joy. In their highly observant and observable world, to bring an emotion to the surface is already to share it deeply. To give physical expression to an emotion – by composure, or gesture, or cry – is both to give up one's inner space, one's private realm, and to impose its contents on others. Crying is repulsive to the Chachi because in their shared and open lives, it becomes too intimate, more than they can handle, like, for us, hearing the neighbors moan during sex. It passes an accepted boundary of the inner components of a life, almost as revolting as opening someone's body up and pulling out its organs. For the Chachi, emotional self-control serves as much to keep oneself whole as to refrain from disturbing others.

Through a process of reflective symmetry, I come to see that for the Chachi there is something wrong, something childlike and undeveloped about the person who cries in frustration. She lacks the knowledge of how to share space with others, how to master her own emotions and keep them out of others' way. For the Chachi, it would not only be distasteful, but ineffectual to respond immediately to her crying. It would only draw farther into the open what must be fundamentally her own efforts to construct a private space. To intervene would be to disrupt everyone's daily routine and to pull the entire community in. Indeed, the Chachi have such a communal medium for addressing cases of extreme disruption and transgression, as when a man continually beats his wife or has left his home for another woman. The Uni, the traditional governor, calls a community meeting. Each party involved speaks his/her piece. The argument continues until every side and angle has been spoken. Often, the trial lasts long through the night. In the end, the Uni issues his verdict, not of "guilty" or "innocent," but, we might say, of *how* guilty and *how* innocent each party is. Then he prescribes a punishment, almost always corporal, to each in accordance with his/her amount of responsibility for the problem.

Perhaps not surprisingly, the Chachi tolerate crying when it is in this kind of communal setting. When a person, especially a woman, experiences extreme grief, she tells her story in a striking, wailing voice. Such a display might move others in her presence, especially other women, to wail with her, in an expression of ecstatic empathy. A drunken man might also cry while talking of his inner pains in a public place such as a dance, and this will not cause immediate repulsion, although at a certain point his family members will feel that it is their duty to bring him to a private space (at home) and end his display (by putting him to bed). Interestingly, these contrasting cases are likely to repulse the Westerner. There is something eerie, pagan, witchlike for us about the wailing Chachi woman, and the drunken man, clearly, is a public nuisance.

As our picture of another way of life deepens, however, we see more than conflicting judgments about what is a right action. We see that life is cut out, described, and prescribed in a different way. We see that our disagreements about what is a right action are at the same time disagreements about what a person is and how the world in which she acts works. Our disagreement with the Chachi is not merely about whether it is right or wrong to help a person who is crying. We disagree, more fundamentally, about whether such a person is, in fact, in need of help. We disagree about what it means to help and how help can be effected. We disagree about the kinds of skills and knowledge a mature adult should possess. We disagree about the moral emotions that a crying person should naturally arouse. And behind these differences lies a host of other conflicting distinctions, about what space is private and what is shared, about how much space is defined by physical boundaries and how much by act, about what types of obligations we have to ourselves and what types we have to others, about what kind of emotions are personal and what kind are communal, etc.

This complexity of conflict reinforces for the deeply engaged person how uniquely each way of life carves out the world. At the same time, it makes the universalist response to cultural diversity much less attractive for her. The universalist would point to some common principle shared by our way of life, the Chachi, and all others, to argue that we really have the same values and truths. He would claim, for instance, that we all believe it is right to help a person who needs help. Of course, he must state this principle using his own concepts, his own grasp of what human life is and how it works. But even if we grant that this principle captures something roughly shared by all human groups, there seems to be a deeper problem. The principle is in itself too thin to provide a standard of evaluation across different ways of life. Outside the context of a particular way of life, it is empty. It carries no content; it tells us nothing about the situation and what is right or wrong. Without the context of a way of life, we do not know whether a person who is crying needs help, or in what such help consists. We do not know whether it is right to rush to her side, or to leave her alone. And yet with context, we have two different, conflicting stories. For us, the crying person initially and generally inspires compassion; it is reasonable, natural, commendable, even rewarding to offer her aid. For the Chachi, the crying person initially and generally inspires repulsion; it is awkward, unnatural, distasteful, and most likely ineffectual to offer her aid. To ask the crying person what is the matter, what we can do to help her, is, for the Chachi, as unnecessary, uncomfortable, and violating as it would be for us to ask a constipated person who is locked up in the bathroom for several minutes the same questions. Of course, we recognize that he is suffering a difficulty, but we believe there is nothing we can do for him. It is certainly not our duty to help him, and it would be both awkward and distasteful to ask for details or to offer assistance.

While universals without the context of a way of life tell us nothing about a situation and what is right or wrong, universals with context describe different situations and point differently to actions as right or wrong. In other words, universals, given the complexity of context, seem only to reinforce relativism. The interweaving of different domains of life within this complexity also suggests why we might want ultimately to consider relativism not with respect to a particular domain in isolation, but more broadly at the level of a way of life. It is not clear that the same domains exist, in the same way, in the same shape, and with the same relations, for every way of life. When we assume that our disagreement about whether it is right to help a person who is crying lies entirely in the moral domain, we overlook all of our other areas of rich difference. We miss the fact that, for the Chachi, responding to the crying person is not a particularly moral issue in the first place. In short, we seem to overload the moral domain with difference.

The moral universalist, on the other hand, seems to run to the other extreme. In order to find agreement in the moral domain, he unloads so much difference that his principles run empty. They mean nothing without the context of a way of life. Of course, since he has unloaded so much difference from the moral domain onto all of the others, he could just claim that there is one right or best way to understand these other domains. We have the same moral principles, and where we disagree in other domains, it is due to mistake or lack of development on the part of other peoples. If only the Chachi understood social space like Western individuals, had private homes like ours, learned to display and talk through their emotions like us, etc., they would see that it is right to help a person who is crying…But for the one who is deeply engaged in Chachi life, it has its own coherence, as our life, too, has its own defects. The complexity of context gives each way of life a shape so penetrating and unique that it seems to contain – to define and not to release – our claims about a situation and what is right.

1.2.5 Dangling Pieces

When we are deeply engaged in another way of life, we run across elements that find no ready equivalent in our own way of life. We seem to lack the immediate resources to characterize, process, and maneuver them; and yet they strike us as present and real. These dangling pieces suggest that there are aspects of human experience which are not in the same way, not to the same degree, or perhaps not at all part of the experience of our own way of life. We have already seen some of these pieces in our discussion of the first three features of deep engagement. Social space, for instance, seems to have different features and contours for the Chachi. Notably, they do not draw the line between public and private space in the same place or in the same way as us.

We have seen, as well, that the Chachi, in their mode of quiet understanding, seem to deploy a faculty and to latch onto features that are underdeveloped in our own way of life. That is, both the ability to recognize them and the recognition itself seem lacking in us. We miss the detail and movement in the people, animals, plants, and natural forces around us. One might think that the difference lies in the fact that the Chachi are familiar with the common situations and environmental features of the rainforest, whereas we are not. But they carry this observational ability into our world. Show them a gadget or machine for the first time, and they seem to under-stand it intuitively. Give them a camera, and the images they capture are, without any training, striking. Take them to the city, and they will point out, across a crowded street, some person whom they once briefly met.

Part of what is distinctive about dangling pieces is that they are difficult to char-acterize, but we can begin to put some of their key traits together by reflecting on our earlier examples. A first trait is that dangling pieces are hard to see. Initially, we may not notice them at all; or, if we do, we may have the sense of seeing something vaguely or confusedly. At a certain point, I notice the grandmother looking at me and I realize that there is something about my bathroom ritual full of meaning for the Chachi, but I do not know what it is. When the children come to me with a cold remedy to treat my crying, I can't figure out how their parents are aware of my state or what it means for them, yet I see that something is awry.

A second trait of dangling pieces is that, even as we become more immersed in another way of life and gain a deeper context in which to situate them, we still find these pieces difficult to articulate and to conceptualize. We have to invent new terms, or to extrapolate from what might be little-noticed or uncommon aspects of our own way of life to what become very basic and fundamental aspects in theirs. Although I describe the elements of Chachi life that center around intuition and

keen observation as a mode of "quiet understanding," this term means nothing specific, or at all essential, in our way of life. It is a term that I invent for the sole purpose of capturing something unfamiliar to us. We might think that a professional
ballerina, at least on the dance floor, has an acute awareness of her own body, and of
the space and movement around her, which is somewhat akin to the awareness of
self, space, and movement that is ubiquitous among the Chachi. Or, we might sense
that a highly trained naturalist, at least in certain environments, possesses something
like the keen observational faculty that is common to all Chachi, and which structures so much of not only their cognitive, but social life. Yet we draw these alleged
similarities from the very margins of our own experience to try to come to terms
with elements that are foundational to theirs. While such descriptions and graspings
by analogy may help us to articulate something about Chachi life, their ad hoc
nature and roughness only reinforce how they dangle outside our own experience,
how they are parts which find no ready equivalent in our way of life.

Finally, a third trait that we can notice about dangling pieces is that, despite the
difficulty we find in conceptualizing them – that is, in both recognizing and articulating them – they strike the deeply engaged person not as imaginary or as inexis-
tent, but as real. We doubt only what they are, not *that* they are. Dangling pieces are
like missing pieces of a puzzle; they interlock with other aspects of a way of life. We
know to look for them because we can see, from the other pieces that we grasp better, that there is a hole where they should fit. When we find them, we see how they
pull disparate pieces of the puzzle together. The elaborate and unique shape of
Chachi social space helps to explain why they are repulsed by my crying, and also
why they find my bathroom ritual somewhat disgusting and silly. Quiet understanding helps to explain why the Chachi don't talk to their children in the canoe, as well
as a host of other observations and pieces of information that I gather while living
among them, like why they don't traditionally greet each other with words or cere-
mony, or why the project workers who visit them have the impression that they are
not as astute as their Afro-Ecuadorian neighbors because they do not ask questions
during workshops together.

Sometimes it is helpful to think of dangling pieces, in the spirit of the Sapir-
Whorf hypothesis, through native words that find no easy translation in our own
language. In the Chachi language, for instance, there exist numerous words that we
might translate as something like "demon," "evil spirit," or "goblin." But in
Cha'palaachi, the words correspond to a detailed ontology of evil spirits, each with
different characteristics and behavior. We could add modifiers or descriptive clauses
to a word like "demon" in order to differentiate them, such as, "water spirit," or
"bird spirit," but there remain two difficulties with such a translation. The first is that
we are not so much finding as creating equivalents in our own language. They fail
to preserve the same relationships and emphasis as they have in Chachi language
and life. As we have seen, this sort of rough, ad-hoc characterization only reinforces
their lack of a ready equivalent in our own way of life. The second difficulty extends
even farther beyond the linguistic. In our way of life, all of these demons are mere
superstition; they correspond to the same null set. But to the Chachi, the supernatural is a vast realm, with different entities and forces that are felt, identified, and acted

upon intersubjectively. How do we account for the actual content that these words seem to need and to have in Chachi life, but not in our own?

We could try to account for this content in terms of purely natural entities and forces that have some equivalent in our own way of life. Perhaps the entities are illusions and the forces boil down to some mixture of suggestion, hysteria, and coincidence. And, perhaps, under certain conditions, this provides what amounts to being what is for us enough actual content to be able to explain how the Chachi can feel, identify and act upon the supernatural with as much discernment as they do. Yet, to the deeply engaged person, these dangling pieces are so rich, effective, and entwined in the native way of life that they suggest another possibility. As Richard Shweder says about his own work in the Hindu temple town of Bhubaneswar on the East Coast of India, he would like to take his informants as meaning something substantial when they talk of death pollution and the transmigration of souls.[31] In our scientific, if not, scientistic culture, we are more comfortable with dangling pieces in the social and practical realms than in the theoretical realm, especially that portion which we deridingly label as, "supernatural." This is the part that we are often afraid to mention, the part we are sure to belittle or brush past, for fear of being labeled, "superstitious," or, "kooky." Evans-Pritchard mentions seeing one night a strange, bright light behind his house. The next morning, the people tell him about a witch that was passing through on his way to feast on a victim's flesh.[32] Although Evans-Pritchard admits that this explanation fits the phenomenon better than any he can himself come up with, he is reluctant to accept it fully.

In my own experience, these dangling pieces that we would call "supernatural" exhibit the same traits as the others we have already discussed. They are difficult to recognize at first; I have the sense of confronting something, but I do not know what it is. When finally I have a better grasp of them, I often have to invent or "slide" my way into terms that seem to fit them. And yet I have no doubt that they refer to something in the world, that they are richly articulated by the Chachi, and that they are interwoven into their way of life in complex, effective ways. Perhaps what is most compelling about these dangling pieces is that they strike me in a completely unsolicited manner. Like Evans-Pritchard, I do not go out into the night looking for witch lights because someone has told me about them. The order of discovery is the other way around. I sense something strange hovering outside my window, and I ask my friend why he has a bad headache. He goes on to tell me an elaborate story about his grandfather, the shaman, and an evil spirit who has followed him down the river to my hut. What is also striking about these dangling pieces is that they are intersubjectively available. More than one person accesses them; and they fit, like pieces of a puzzle, into different narratives, observations, and pieces of information across different locations, narrators, and times.

---

[31] Richard A. Shweder, "John Searle on a Witch Hunt: A Commentary on John R. Searle's Essay 'Social Ontology: Some Basic Principles'," *Anthropological Theory* 6, no. 1 (03, 2006), 106–108.

[32] Evans-Pritchard, *Witchcraft, Oracles and Magic among the Azande,* 34.

I believe that these "supernatural" dangling pieces are so taboo for us, especially in a context like academic philosophy, that it would not at all further my argument to belabor any of my examples in detail. Suffice it to say that I ended up living with a family that, shortly before my arrival, had lost its fifth and last generation of shamans, and that I came to appreciate the richness and integrity of this aspect of their lives. Yet, perhaps the fact that these examples seem to have no rightful place in my own work speaks even more profoundly than the content of the examples themselves. That is, if I want to treat them not as superstitious, confused, or incomplete, but as world-referring, coherent, and effective, then there seems no respectable, serious way to go about it. And this fact about our own way of life underscores beautifully with what severity such dangling pieces lack a ready equivalent, or any kind of place at all, in our way of life. Yet, to the same degree, it provides impetus to the deeply engaged person to find some way to reconcile this difference, to be able to say that each way of life grasps ahold of the world, without excluding or diminishing the grip of the other.

Dangling pieces, like all the features we have seen so far, reinforce the uniqueness of the shape of each way of life. As they motivate relativism, they also complicate the alternative ways that we have seen to account for cultural diversity. In particular, dangling pieces frustrate the reductivist move that lies at the heart of nearly all the alternative accounts. Crude absolutism and the various forms of evolutionism would have that our different claims – about whether it is good to talk to your children in the canoe, whether it is right to offer help to a person who is crying, whether it is a good habit to wash your hands after going to the bathroom, whether there can be such things as evil demons, let alone whether specific statements about such demons are true – conflict with each other because other ways of life are mistaken, or less developed and less enlightened than our own. In other words, these responses reduce the differing claims of other ways of life to inferior variations of our own, familiar claims. Dangling pieces, on the other hand, show how much is left out of that reduction, what does not readily fit from another way of life into the terms of our own. To take Chachi practices and beliefs without a space for something like what we might call a mode of quiet understanding, a faculty of keen observation, a highly developed social space with minimal physical markers, a rich "supernatural" domain, is to draw a caricature of their way of life. And it is because of this lack of match or fit between caricature and that way of life itself that the deeply engaged person tends to reject these other solutions to the problem of cultural diversity.

Universalism, perhaps, seeks to belittle the differing claims of another way of life less than the absolutist and evolutionist responses to cultural diversity. It wants to say that differing claims are not inferior to ours, because, in essence, these claims are not really different from ours. Dangling pieces, however, emphasize how much difference universals must take into account. We cannot simply equate a way of life that is richly structured by a mode of quiet understanding, or that contains a vast "supernatural" realm, with one in which both of these features are missing. They are not simple variants of each other, in which similar shapes have been built out of the same blocks, but are unique structures, in many cases, built out of different, incompatible blocks. Dangling pieces, like the complexity of conflict, stress how thin universals must be to stretch across different ways of life. They might reveal something about us, about how we find other ways of life to be like our own, but they fail to capture the richness of cultural diversity. They do not so much grasp the phenomena as wash them away, and it is this cleansing of difference, like the belittling of difference that we saw earlier in the reductivist move, that the deeply engaged person cannot accept. She cannot make less of the difference because she is immersed in it and sees it so well.

1.2.6 The First Person

The deeply engaged person does not stand in an abstract relation to the facts of cultural diversity. She lives and breathes them. There is no place where she leaves her daily acts, thoughts, and feelings behind. She need not look far for the facts of cultural diversity because she walks, sleeps, bathes, laughs, and gets sick amidst them. She finds them when her own life unwittingly stumbles upon, or crashes into, them. They appear as the riddles that she cannot help but turn round in her head. She learns them through her own embarrassment, frustration, and wonder. They are the fruit of her own insight and misadventure. Malinowski explains that it is improper for a Trobriander child to be said to look like his mother, or his maternal kinsmen. And he specifies: "I was introduced to this rule of *savoir vivre* in the usual way, by making a *faux pas.*"[33]

It is through lived context and shared acts that the deeply engaged person acquires knowledge of another way of life. Over the course of preparing food and sharing meals together, joining ceremonies, and attending meetings together, washing clothes and bathing in the river together, rowing canoes and running for shelter from storms together, she builds relationships with the people. This is what leads a participant observer like Malinowski to call the Trobrianders closest to him not merely, "informants," but, "friends." The deeply engaged person discovers the facts of cultural diversity and synthesizes them through these rich interpersonal exchanges. "It would have been impossible for me to ascertain the rules of custom and the moral ideas of the natives," Malinowski acknowledges, "without the subjective outpourings of these friends of mine."[34]

Often, the circumstances of deep engagement are not simple, and the interpersonal relations that we develop do not rest on friendship alone. Evans-Pritchard was a government worker, Malinowski was a refugee from world war, and I myself was a teacher, a conservation worker, a mother, a wife. Geertz expresses doubt about the deeply engaged person's success in fostering authentic relationships with the

---

[33] Malinowski, *The Sexual Life of Savages in North-Western Melanesia: An Ethnographic Account of Courtship, Marriage, and Family Life among the Natives of the Trobriand Islands, British New Guinea,* 204.

[34] Ibid., 284.

people. "[S]o many anthropologists leave the field seeing tears in the eyes of their informants that, I feel quite sure, are not really there."[35] His concern has to do, in part, with the instrumentality of the informant-anthropologist relationship. The anthropologist uses the natives to study their culture, while the natives use the anthropologist to gain prestige, employment, or other goods. It seems to me, however, that same-culture friendships, just as often as their cross-culture counterparts, serve personal interests and stem from circumstantial beginnings. But it would be unjust if we reduced our characterization of either kind of friendship to merely these instrumental aspects.

Although he is pessimistic, Geertz does not preclude the possibility of genuine intercultural, interpersonal relationships. In his wryness about the tears, he means to draw attention to the asymmetry in the power relations between the local people and the Western outsider.[36] It has often struck me that the role of the deeply engaged person is something like that of an infant prince.[37] In one sense, I have far more power than the local people. The mere fact that I have the resources to make the long journey from my home to their territory already sets us apart. I have the freedom, money, food, means of transportation, and savoir-faire to explore the world, while this has never been an option for them. I bring with me food, clothes, and medicine of a quality and variety they have never seen. I speak the lingua franca of the most powerful nations of the world. I have dollars in my pockets that can buy me food when I am hungry, medicine when I am sick, and help when I am overburdened.

We could imagine situations in which the relations of power at play in deep engagement were more balanced. Perhaps something like an intercultural exchange would be the most equal arrangement, where people from my culture visit the Chachi, and vice versa, in turns. Supposing there were a way to arrange and agree to all this, that it didn't compromise the integrity of either culture, that the resources for the program came from some outside, impartial source, there would still be difficulties. For instance, those who went first, or those who were currently having their turn, would be at an advantage over the rest. Certainly, we could also imagine instances of something like deep engagement in which the dominant power ran the other way around, in which the deeply engaged person was powerless, immersed in another way of life entirely against her will. This is the situation of a prisoner of war, or of a captured slave. But the deep engagement that we are concerned with in

---

[35] Clifford Geertz, "Thinking as a Moral Act: Ethical Dimensions of Anthropological Fieldwork in the New States," in *Available Light: Anthropological Reflections on Philosophical Topics* (Princeton, NJ: Princeton University Press, 2000), 33.

[36] His purpose, specifically, is to address the ethical irony of this asymmetry in a globalizing world. There is much to say about this, and I am sorry not to have the space to address it here.

[37] While I have used the feminine gender for all of my generic statements about the deeply engaged person, I cannot bring myself to write "princess" here. For one reason, "princess" incorrectly connotes the image of a spoiled person with frivolous beauty. More importantly, I distinctly experienced this particular power relation with the Chachi, and also with more Westernized Ecuadorian groups, as an instance of masculinization. In the situations where this relation was most apparent, there was no feminine role that could hold as much power as my U.S. status afforded me, and so it seemed I was slipped into a masculine role by default.

this chapter, the kind that is voluntary and leaves ample space for anthropological reflection and analysis, is clearly a privilege; and the asymmetry of power arises from this basic fact.

Nonetheless, there is a sense in which the (willingly) deeply engaged person is also powerless. She is an *infant* prince. And this sense, surprisingly, ends up being very useful to her in grasping the other way of life. As we have seen in our discussion of reflective symmetry, among the Chachi, I am childlike. I do not observe well, contain my emotions, or move my body carefully like an adult. I also cannot perform the work of an adult. I cannot carry two buckets of water up from the riverbank without spilling, balance the weight of a trunk of plantain using a strap across my forehead, or even row a canoe without turning in circles. I know, moreover, nothing about my environment. I have no idea that the thick, giant spider hanging by my clothes is harmless, and actually helps people out by eating the cockroaches, or that the cute millipede curled up on the forest floor can shoot venom in my eye if I get too close. I have, at the same time, no idea who the important people are or how the social systems and conventions work. I do not understand why it is disgusting to wash my hands after going to the bathroom, or silly to walk through the village saying, "good morning," in Cha'palaachi to all of the villagers.

Some kind people may try to help me in my weakness, out of what we might label personal interest, pity, curiosity, or perhaps a love of teaching and sharing. But this is good for the deeply engaged person. This is the same set of motivations (though without the familial ties) that would lead the local people to rear a child of their own kind. And it is from a childlike state that the deeply engaged person must construct the knowledge of a mature, acculturated adult in the other way of life. So, it is helpful that she finds herself in a helpless state. It sets out exactly the right conditions and relations for her to grow into an understanding of that way of life.[38] She never learns exactly like a native; she never sheds her previous knowledge and experience in order to start "fresh," "like a baby." But she does revisit those earlier stages of learning in an abbreviated and approximated sort of way. And it is this new construction, this new growth in her own person, that allows her to wiggle her way into a life that may be radically different from her own, with domains of action and thought drawn as she could not otherwise fathom, and pieces of experience that find no ready expression in her native terms.

We have seen that the deeply engaged person comes across the facts of cultural diversity not as obscure tidbits in a text, but as rich experiences integrated and interwoven in the context of a way of life. Her upfront, in-the-fire involvement forces onto her the punctuated detail that brings out the coherence of attributive symmetry,

---

[38] "[O]ver and again, I committed breaches of etiquette, which the natives, familiar enough with me, were not slow in pointing out. I had to learn how to behave, and to a certain extent, I acquired 'the feeling' for native good and bad manners. With this, and with the capacity of enjoying their company and sharing some of their games and amusements, I began to feel that I was indeed in touch with the natives, and this is certainly the preliminary condition of being able to carry on successful fieldwork." Malinowski, *Argonauts of the Western Pacific; an Account of Native Enterprise and Adventure in the Archipelagoes of Melanesian New Guinea,* 8.

the irony of reflective symmetry, the insolubility of complex conflict, and the weight of dangling pieces. Her experiences etch the unique shape of another way of life onto her own awareness and keep the impression so vivid, so rich and central that she is compelled to find a consummate characterization for the facts of cultural diversity. She cannot simply reduce, water down, or ignore them. In this sense, the first person reinforces all of the other features of deep engagement and their effects that we have previously seen.

Yet, the first person accomplishes something beyond motivating relativism and complicating the alternative views. It helps to dissolve a sort of riddle commonly brought up against relativism. Or, perhaps more accurately stated, it explains how this was never any kind of difficulty, or obstacle in the first place. As we will discuss in more detail in the following chapter, relativism is often accused of being an incoherent view. Part of this challenge has to do with the perspective of relativism itself: How can you know of ways of life that are significantly different from your own, if you have nothing but relative concepts and relative standards of evaluation to go by? Or, if there is no absolute perspective, how do you grasp truths that are not your own?[39] The perspective through which this is possible is precisely that of the deeply engaged person. With the first person feature, we see how the relativist can grasp a radically different way of life without owning it, how she can have a sense of its content and shape without fully translating or adequately rendering them in the terms of her own way of life. Her understanding is never an abstract exercise of analysis. She never ceases to be herself or to inhabit her perspective. The explanations she offers must be tethered back to the terms and ideas of her own way of life. For better or for worse, her grasp is never that of a native. Yet, through lived experiences, shared relationships, and a return to a more childlike state, she builds a bridge to a very different way of life and earns an understanding of its integrity, richness, and difference.

1.3 How Close Does This Get Us to Relativism?

We can see in Table 1.2 a summary of the distinctive features of deep engagement and the ways in which they complicate the alternative accounts of cultural diversity, on the one hand, and motivate relativism, on the other. Deep engagement brings out the coherence of another way of life (attributive symmetry), the inconsistencies of our own way of life (reflective symmetry), the radical difference between our conflicting claims with other ways of life (complexity of conflict), the important elements in other ways of life that find no ready equivalent in our own (dangling pieces), and the rich, experiential learning that brings the facts of cultural diversity to light (first person). This makes it difficult for the deeply engaged person to accept

---

[39] I address these concerns, as well as some of the related literature, in more detail in Chap. 2. I also elaborate further on the relativist's response to them in Chap. 4.

Table 1.2 Distinctive features of deep engagement

Feature	Complicates Crude Absolutism	Complicates (Classic) Evolutionism	Complicates Pragmatic Evolutionism	Complicates Universalism	Reinforces Unique Shape of Other Way of Life	Validates Coherence and Effectiveness of Other Way of Life
Attributive Symmetry: Practices and beliefs of other way of life seem coherent and reasonable in context.	Yes. It is hard to claim that divergent practices and beliefs are inferior or mistaken once they appear coherent and reasonable in context.	Not necessarily. Inasmuch as other ways of life are somewhat evolved, (Classic) Evolutionism expects them to be coherent and reasonable.	Not necessarily. Inasmuch as other ways of life are somewhat evolved, Pragmatic Evolutionism expects them to be coherent and reasonable.	No. Universalism expects other ways of life to be coherent and reasonable inasmuch as they embrace universal practices and beliefs.	Yes. It appears that what allows another way of life to be coherent and reasonable, despite divergent practices and beliefs, is its unique shape.	Yes. Attributive Symmetry underscores coherence and effectiveness of other way of life.
Reflective Symmetry: Our own practices and beliefs seem less coherent and reasonable from the perspective of another way of life.	Yes. Throws into question the superiority of our way of life.	Yes. Throws into question whether one way of life is more developed than others.	Yes. Throws into question whether one way of life is more developed than others.	Not necessarily. Universalism does not require our practices/beliefs to be more developed than others. However, too much reflective symmetry might suggest that we ourselves have a poor grasp of universals.	Yes. It appears that each way of life organizes life with its own set of advantages and disadvantages.	Yes. Places other ways of life more on a par with our own.

(continued)

Table 1.2 (continued)

	No. Crude Absolutism	No. (Classic)	No. Pragmatic Evolutionism	Yes. Universals	Yes. Complexity of Conflict	Somewhat.
Complexity of Conflict: Disagreement between two different ways of life stretches across different domains, which are themselves carved out differently by each way of life.	Absolutism can insist that other ways of life are simply wrong for carving out domains differently than us.	Evolutionism can insist that other ways of life are simply less developed because they carve out domains differently than us.	Evolutionism can insist that other ways of life are simply less developed because they carve out domains differently than us.	Universals without cultural context are too thin to evaluate divergent practices/beliefs. With context, they reinforce the radical difference between our practices/beliefs.	Complexity of Conflict defines the unique shape of another way of life.	Complexity of Conflict validates the coherence and effectiveness of another way of life inasmuch as it elaborates on the structures recognized through Attributive Symmetry.
Dangling Pieces: Meaning and content are left out of our analysis of another way of life when their practices and beliefs are reduced to the familiar terms of our own.	Yes. Highlights the important aspects of another way of life that are left out when it is reduced to the terms of our way of life.	Yes. Highlights the important aspects of another way of life that are left out when it is reduced to the terms of some "best" way of life.	Yes. Highlights the important aspects of another way of life that are left out when it is reduced to the terms of some most successful or "best" way of life.	Yes. Emphasizes how thinly universals must stretch in order to encompass the divergent practices/beliefs of other ways of life.	Yes. Underscores the depth of uniqueness in the shape of another way of life.	Somewhat. Draws attention to pieces critical to understanding coherence and effectiveness of other way of life.
First Person: One who is deeply engaged in another way of life experiences it in her own person, through lived experiences and relationships with others.	Yes. Fills out context of other way of life too vividly to be able to claim that divergent practices/beliefs are simply wrong.	Somewhat. Fills out context of other way of life vividly enough that it is tricky (but not impossible) to claim that divergent practices/beliefs are incorrect/less developed.	Somewhat. Fills out context of other way of life vividly enough that it is tricky (but not impossible) to claim that divergent practices/beliefs are incorrect/less developed.	Somewhat. Fills out context of other way of life vividly enough that universals must be very thin to encompass divergent practices/beliefs.	Yes. Vividly emphasizes the unique shape of another way of life.	Yes. Explains how coherence and effectiveness of other way of life can be grasped without violating relativistic constraints.

a view which states that the conflicting practices and beliefs of another way of life are simply mistaken (absolutism), less developed and incomplete (evolutionism), or really just the same as our own (universalism). Instead, she sees that each way of life has its own unique shape, its own share of what we might call coherence and effectiveness. And she is led to the thought that outside a particular way of life, our normative claims cannot stand. This holds as much for our practical normative claims about how the world should be, as for our theoretical normative claims about what the world is. It solves the puzzle that deep engagement makes so pressing, the puzzle of how we can acknowledge the integrity of practices and beliefs that conflict so deeply with our own. It is, at the same time, the kernel of relativism.

The exposition of the key features of relativism is not in itself an argument for relativism. It is an explanation of why we might consider relativism in the first place. Certainly, it will not and cannot sway everyone. Some will disagree that these are the features and effects of deep engagement. Others will claim that since they have no experience of deep engagement, the argument simply has no context or sway with them. But the point is not that some random experience, like wearing green hats on Mondays, makes relativism a compelling response to the facts of cultural diversity and the alternative views less attractive. Rather, the point is that the experience of cultural diversity itself, first-hand, in all its complexity and richness, is what makes relativism more compelling. That is, the very act of uncovering, exploring, and thinking through the detail of cultural diversity, pushes us to deal with it in relativistic terms, in terms that would grant autonomy and integrity to the practices and beliefs of other ways of life, without belittling this difference as insignificant (universalism), or as due to inferiority (absolutism and evolutionism).

Surely, a contingency like engaging deeply with another way of life is one that matters. And in our global world, it is not a contingency that we can easily ignore. We are well aware of other ways of life and their divergent practices and beliefs. We also generally have great respect for specialists and studies of detail. The features of deep engagement might not cut through all of the resistance that we have to the very idea of relativism, but they should be enough to convince us at least to keep relativism on the table, to consider it as a possible view among others. And so now we should be ready to move on in our subsequent chapters to examine the coherence, power, and fruitfulness of relativism.

Chapter 2
The Relativist, Anti-relativist Dance

2.1 Introduction

Relativism emerges as a response to both the diversity and dissonance that we find in the ways that different groups of people order, describe, and engage with the world.[1] It stems from the thought that not only are each group's ideas of what is good, right, true, etc. relative to factors such as language, culture, historical epoch, etc., but that there is no ultimate standard or neutral way of measuring such ideas against each other. There is something intuitive, and yet, at the same time, radical and unsettling about relativism. How can we assert anything at all, if even the theory of relativism itself must stand on relative ground? It seems to embrace diversity at pain of undermining our own claims to truth, knowledge, and rightness.[2] This is one reason why many thinkers have reacted against relativistic theories, accusing them of being self-refuting and/or incoherent.

We find an early example of the anti-relativist charges of self-refutation and incoherence in Plato's criticism of Protagoras, the sophist whose famous dictum was that, "Man is the measure of all things."[3] Although responses to relativism, such as Plato's, have played an important role in the development of Western philosophy, relativism itself has much more infrequently been the subject of careful elaboration.[4] It has more commonly been a negative point of reference, a strawman in

---

[1] See Chap. 1.

[2] Michael Krausz and Jack W. Meiland, "Introduction," in *Relativism: Cognitive and Moral*, eds. Michael Krausz and Jack W. Meiland (Notre Dame, IN: Notre Dame University Press, 1982), 5.

[3] Socrates summarizes Protagoras' position for Theaetetus: "Man is the measure of all things: of things which are, that they are, and of things which are not, that they are not." Plato, "Theaetetus," trans. M.J. Levett, revised by Miles Burnyeat, in *Plato Complete Works* (Indianapolis, IN: Hackett Publishing Company, 1997), 169 (151e–152a).

[4] Cf Chris Gowans, "Moral Relativism," *The Stanford Encyclopedia of Philosophy (Fall 2010 Edition)*, ed. Edward N. Zalta. http://plato.stanford.edu/archives/fall2010/entries/moral-relativism/.
Gowans, "Moral Relativism," introduction.

© Springer Nature Switzerland AG 2020
A. Luboff, *Facing Relativism*, Synthese Library 425,
https://doi.org/10.1007/978-3-030-43341-3_2

relation to whom contrasting, positive content is developed. In fact, the label, "relativism" has such a pejorative connotation that contemporary theories such as pragmatism, which in many ways might be considered mature versions of relativism, rarely go by that name. Relativism has been more frequently developed and embraced, at least in an open way, on the fringes of traditional philosophy, in areas such as anthropology, literary theory, the social sciences, and popular culture.

Because charges of self-refutation and incoherence target the very formulation and formulability of relativism, they are often used to justify its strawman treatment. They stand behind a poorly developed, yet all too common, reaction to relativism, which is the immediate and wholesale rejection of its very idea.[5] But such a knee-jerk reaction is usually a good indication that much more lies beneath the surface. And so, in this chapter, I will urge that we look with more careful attention at the coherence of relativism. I will ask that even those repulsed by the view suspend judgment for a moment and lean in to the discomfort that it raises. Let us explore in detail the dance back and forth between the relativist and the anti-relativist. Let us look at the moments in their argument not for the mere sake of winning the argument, but for the greater benefit of growing from the dialogue.

Rather than turning away from relativism, my intention in this chapter is to use the charges of self-refutation and incoherence as an occasion for elaborating some of the view's positive content. In part two, I will examine some contemporary examples of the charges of self-refutation and incoherence in order to give a fuller sense of the relativist, anti-relativist dialectic. While there are certainly self-refuting and incoherent formulations of relativism, I will propose that these alleged paradoxes are not inevitable pitfalls, inherent in relativism itself. Relativists often complain that the said inconsistencies and incoherence are generated by forcing their statements into the language and perspective of the absolutist.[6] The anti-relativist responds, characteristically, that the relativist must give a fuller picture of the alternate meaning which her statements are instead supposed to have.[7] I will offer this fuller picture and suggest how the relativist can escape the paradoxes, by appealing to three core ideas: a relativistic distinction between internal and external claims, analogical thought as the key to grasping alternatives from a relativist perspective, and resistance as a relativistic indicator of world-determined content. In this first section, I will begin with a more basic exploration of the idea of relativism, and of the class of objections associated with self-refutation and incoherence.

---

[5] Jack W. Meiland, "On the Paradox of Cognitive Relativism," *Metaphilosophy* 11, no. 2. (1980): 115.

[6] Siegel considers this objection as made by Harold I. Brown, Jack W. Meiland, Chris Swoyer, James N. Jordan and M.F. Burnyeat. See Harvey Siegel, "Relativism, Truth and Incoherence," *Synthese* 68 (1986): 225–259. Reprinted as "The Incoherence Argument and the Notion of Relative Truth" in Harvey Siegel, *Relativism Refuted* (Boston: D. Reidel Publishing Company, 1987), 3–31.

[7] See, for example, Siegel, "Relativism," esp. 234–40.

2.1.1 A Definition of Relativism

Relativism in its various forms targets the key elements with which we act and understand ourselves in the world: truth, rightness, knowledge, reality, values, goodness, etc.[8] About such elements it makes two important non-absolutist claims: (1) that they are relative to contingent or contextual factors such as perspective, conceptual scheme, culture, historical epoch, etc. – what we might call "frames of reference"[9] by way of shorthand; and (2) that they are inevaluable both independently of frames of reference and across one frame to another.[10] (1) is the part of our definition which contains the word "relative" and is perhaps most often associated with the label "relativism." The restrictions in (2), on the other hand, are the part which assures that relativity is more than a mere transitory phenomenon and that the theory does not resolve into a form of absolutism.[11] In some definitions, these restrictions may be represented as incompatibility or untranslatability.[12]

Absolutism, like relativism, may best be distinguished as a family of views, and variants from the two families may clash in several ways. The greatest point in contention between the two sides is whether key elements such as truth, rightness, knowledge, reality, values, goodness, etc. *have any status* which is determined independently of frames of reference. Absolutism in its variations can concede a number of points to relativism while holding onto an ultimate sense in which key elements enjoy some status beyond frames of reference. In what we might think of as a

---

[8] A particular version of relativism may target any or all of these elements.

[9] Both frames of references and the groups to which they apply are idealizations. Their boundaries are variable and fluid. The most interesting cases of relativity will be when we are comparing groups with more than one member each, and between which there is substantial divergence in their key elements. Otherwise, relativistic analysis may still apply, but a different question surfaces: Why resort to relativistic analysis? Why bring in such a radical theory for what can be explained just as easily with milder and more common means? Absolutist theories can accommodate these cases of relativity with simple means, for example, by granting differences of opinion within a group, or acknowledging sensitivity to context, as in the case of indexical expressions.

[10] There is no standard definition of relativism. The reader may wish to compare this definition with others, e.g. Krausz and Meiland, 3; Chris Swoyer, "Relativism," *The Stanford Encyclopedia of Philosophy* (Spring 2014 Edition), ed. Edward N. Zalta, http://plato.stanford.edu/archives/spr2014/entries/relativism/, Sect. 1; Carol Rovane, "Did Williams Find the Truth in Relativism," in *Reading Bernard Williams,* ed. Daniel Callcut (New York: Routledge Taylor & Francis Group, 2009), 43–69; and Carol Rovane, "Why Scientific Realism May Invite Relativism," in *Naturalism and Normativity,* eds. Mario de Caro and David Macarthur (New York: Columbia University Press, 2010), 100–09.

[11] Cf Krausz and Meiland, "Introduction," 2.

[12] I have chosen here "inevaluability" over these other possibilities because it veers less toward the paradoxical formulations of relativism. Terms such as "incompatibility" and "untranslatability," by negating a dimension in which alternatives are compatible and translatable, could appear to be making an implicit (and ultimately self-refuting or incoherent) use of a universal perspective within relativism itself. Although I believe that the solution I offer in the second part of this chapter can overcome the potential difficulties of these terms, I have at this point, for ease of exposition, avoided them.

classical absolutist view,[13] the absolutist concedes none of these points; he disagrees with all of our definition of relativism. The status of key elements is determined entirely outside of frames of reference; the latter, if they play any kind of important role, tend only to confuse us about the real nature of truth, rightness, knowledge, etc. So, for example, neck elongation, as practiced by the Padaung tribes of Southeast Asia, is not beautiful for them because of its social and historical context – the stories they tell about it, the meaning they describe to it, the forms of power and relationship that it encodes. Rather, it is beautiful for anyone – of the Padaung or another culture – only inasmuch as it captures the ultimate and immutable form of Beauty itself.

On the other hand, a contextualized or perspectival absolutism can grant all of part (1) of the definition of relativism and still maintain that key elements are determined in an important way outside of frames of reference.[14] According to this view, key elements ultimately depend on a reality which transcends frames of reference, but this reality is grasped incompletely by each frame, through the contingencies of a particular context or lens. In this way, key elements are relative to frames of reference. However, since the ultimate sense of key elements lies beyond frames of reference, there are grounds for comparing and unifying relative key elements from different frames. This conflicts with part (2) of our definition of relativism in its entirety. The perspectival absolutist may admit that his grasp of these neutral grounds is imperfect or incomplete, but because his key elements aim towards an ultimate reality, he can still use them as a standard for evaluating key elements across frames of reference. On this view, for example, we might say that neck elongation is beautiful for the Padaung inasmuch as their social and historical context captures aspects of absolute Beauty itself. However, when we compare neck elongation with the Western practice of not altering neck length, we might still say that an unaltered neck is more beautiful, not only for us, because of our social and historical context, but for anyone, because an unaltered neck comes closest to the absolute form of Beauty. We might add, moreover, that anyone who has arrived at true and deep understanding of Beauty can appreciate this truth.[15]

Finally, we might note that there is a variety of perspectival absolutism which grants all of part (1) of our definition, and the first half of part (2). According to pragmatic fallibilism, key elements are relative to frames of reference, and they are inevaluable independently of them; but, there is still a way of evaluating key elements across one frame to another that is importantly non-relative. Pragmatic fallibilists espouse a (somewhat dogmatic) faith in the progress of science and the key

---

[13] For instance, the Platonic theory of forms.

[14] Cf Krausz and Meiland, "Introduction," 1; Siegel, "Relativism," 232; and Rovane, "Did Williams," 45–46, 49–50.

[15] Of course, the dispute does not have to be resolved in this way. For instance, a perspectival absolutist who is impressed by Padaung culture might instead claim that elongated necks are more beautiful because *they* come closest to the absolute form of Beauty.

elements it uncovers.[16] So, even though we cannot evaluate alternative key elements from outside our own framework, we can affirm that our own key elements improve over time. History provides us with a route of escape from the contingencies of historicity itself. Although we cannot step outside our own lives to grasp or make sense of absolutes, we can, over time, perceive ourselves converging toward them. We can calibrate *through* our contingencies to a convergent, absolute plain which, although we do not grasp it perfectly, allows us to evaluate alternatives in a non-relativistic way. Ultimately, some truths, values, etc. reach closer to this Archimedean point. They advance farther in the trajectory of progress, and they simply are, by virtue of their closeness, better than others.[17] We might say, then, that, while elongated necks are traditionally beautiful for the Padaung, unaltered necks are ultimately more beautiful, because they come closer to Beauty itself. Unaltered necks are a less complete and accurate expression of beauty. Although, as humans, we cannot quite fathom or express absolute Beauty, we can see, by virtue of the fact that most contemporary and successful cultures, and even some contemporary members of the Padaung themselves, find unaltered (not elongated) necks beautiful, that they are, in fact, more truly beautiful.[18]

The purpose of our definition of relativism, in all of its parts, is to distinguish it from any form of absolutism. After all, a possible response to the charges of self-refutation and incoherence is simply to give up relativism. These variations of absolutism give us a sense of the various points at which the relativist can give up and the absolutist can give in. What I hope to show, however, is that the relativist can defend herself against the anti-relativist's charges without at any point giving up her view.

---

[16] For a clear expression of this view, see Karl Popper, "Facts, Standards, and Truth," in *Moral Relativism a Reader*, eds. Paul K. Moser and Thomas L. Carson (New York: Oxford University Press, 2001) 32–52 (esp. 36–39). Putnam also seems to have a similar view. See, for example, Hilary Putnam, *Ethics without Ontology* (Cambridge, MA: Harvard University Press, 2005), 121–29. Although these examples are part of a different literature, what we are calling here, "pragmatic fallibilism," is quite close in structure to the "pragmatic evolutionism" discussed in Chap. 1.

[17] Relativity and inevaluability are expressed together on this view as fallibility; they are, given the contingencies and limitations of human experience, the inevitable failure of each group's key elements to reach absolute truth, rightness, knowledge, reality, values, goodness, etc. Pragmatism, on the other hand, is what captures the absolutist aspect of this view; it is the lived experience of working – through force, intellect, trial and error, perseverance, etc. – that paves a path closer and closer to such absolutes.

[18] This particular example may be unfair for a pragmatic fallibilist such as Popper, because it focuses on aesthetic, not empirical, truths and measures success by social, not narrowly scientific, progress. However, the form of the example remains broadly the same in either domain, and the reader may find it instructive to consider any differences in the way our intuitions play out between the two.

2.1.2 Details of the Accusations

There are countless varieties of relativism, depending on which key elements are
taken as relative and to what factors.[19] In this chapter, I will focus in particular on
ethical and epistemic relativism, two general varieties of relativism that are common targets of the charges of self-refutation and incoherence. These two types, as
should be obvious from our definition, bear a structural similarity, and so we might
expect to find similarities between them at the level of both criticism and defense.[20]
In considering them together, I hope to be offering a model of anti-relativist accusations and relativist responses that can be easily extrapolated and applied to other
varieties of relativism. At the same time, I intend to leave room for a very broad kind
of cultural relativism, in which ethical and epistemic dimensions, along with others,
are interwoven.

Most importantly, in addressing these two types of relativism together, I hope to
stave off what strikes me as another unfortunate strategy in responding to the charges
of self-refutation and incoherence. Quite often, a thinker will defend a relativist
position in one domain by supporting it with absolutist assumptions in another.
Indeed, the buttressing relationships between forms of absolutism and relativism
across domains such as the epistemic and the ethical are quite interesting. Yet what
I aim to show is that this strategy is at a certain level unnecessary: on its own, relativism has an adequate response to the challenges of self-refutation and incoherence, without fleeing to forms of absolutism in any domain.

Self-refutation, inconsistency, and *incoherence* are interrelated terms. A charge
of one often leads to the charge of another, and they are sometimes used inter-
changeably in the literature. Moreover, those who do make the effort to distinguish
carefully between the terms do not necessarily differentiate them in the same way.
While I will not claim to give a comprehensive or ultimate definition of any one of
these terms, I would like to distinguish among them in order to discuss different
aspects of the accusations leveled against relativism. Although these terms are common in formal logic, and indeed part of the argument against relativism seems to
rest on the idea that there is something formally or foundationally wrong with it, I
shall try to use fairly broad language in order to avoid the impression that the problem is reducible to *mere* logic. I will thus define the terms as follows:

Inconsistent: within the theory itself, and/or that which is directly entailed by
                     the theory, a particular statement or position and its contradiction
                     are both upheld.
Self-refuting: the theory implies its own falsity.
Incoherent: the parts of the theory do not hold together, either logically or
                     conceptually.

---

[19] Chris Swoyer, "Relativism," Sect. 1.5, sets out a very helpful framework for relativism and cal-
culates that, given rather coarse distinctions, there are 162 varieties of relativism. "With finer distinctions, or with combinations…the number climbs well into the thousands."

[20] Krausz and Meiland, "Introduction," 8–9.

It may help first to think of these terms with respect to a simpler theory than relativism. Imagine that we have a very limited color theory called, "Orange," which states that, "All entities are either red or yellow, but not both." Further, imagine that we use this theory to describe very simple entities of one color, such as, "The apple is red," and, "The sun is yellow." Up to this point, we might not recognize any problem with the theory. Imagine, however, that the theory also claims both that, "The stoplight is yellow," and that, "The stoplight is red." We can see right away, then, that the theory is inconsistent. We know from the definition of the theory that all objects are either yellow or red, but not both. Using this definition, we can infer from the statement, "The stoplight is yellow," that, "The stoplight is not red." However, we already saw that the theory contains the statement, "The stoplight is red." Since the theory directly entails both a statement and its contradiction (the stoplight is and is not red), it is *inconsistent.*

If we look more closely at the definition of the theory itself, we might discover a new worry. According to Orange, "All entities are either red or yellow, but not both," but what about the theory Orange itself? What color is it? If we stipulate that Orange is red, then how do we account for the fact that it contains, "yellow"? And if we stipulate that it is yellow, how do we account for the fact that it contains, "red"? If it is both red and yellow, then something *does* exist that is both red and yellow, namely, the theory itself! If it is neither red nor yellow, but some separate color (orange?), then the theory itself proves that an entity of another color exists.[21] Since the very statement of Orange demonstrates that an entity that is not exclusively either red or yellow exists, it is *self-refuting.*

Finally, as we look over the theory Orange, we may start to notice that it contains much more than a simple contradiction that can be neatly fixed. From the stoplight example, we can generate many more contradictions, such as, "The stoplight is and is not yellow," and, "The stoplight is and is not both yellow and red." From the self-refutation example, we see that the theory itself is not well-formulated. In this case, then, the theory does not hold together either logically or conceptually, and we may claim that it is not only inconsistent and self-refuting, but *incoherent.*

We may begin to notice from this example that the three charges against relativism are interrelated. If, for instance, the inconsistency we identify involves the definition of the theory itself, this may lead to a charge of self-refutation. On the other hand, if a part of the theory (its definition, the statements it contains, or those it directly entails) is inconsistent, it may break apart with contradictions and lead to a charge of (logical) incoherence. However, the three charges do not always imply each other. A charge of self-refutation usually means that we can generate an inconsistency, but it need not be based on one, as we will see in the case of Maurice Mandelbaum's criticisms.[22] Although it is easy to develop the charge of logical

---

[21] At this point, the reader may be noticing many ways to save our poor theory (for example, by introducing a distinction between first and second order statements), or the reader may be thinking that it was quite ill defined to begin with. These both seem to me to be fair responses to the example, which, nonetheless, captures the sorts of complications that relativism tends to find itself in.

[22] Section 2.2.

incoherence from inconsistency, we will also find that the related charge of conceptual incoherence runs much deeper.[23]

2.2 The Relativist ~ Anti-relativist Dance

2.2.1 Preface

Now that the preliminaries are out of the way, let us explore the accusations of self-refutation and incoherence through the dynamic argument back and forth between the relativist and the anti-relativist. The dialectic may proceed in any number of ways, not necessarily as described below. There may be different arguments, or the arguments may be articulated and grouped together in other ways. Some moments of the dialectic may be omitted, or it may take turns other than those we envisage here. My purpose here is not so much to give a fully comprehensive account of the dialectic, as to show a general course of argument, the most common steps in the dance – to give a sense of the anti-relativist accusations as they arise, and of how the relativist may with integrity respond. Charges of self-refutation and incoherence are often addressed as just one aspect of an argument for or against relativism. Although these charges tend to take center stage, the examples below are not meant to represent any of the thinkers' views on relativism comprehensively.

For the purpose of exposition, I will focus on four moments in the relativist ~ anti-relativist dance:

(1) **The anti-relativist's initial charge of self-refutation:** by its own lights, relativism is false (Sect. 2.2). Ethical relativism blatantly contradicts itself (Sect. 2.2.1), and epistemic relativism either implies its own falsity or relies on absolutist assumptions, thereby tacitly refuting itself (Sect. 2.2.2.)
(2) **The relativist's first response:** Relativism does not rely on absolutist assumptions or refute itself as long as it maintains a distinction between internal and external claims (Sect. 2.3).
(3) **The anti-relativist's charge of incoherence:** the theory of relativism cannot hold itself together (Sect. 2.4). Epistemic relativism cannot be formulated without making implicit use of an absolute perspective and collapses into arbitrariness (Sect. 2.4.1), as does ethical relativism (Sect. 2.4.2).
(4) **The relativist's more complete response:** analogical thought and world resistance give coherence and content to the relativist's view without appealing to an absolute perspective in a self-refuting or obfuscating way (Sect. 2.5).

---

[23] Section 2.4.

2.2.2 The Charge of Self-Refutation

2.2.2.1 Against Ethical Relativism

Let us begin round one of the dance by looking at how the charges of self-refutation emerge. In a short chapter in his concise, semi-popular work, *Morality: An Introduction to Ethics,* Bernard Williams identifies a clearly inconsistent form of ethical relativism. He defines this theory by three propositions:[24]

(1) 'right' means (can only be coherently understood as meaning) 'right for a given society';
(2) 'right for a society' is to be understood in a functionalist sense;
(3) (therefore) it is wrong for people in one society to condemn, interfere with, etc. the values of another society.

As should be obvious from Williams' formulation, the inconsistency arises between the first and third propositions of the theory. While the former limits the use of 'right' to a particular society, the latter uses 'right' in a universal sense to prescribe tolerance across different societies.[25] So, 'right' is both restricted and cannot be restricted to a particular society. Because the theory upholds two mutually contradictory positions, it is inconsistent. Moreover, because the inconsistency involves the major propositions of the theory itself, it is also self-refuting.

Williams admits that this is a vulgar, unsophisticated formulation of relativism.[26] We might also note that it is rather different from our definition of relativism in Sect. 1.2 above. Although proposition (1) fits part (1) of our definition fairly well, we do not have the functionalist qualifications of proposition (2).[27] Moreover, proposition (3) establishes a much stronger result than the inevaluability in part (2) of our definition. Indeed, it is the strong normative dimensions of proposition (3) that seem to get the theory into trouble. Yet we would be wrong to conclude from this that the inconsistency which Williams highlights is peculiar to just one form of relativism and that it can be avoided with a simple reformulation of the theory. It is, in fact, a specific instance of a more general problem. Relativism must be very careful in how it navigates the relationship between what we might call the particular and the universal, the internal and the external, or the local and the global.[28] While some

---

[24] Bernard Williams, "An Inconsistent Form of Relativism," *Relativism: Cognitive and Moral,* eds. Michael Krausz and Jack W. Meiland (Notre Dame, IN: University of Notre Dame Press, 1982), 171. Reprinted from Bernard Williams, *Morality: An Introduction to Ethics* (New York: Harper & Row, 1972), 22–26.

[25] *Ibid.*

[26] Still, Williams argues, it is an appropriate target of critique because it is the most pervasive and influential form of relativism, p. 171.

[27] I do not see how functionalism matters here (in this chapter) as far as inconsistency is concerned. Williams, however, has a further goal of demonstrating the *inadequacy* of functionalism, p. 172.

[28] I do not mean to imply that these expressions are equivalent or that any one of them adequately captures the problem. The point is that relativism must be very careful in delineating what is relativistic and what – if anything – is not. See Sects. 2.4 and 2.5 below.

element in the formulation of relativism must make alternatives separate and distinct, it is difficult to articulate this element without violating the relativistic constraints of the theory itself.

When what separates alternatives is a normative element (such as the impermissibility to condemn or interfere with other societies) in a theory of ethical relativism (which constrains normative force to particular societies), then the inconsistency strikes us right away. We cannot assert a normative claim non-relativistically; that is precisely what our theory forbids. But how can relativism tell us anything about the force of claims across different societies if it does not make just that sort of non-relative normative claim? If, on the other hand, what separates alternatives in a theory of ethical relativism is not a directly normative claim, but a more descriptive one, then the inconsistency still does not disappear. As we will see, it is merely displaced to a more general level.

Consider, for example, the descriptive claim that societies are constructed differently from their most basic ideas and ways of interacting with the world on up. This descriptive claim, together with part (1) of our definition of relativism, also establishes normative insularity. If key ethical elements only have meaning relative to particular societies, and if different societies are constructed differently from their most basic ideas and ways of interacting with the world on up, then the ethical claims of one society have no grounds of applicability in another. There is no common standard for evaluating ethical claims across societies. While such inevaluability does not establish quite the same kind of normative insularity as Williams' (inconsistent) appeal for tolerance, it does at least imply that we have to think carefully about our own key elements and what kind of foundation they have in our interactions with other societies. So, it seems to be an ethically significant form of relativism which falls out of this more descriptive claim.

The difficulty, however, is that in appealing to this kind of constructivism, the relativist inherits a much broader relativism. While she has cleared the ethical domain of inconsistency, she is also no longer entitled to think narrowly of the ethical as such an independent domain. The alternatives in question are now more aptly distinguished globally as worldviews, not narrowly as codes of ethics. At such a global level, the line between the ethical and the epistemic is blurred; how a people describe the world and what they believe about it is intimately tied to their judgments about what is good, right and important.[29] So, the ethical relativist must also consider the charges against epistemic relativism, and it is here that she finds the problem of inconsistency has re-emerged.[30] If what insulates the claims of societies from each other is their most basic ideas and ways of interacting with the world on up, then what kind of status can the theory of relativism itself enjoy? If relativism transcends societal boundaries, then is it not itself an exception to its own truth?

---

[29] Although I will not be discussing this here, it is worth noting that at this global level not only are the epistemic and the ethical entangled, but other domains are part of the interweaving as well, such as the aesthetic and the emotive.

[30] Sections 2.2.2 and 2.4.

And if it does not, then what kind of truth could it have? How could it say anything meaningful about any society, any reality beyond its own? Not only is the problem of inconsistency still present, but it has grown from the formulation of relativism to the very formulability and conceivability of the theory itself.

2.2.2.2 Against Epistemic Relativism

Let us turn now to epistemic relativism. A convenient way to begin to get a sense of the challenge it faces is to frame the anti-relativist's question in terms of truth relativism: If truth is relative to contingent or contextual factors such as perspective, conceptual scheme, culture, historical epoch, etc. and is inevaluable independently of them, then is relativism only relatively true? What is the status of the theory itself? Can it place such severe limitations on knowledge and still be a piece of knowledge itself?[31] Harvey Siegel, in his contemporary re-construction of Plato's original arguments against Protagoras, distinguishes two prongs of the anti-relativist attack:[32]

(1) [Relativism] **Undermines the Very Notion of Rightness (UVNR):** If relativism is right (or true or cognitively superior), it is not right at all.
(2) **Necessarily Some Beliefs Are False (NSBF):** If relativism is true, it must acknowledge that it is (relative to alternative standards) also false.

We will see that these slogans take on various meanings at different moments in the relativist ~ anti-relativist dialectic, as the anti-relativist charge deepens from self-refutation to logical and finally conceptual incoherence.[33] At this initial stage, however, we may take UVNR at face value, as a charge of obvious self-refutation. If relativism is supposed to be true *non-relativistically*, then it implies its own falsity. There is, it turns out, a piece of knowledge which transcends the limits of contingent and contextual factors, and this piece is relativism itself! On the other hand, argues the anti-relativist, if relativism is only *relatively* true, then we lose our grip on the very notions of truth and rightness.[34] After all, how can we make sense of the idea that truth is always relative to contingent and contextual factors, when

---

[31] Cf Meiland, "On the Paradox," 115–16, and Siegel, "Relativism," 241–45.

[32] Siegel, "Relativism," 226–31. Siegel's work is not so much a commentary on Plato as an attempt to argue against the contemporary epistemic relativist (whose view is related to but more sophisticated than Protagoras') in the spirit of the *Theaetetus*. I have found his discussion helpful not only for its contemporary focus and argumentative detail, but for the real-life dialectic between Siegel and the relativist Jack W. Meiland, which shines through their respective works at various points.

[33] Sections 2.3 and 2.4.

[34] Cf Meiland, "On the Paradox," 116. As Meiland points out (119–20), a third option is for the relativist to adopt a qualified view, by which everything *except* relativism itself – for instance, because of its meta-epistemological status – is relatively true. Like Meiland, I see no point in following this possibility; the relativist's position is stronger and more consistent when she accepts and makes sense of the notion of relative truth across the board.

our very knowledge of what truth is and how it works is subject to the same relativistic constraints?

From this line of argument, we can see that the initial charge of self-refutation already suggests another of incoherence.[35] Yet, at this point, the relativist may easily counter that there only appears to be a dilemma because we have presupposed an absolutist conception of truth: we are mistaken in desiring or even considering the possibility of a kind of truth or knowledge which transcends relative factors; such constraints are the very point that relativism aims to establish. This counter, however, does not put an end to the anti-relativist's objections. He can, in fact, grant the notion of relative truth and still arrive at the charge of self-refutation. This is where the NSBF argument comes into play.[36] Relativism may by a certain set of standards be true, but its very definition implies that there must be different sets of standards by which it is also false.[37] Moreover, the absolutist himself seems to possess exactly such an alternative set of standards. In this way, the very truth of relativism leads to its own falsity and supports the anti-relativist's views.

In the next section, we will consider how the relativist might respond to the charge of self-refutation. At this point, however, it is worth mentioning a slightly different line of attack, which aims to show that the relativist refutes herself not by treating her own thesis non-relativistically, but by treating at least some of the evidence which she uses to support her thesis non-relativistically. Maurice Mandelbaum in his article, "Subjective, Objective, and Conceptual Relativisms," carefully divides up different species of relativism and considers examples from the work of John Dewey, Charles A. Beard, Benjamin Lee Whorf, and others in order to argue that in every case the relativist falls to what he calls the "self-excepting fallacy."[38] Mandelbaum points out, for example, how Whorf, in building his case for a conceptual linguistic relativism, describes the worldview associated with radically different languages. So, concludes Mandelbaum, at least Whorf "was not bound by his own grammar, but stood outside both his own language and theirs."[39] In demonstrating conceptual linguistic relativism, Whorf himself became an exception to conceptual linguistic relativism.[40]

---

[35] I discuss this charge in Sect. 2.4.

[36] I return to this argument in more detail in Sect. 2.4.1.

[37] Siegel, 227–31.

[38] Maurice Mandelbaum, "Subjective, Objective, and Conceptual Relativisms," in *Relativism: Cognitive and Moral,* eds. Michael Krausz and Jack W. Meiland (Notre Dame, IN: University of Notre Dame Press, 1982), 34–61. Reprinted from *The Monist* 62, no. 4 (1979): 403–23.

Meiland mentions a similar argument by Husserl in "On the Paradox," 117.

[39] Mandelbaum, "Subjective," 48–49.

[40] Mandelbaum's use of real works and figures presents an interesting challenge. If these figures did not, in fact, consider themselves to be embracing and/or elaborating a theory of relativism, then they are not guilty of the self-excepting fallacy. Or, if they were careful at some point to qualify their descriptions of alternative worldviews as relative and non-neutral, then again Mandelbaum's charges do not apply. In this way, Mandelbaum's argument, in order to go through, demands very careful textual research and analysis. Nevertheless, even if Mandelbaum turns out to be mistaken

2.2.3   The Relativist's Response

Now that the charges have been laid out, it is time in the dance for the relativist to begin developing a response. In the previous section (Sect. 2.2), we saw that the charge of self-refutation against the epistemic relativist involves at least four complaints:

(1) In asserting the truth of relativism, the relativist shows us that at least one piece of knowledge is non-relative (namely, her own theory).
(2) If relativism is only relatively true, then it is not true at all.
(3) If relativism is relatively true, then it must also acknowledge that it is relatively false.
(4) In arguing for relativism, the relativist treats at least some of her evidence non-relativistically.

We also saw a charge of self-refutation against the ethical relativist:

(5) In prescribing tolerance, relativism treats at least one value non-relativistically.

These complaints fall into two broad categories. (1), (4), and (5) claim that relativism refutes itself by unwittingly taking an (albeit limited) absolutist stance. (2) and (3), on the other hand, accuse relativism of self-refutation only by themselves assuming an absolutist point of view.

Let us consider the second category first. At least on the surface, the relativist seems to have an easy and immediate response. She is not self-refuting because she does not subscribe to an absolutist conception of truth. For her, there is no truth besides relative truth; relativism is as true as true can be. She can even concede that, relative to other factors, factors which are not her own, relativism may be false. This does not refute, but rather reinforces her view.[41] After all, the non-relativist's view is just another example of the kind of alternatives which relativism already predicts and describes. Relative truth is not self-refuting, but radical, in that it both revises and limits our traditional concept of truth. While the absolutist may complain of the impotency of relative truth in its ability to warrant belief and justify claims to knowledge,[42] this is only in contrast to a kind of potency which the relativist does not believe that any theory can actually have. As Krausz and Meiland point out in their introduction to Mandelbaum's article, for the non-relativist to be unconvinced by the relativist's arguments is quite different than for the relativist to be self-refuting: "Relativism may be more appropriately considered as a world-view which generates its own goals and standards."[43]

---

about these historical figures, he does seem to have a valid point to which the relativist must respond: how does she articulate relativism from a relativist point of view?

[41] Krausz and Meiland make this point with respect to Goodman. See Michael Krausz and Jack W. Meiland, "Introduction to 'Fabrication of Facts,'" in *Relativism: Cognitive and Moral,* eds. Michael Krausz and Jack W. Meiland (Notre Dame, IN: University of Notre Dame Press, 1982), 16.

[42] Siegel, "Relativism," 242.

[43] Michael Krausz and Jack W. Meiland, "Introduction to 'Subjective, Objective and Conceptual Relativisms,'" in *Relativism: Cognitive and Moral,* eds, Michael Krausz and Jack W. Meiland (Notre Dame, IN: University of Notre Dame Press, 1982), 30–31. Cf Meiland, "On the Paradox," esp. 121–22.

Although relative truth may help the relativist to escape charges of self-refutation, it opens up questions of its own, paving the way for new charges of incoherence: How can the same claim be both true and false, or right and wrong? What exactly is the relativist world-view like, and how do we get a grip on it without again presupposing an absolutist picture? The remaining two sections of part 2 will attempt to explore and respond to these questions. Before moving on, however, we must address the first category of self-refutation complaints mentioned above.

If, indeed, the relativist means her theory as naively as the anti-relativist construes it, then it *is* self-refuting. Relativism cannot be true in the absolutist's sense of truth. The relativist's own arguments and evidence for relativism do not escape the relativistic limits of knowledge. The relativist cannot consistently prescribe tolerance as a non-relative value. However, there is another meaning which the relativist *could* and, I believe, the sophisticated relativist *does* have: she already accepts relativism and so implicitly takes all of her claims as internal to factors such as her perspective, conceptual scheme, culture, historical epoch, etc. Given what she can and does know of the world, relativism is true. There is no "external" sense for her in which relativism, independently of such an experience of the world, could be true. When she encounters and attempts to describe what she deduces to be an alternative experience of the world, she does so from within her own experience, using her own terms and powers of description.[44] She does not inhabit the alternative experience or describe it from a transcendent point of view.

Likewise, we might understand the ethical relativist's prescription for tolerance as addressed only to members of her own social group: given our understanding of the relativity of rightness to a particular society, we should not condemn or interfere with the practices of other societies. Such a prescription is internal to a particular experience of the world and does not make relativism self-refuting by appealing to a universal and non-relative sense of rightness.[45] However, it also does not necessarily follow from the other premises of ethical relativism (by Williams' definition or mine). It is equally consistent for a relativistic view to prescribe, for instance, conversion and intervention instead of tolerance: our sense of rightness cannot transcend the social and cultural conditions of our experience of the world, but that does not condemn us to inaction; we must embrace rightness as we know it, and fight for and promote it across the board. On an internalist conception, tolerance is both

---

[44] See Chap. 1, esp. Sect. 2.6.

[45] We might imagine, as an anonymous reviewer mentioned to me, a sense of rightness that is both universal *and relative*. For instance, it might just so happen that all ways of life agree that a particular action is right for them. Such a *contingent universal*, as we might call it, does not open relativism to charges of self-refutation or incoherence, and so is not much of a concern here. Moreover, it seems to me that, besides any conceptual or linguistic difficulties, we currently have serious historical, political, and economic barriers to any system that might be used to verify such a universal. A U.N. resolution, which might come closest to such a system, is rife with complicating factors, such as who is chosen to represent a country (and, if there is internal deliberation, who is chosen to represent the further groups within a country), how power is distributed over countries within the U.N., and how economic aid and other forms of support are contingent upon declarations and their enforcement.

consistent with ethical relativism and not an essential part of ethical relativism. While this may be a disappointing consequence for vulgar relativism, it does not affect ethical relativism such as we defined it in Sects. 1.2 and 1.3.

If the relativist carefully qualifies all of her claims as internal to her own relative factors such as perspective, conceptual scheme, culture, historical epoch, etc., she avoids making or appearing to make any absolute claims and so does not refute herself in stating relativism.[46] She can embrace the truth of relativism, put forth descriptive evidence for relativism, and make prescriptions based on the fact of relativism without inconsistency. Yet, as we will see in the following section, she solves the problem of self-refutation at the price of an even deeper problem of incoherence. As the anti-relativist sees it, self-refutation and incoherence are two horns of a dilemma.[47] If the relativist makes use of any kind of absolutist view in formulating relativism, she is self-refuting. If, on the other hand, she embraces a thoroughgoing relativism, she is incoherent. An internalist picture of truth and value may help us to solve the problem of self-refutation, but how does it allow us to hold onto the notion of alternatives, which is so vital to relativism? What, moreover, gives substance to notions like relative truth and relative value so as to prevent them from collapsing into merely consistent belief?

2.2.4   The Charge of Incoherence

2.2.4.1   Against Epistemic Relativism

At this point in the dance, the relativist has opened herself to new charges. Let us look at the case against epistemic relativism first. There is a straightforward kind of logical incoherence that is very closely tied to inconsistency and self-refutation. When the parts of a theory cannot stand together logically, we may say that the whole theory comes apart, or is incoherent. The same claim in a theory, or the very statement of the theory itself, cannot be both true and false. At the point where we discover such internal contradiction, the theory ceases to make sense. In this way, a theory that is inconsistent, and especially one that is self-refuting, tends also to be incoherent. A response to the charge of such inconsistency is at the same time in many respects a response to the charge of logical incoherence as well.

We can see the relationship between self-refutation and logical incoherence clearly in the NSBF argument and the UVNR argument which follows on its heels. In the first step of the NSBF, the anti-relativist asks us to assume that relativism is true. Let's even grant, he adds, that relativism is relatively, not absolutely, true. This means that relativism must be true relative to a particular perspective, conceptual scheme, culture, historical epoch, etc., or "frame of reference," for short. Let's say that Frame A is an example of such a frame of reference in which relativism is true.

---

[46] Cf Meiland, "On the Paradox," 120–21; 235.

[47] Meiland, "On the Paradox," 116; Siegel, "Relativism," 231.

Now consider any other frame, X. Is relativism also true in X?[48] The very definition of relativism tells us that the truth status of relativism in X will be determined entirely in X, regardless of the status of claims in A. In fact, it is just as likely that relativism will be false in X as it is that it will be true. So, says the anti-relativist, let B be some such X in which relativism is false. But for relativism to be false in some B is just what it means for relativism to be false simpliciter. In other words, the assumption that relativism is true leads to the conclusion that relativism is false. Therefore, he determines, relativism is self-refuting.[49]

The anti-relativist's stream of argument, however, does not stop at self-refutation. In fact, the conclusion of the NSBF throws him straight into the UVNR. As he sees it, we have identified not only a flaw in the argument, but a seam at which it unravels entirely. This is a grand case of self-refutation, he exclaims. How can a theory of truth undermine its own truth? If the truth of relativism entails its falsity in certain frames, then from what standpoint are we to assent to it as a rationally justifiable theory? Why should claims in A carry any more weight than those in B? Isn't relativism just as false as it is true?[50] He now confronts the relativist with the charge of logical incoherence: her theory falls apart at the point of contradictory claims. In such a case of self-refutation, the point is its very heart – the assertion of relativism's own truth.

Fortunately, the relativist has already responded to the first charge of self-refutation, and to a great extent, that response helps her with the concomitant charge of logical incoherence as well. Recall our earlier discussion in Sect. 2.3. The relativist's conception of internal truth dissolves the inconsistencies in an argument such as NSBF by allowing the same claim to be true (or false) in incomparable ways. For the relativist, key elements such as truth are not only relative to particular frames, but they have no sense external to such frames. Relativism is true in A, and relativism is false in B; it is not both true and false in the same frame. Because there is no logical context in which we can juxtapose truth in A with falsity in B, relativism is not self-refuting.[51] And because relativism is not self-refuting, it is not, at least at

---

[48] The anti-relativist is assuming here that the same theory is expressible in both A and B. In some cases, the relativist may want to deny this possibility. For example, a global relativist may insist that different frames involve incompatible basic terms and concepts and so cannot be used to construct the same theory. This amounts to a more radical internality than that of internal truth, although it is a similar strategy. While it may help the relativist avoid the charge of logical incoherence, she must still respond to the anti-relativist's deeper charge of conceptual incoherence. See text below.

[49] For a version of this argument, see Siegel, "Relativism," 229–30.

[50] Cf Siegel, "Relativism," 229–30 and 240–43.

[51] Those who take into account the fact that frames such as cultures are fluid, and that a single individual may be able to move agilely through more than one of them, might at this point consider a third, hybrid frame C, which is a conjunction of A + B. Could C then provide a logical context for juxtaposing the truth and falsity of relativism that we find in A and B? As far as I can tell, this still would not render relativism incoherent. If C is truly its own frame, then relativism should have its own truth status relative to it. An agent of C, despite his ability to move through A and B, will still have his own over-arching view regarding relativism. Relativism will not be both true and false

this logical level, incoherent. Truth in A and falsity in B do not cause relativism to fall apart because its truth status does not transcend the frames in the first place; what turns out to be incoherent is not relativism, but rather the very idea that truth could be evaluated across frames.

While internal truth helps the relativist to avert the charge of logical incoherence, it only aggravates the anti-relativist's deeper worries about conceptual incoherence, which are to some extent already apparent in his evocation of UVNR: *From what standpoint is relativism rationally justifiable?* How do we latch on to relative truth? How can we assent to it? And how is it useful? How does it fulfill the functions we formerly assigned to truth before the relativist came by and revised our very notion of truth?

In many ways, the force of UVNR comes from its absolutist understanding of transcendence: We must be able to identify truth as something which extends beyond our frames of reference; otherwise, it is as contingent and arbitrary as they are. As far as the anti-relativist can see, to say that a claim is true without such transcendence is to say no more than that it is consistent with other claims that are made in the same frame as it. And this, he believes, offends our sense that truth must be something necessary and world-determined. Moreover, it is precisely this sense which leads him to believe that when we assess truth, we must not look to our frames, but beyond them. For him, the very idea of truth demands that there be neutral grounds on which we can evaluate truth claims independently of frames. And so, the very idea of truth allows for the NSBF argument to go through – for us to place the truth and falsity of relativism side-by-side.[52, 53]

It may seem that the relativist and anti-relativist are merely begging the question against each other by disputing the nature of truth. Yet there is more to the anti-relativist's arguments than a metaphysical predilection for absolute truth. His point is not merely that truth must be something which transcends frames and can in some way be evaluated independently of them, but that the relativist's own story seems,

---

in C. If, on the other hand, C is just the state of being sometimes in A and sometimes in B, then, relativism still will not be true and false at the same time, and so avoids incoherence. If, however, C is just an overlay of A and B which does not allow for them in different moments but brings them together simultaneously, then I think that it is the frame itself, not relativism, which is incoherent. Indeed, cross-cultural lives do sometimes lead to this kind of confusion and incoherence. The result of working through such conflict, however, does not seem to be so much the union of A and B as the genesis of a new frame which is no longer hybrid, but its unique self. And so, again, we do not have a single frame in which relativism's variability across frames renders it logically incoherent.

[52] Of course, the kind of pragmatic absolutist whom I discussed earlier would not agree with the picture we have drawn here of absolute truth. In fact, he embraces the relativist's conception of internal truth and stands, as far as the NSBF and UVNR are concerned, on the relativist's, not the anti-relativist's, side. His dispute with the relativist (that is, with the sophisticated relativist of our dialectic, not with the strawman caricature of a relativist who comes up so many times in the literature) centers on the possibility of transcendent relative knowledge, not on the charges of self-refutation and incoherence that are at issue here.

[53] Siegel, 230–43, expresses many of the anti-relativist ideas in this paragraph, especially in his response to Jack W. Meiland, "Concepts of Relative Truth," *The Monist* 60, no. 4 (1977): 568–82.

contradictorily, to depend on truth ultimately possessing these qualities. Furthermore, he sees this dependence in two distinct aspects of the relativist's theory. First of all, the relativist must be able to explain how her theory is about something that can interestingly be called "truth" – if no aspect of relative truth transcends frames of reference, then how is it different from mere convention, or consistent belief?[54] There is nothing particularly radical or revealing about the idea that conventions and beliefs are relative to frames of reference. Relativism, in order to be robust and worthy of our attention, must explain to us how relative truth is at a deeper level world-determined and world-informing. But how can the relativist do that without talking beyond frames of reference? And if she does talk beyond them, then how does she avoid the anti-relativist's charges as he has already laid them out? It seems that in so talking, the relativist is identifying some aspect of truth which is external and non-relative. At the very least, she seems to be giving us enough neutral grounds to hold the two mutually contradicting statements in the NSBF together. How can the relativist give content to the concept of relative truth without evoking transcendence in a self-refuting and self-defeating way?

Secondly, the relativist must be able to formulate alternatives.[55] Her theory is about the relativity of key elements such as truth to different frames of reference. If, however, she cannot establish that there are, in fact, different frames in which such elements vary, then her theory fails to isolate a phenomenon which can interestingly be called "relativity." It collapses into a view which has no tension with the anti-relativist's: truth is determined by the way the world is, period. There is no reason to introduce the concepts of alternative truths and relativity to frames if we cannot identify more than one frame. As the anti-relativist understands it, the internality of key concepts like truth is so strong that it, in fact, places the relativist in precisely this predicament. The relativist avoided the charges of self-refutation and logical incoherence by insisting that truth has no sense external to frames of reference, and that there is no shared logical context in which to evaluate the truth claims of different frames. How, then, can the relativist tell us anything interesting about an alternative frame to her own? If her whole understanding of truth is restricted to her own frame, how can she even suppose that something like truth re-emerges in another frame? Must she not assume that her own understanding somehow transcends its relative limits in order to assess and comprehend alternatives? And if she can inhabit such a minimally transcendent stance, then why does that stance not provide sufficient logical grounds for juxtaposing the two mutually contradicting statements in the NSBF? Don't the very grounds on which she formulates her theory at the same time pull it apart? Either she is so restricted to her own frame that she can give no

---

[54] Cf Siegel, "Relativism," 236–45.

[55] I believe this problem lies in part behind Bernard Williams' criticism that relativism, in the very process of becoming clearer, slips away from us. See Chap. 9 in Bernard Williams, *Ethics and the Limits of Philosophy* (Cambridge, MA: Harvard University Press, 1985), esp. 156–57. I return to this point in Sect. 2.5. Mandelbaum, "Subjective," as we discussed earlier in Sect. 2.2, also has a similar point: how does the relativist describe relativism without inhabiting a space which is not itself an exception to relativism?

content to the idea of alternatives and her theory collapses into the anti-relativist's theory of singular, non-relative truths, or she must presuppose some kind of neutral, non-relative grounds on which not only does she elaborate her theory, but that very theory comes apart.

The anti-relativist has now sharpened two new horns of what is in many ways the same dilemma. Earlier, he insisted that either the relativist must assert the truth of relativism absolutely and so refute herself, or she lapses into general incoherence.[56] Now he proclaims that either the relativist gives content to the concepts of alternatives and relative truth by presupposing non-relative grounds, thereby opening herself up to charges of both self-refutation and incoherence; or, she fails to give these concepts substantial content and her theory collapses into one which is uncontroversial and, in fact, compatible with the anti-relativist's own absolutist views. While the horns of the first dilemma were self-refutation *and* incoherence, this second time around the problem they are self-refutation + incoherence *and* meaninglessness, or uselessness. The relativist escaped the first dilemma with her concept of internality. This time, in order to escape the dilemma, she must show that she can give content to relative truth and to alternatives without presupposing neutral, non-relative grounds.

2.2.4.2 Against Ethical Relativism

The charge of incoherence against ethical relativism in many ways parallels the charge of incoherence against epistemic relativism. Ethical relativism, however, does not share epistemic relativism's problem of formulating alternatives, since it does not limit our possibility of knowledge as broadly.[57] The threat of incoherence also does not strike ethical relativism as close to home as it does epistemic relativism, which it hits at the very truth of relativism itself. Still, something like the UVNR argument re-emerges in the ethical case, and it follows from considerations which we might think of as a weaker version of the NSBF.

In epistemic relativism, we found the problem that both the claims "relativism is true" and "relativism is false" follow from asserting the truth of relativism.[58] This is really just a special case of the more general problem that relativism allows the same claim to be both true and false. Relativism allows this, of course, not only in the harmless sort of indexical cases where claims such as, "I am four feet tall," can be true or false in the mouths of different utterers, but in much more controversial cases, where claims such as, "A demonic force is causing her to scream uncontrollably," can be both true and false, relative to different frames of reference. In the

---

[56] Section 2.2.

[57] At least, ethical relativism does not immediately have this problem. However, as I discussed in Sect. 2.2.1, if we are considering a form of ethical relativism that is dependent on a broader relativism in which the ethical and the epistemic are entangled, then ultimately ethical relativism inherits all the difficulties of epistemic relativism as well.

[58] Section 2.4.1.

face of this more general problem, we can still pose a more general version of the
question in the UVNR argument: what is truth if it can vary so widely from frame
to frame? Is it dependent on anything but the frame itself? If it is not, then how does
truth differ from mere convention? And if it is, then how is there not a frame independent, non-relative way in which we can talk about truth?

It is precisely this more general version of the problem which arises in the case
of ethical relativism. The same action, according to ethical relativism, can be both
right and wrong. Again, this not only holds for harmless cases where, for example,
telling a lie can be both right and wrong, given varying circumstances, but for more
controversial cases where, for instance, the Chachi cutting their trees in the community of Loma Linda on December 8, 2010 is both right and wrong, relative to
different frames of reference. Here we find the more general problem behind the
UVNR argument re-emerging in the ethical case[59]: How can the same action be both
right and wrong? What is rightness, if it can vary so widely from frame to frame?

Of course, "UVNR" is a rather dramatic acronym, but again, there is more to the
anti-relativist's charge than sheer absolutist bias. As far as he can see, the ethical
relativist is stuck in a dilemma quite similar to the epistemic relativist's at the end of
Sect. 2.4.1 above. On the one hand, if she insists that a concept such as "rightness"
has no frame-independent content, then it is as contingent and variable as frames
themselves. Rightness reduces to nothing more than convention, and certainly the
idea that conventions vary from frame to frame is neither controversial nor enlight-
ening. Why even bother talking about a concept as thin as "relative right" in the first
place? If ethical relativism is merely a deflationary theory, then how is it different or
better than other varieties of subjectivism or non-cognitivism? What is the point of
relativistic analysis in the first place?[60]

On the other hand, if the relativist concedes that a concept such as "rightness"
has frame-independent content, then she must explain how this content fails to be a
means for determining rightness non-relativistically. According to the anti-relativist,
if there is something that makes cutting the trees in Loma Linda right or wrong
independently of the frame in which we understand and assess that action, then it
must be some objective fact about the world itself, or about human life in particular.
Perhaps it is not enough in itself to determine the correctness of a specific action,

---

[59] Siegel, incidentally, is only concerned with the epistemic case. "Rightness" for him in the UVNR
refers exclusively to epistemic truth. For this kind of incoherence argument in the ethical case, see
David Lyons, "Ethical Relativism and the Problem of Incoherence," in *Relativism: Cognitive and
Moral,* eds. Michael Krausz and Jack W. Meiland (Notre Dame, IN: University of Notre Dame
Press, 1982), 209–225. Reprinted from *Ethics* 86 (1976): 107–21.

[60] Some relativists may just want to bite the bullet here and say that ethical relativism is not significantly different or better than other deflationary ethical theories, but that relativity is still not superfluous because it specifies and elucidates the mechanisms by which convention works. I do not,
however, believe that ethical relativism *requires* such a deflationary interpretation, which is why I
go on to suggest a positive response to this objection in Sect. 2.5. Although both ethical and epistemic relativism are consistent with forms of subjectivism, they are much broader, and to insist on
interpreting relativism exclusively through the lens of subjectivism is only to incite and increase its
pool of dissenters.

independently of frames, but it must at least give us some guidelines, some general picture of what is right and wrong non-relativistically. So, at least at this abstract level, relativism breaks down. But what more, the anti-relativist might ask, is an ethical principle than such a general guideline for action? Even an absolutist can grant that, in the specific application of general principles, contextual and contingent details will have some effect on what is right and wrong. For the anti-relativist, the inevaluability of rightness across frames reduces to this rather harmless variability of ethical principles in their specific application. He insists that the relativist's picture only appeared different than the objective non-relativist's at first because she magnified this variability. The important point, for the anti-relativist, is that all groups of people, from all frames, share a common, general picture of what kinds of action are right and wrong. And so, in guiding action and arbitrating conflict, we have a single, non-relative standard for determining what is best.

2.2.5   *Tools for a Relativistic Picture*

We have now arrived at the final moment of our dance. The relativist has escaped the anti-relativist's initial charges of self-refutation and logical incoherence by insisting that key elements such as truth and rightness only have meaning relative and internal to frames of reference.[61] The anti-relativist has argued in response that accepting such a thesis of internality opens the door to even greater problems of conceptual incoherence. As far as he can tell, relativism is left with two equally unappealing alternatives. Either it collapses into a meaningless, uninteresting theory, or it must presuppose some form of non-relativism and thereby refute itself.[62]

The relativist now confronts two new challenges: she must show (1) that her own point of view, in embracing alternativeness, does not occupy a non-relative space; and (2) that she can distinguish notions such as relative truth and relative rightness from mere convention without giving them non-relative content.[63] If she succeeds, she may not have persuaded the anti-relativist to accept her view, but she will at least have shown that she does not defeat herself on her own terms. In that sense, she will have conquered the charges of self-refutation and incoherence. If she fails, on the other hand, her first defense will collapse and she will fall to all of the anti-relativist's charges. In the following two sub-sections, I develop the concepts of analogical thought and world resistance as a response to these challenges on the relativist's behalf.

---

[61] Sections 2.2, 2.3, and 2.4.

[62] Section 2.4.

[63] Section 2.4.

2.2.5.1   A Relativist Point of View

As Bernard Williams has pointed out, the problem with the idea of relativism is that in the very process of becoming clearer, it slips away from us.[64] Relativism must in fact hold onto two nearly contradictory ideas: one of commonality, which provides the context for the formulation of the theory in the first place, and the other of locality, which creates limits and difference. Without commonality, we have no common denominator with which to talk about alternatives. Without locality, on the other hand, we cannot isolate one alternative from another. But how do we establish significant difference and commonality without the two canceling or contradicting each other? The dynamic opposition between these two ideas lies at the heart of Williams' critique. But what he fails to see is that the two can be grasped *in different ways*, so as to avoid incoherence.

The relativist's grasp of all key elements (truth, rightness, goodness, etc.) is always internal to her frame of reference. This is how she avoids problems of logical incoherence; these elements for her have no external sense.[65] Yet such a constraint on meaning does not prevent the relativist from acknowledging alternatives. For her, the internal world in which she knows truth and embraces rightness is of a different character than the external world in which she recognizes alternative truths and alternatively right actions. The internal world is what she claims for her own. It is the world in which she explores and comes to know through her own experience.[66] The external world, on the other hand, is one she reaches only through exercises of imagination, extrapolation, and inference. In other words, the external is an extension of the internal world which remains tightly tethered to it and does not fully reach beyond it. Yet the external's highly analogical character makes it a very distinct part of the internal with which the relativist can interact in different ways.

The relativist does not need to believe an alternative truth or endorse an alternatively right action in order to conclude from an encounter (be it of a physical, historical, literary, or other nature) with (what strikes her as) a differently constructed frame of reference that, in their own context, such truth and such rightness may be as solid as her own. She can recognize alternatives without inhabiting them in the same way that we commonly recognize other persons as such without in fact becoming them. Of course, she could (at times, or across the board) refuse to grant alternative status, in the same way that we sometimes refuse to grant personhood. This, however, does not make the relativist's position any more or less self-refuting. We may think of it, rather, as how we construe the principal of charity – whether the goal is to interpret another's truths and values to be as much like our own as possible, or whether we should strive instead to grant him an epistemic condition and status like our own. According to the former strategy, most disagreement is caused

---

[64] Williams, *Ethics,* 156–57.
[65] Sections 2.3 and 2.4.
[66] See Chap. 1, esp. Sect. 2.6.

by error (usually on the other side); according to the latter, it is caused by (often irresoluble) difference.

While the relativist may attempt, in her own terms, to identify and describe such difference, this does not amount to the claim that alternatives are reducible or equivalent to anything in her own experience and powers of description.[67] Unless the relativist is in fact the uncritical, vulgar opponent imagined by so many anti-relativists, she is careful to qualify her characterizations of alternatives as the closest she can come to approximating what otherwise does not fit into her realm. Because the relativist does not leave the internal world to contemplate and describe the external, she does not refute herself. She constructs a realm of alternatives without quite reaching them. They are points at the outer limits of her own knowledge and experience. She gives them dimensions and fills them in not by leaving her own perspective or jumping to neutral ground, but by relating them to her own experience.[68] She extrapolates what seems most basic both to her own world and to the one she is confronting, while trying to imagine what, in order to square the picture, must be radically different. Of course, she may see that such confrontation and exercises of analogical thought cause her own perspective to evolve and grow, but at no moment does she find herself inhabiting any perspective other than her own.

The line between locality and commonality is a choice. The relativist decides, based on her own experience, when she has confronted an alternative; and in exploring that alternative, she determines what it shares with her own frame and, how, in order to fit these common terms, it must at the same time be radically different. The anti-relativist complained in Sect. 2.4 that the relativist cannot grasp alternatives without contemplating key elements such as truth from an external perspective. He thought that in order for relative truths to count as variants of the same kind, they must share some common, *neutral* ground, and it was precisely on such ground that he found a problem with the contradictory statements, "Relativism is true," and, "Relativism is false," standing side-by-side. What he failed to see, however, is that commonality for the relativist comes from within her own perspective. She does not look outside for common ground, but reaches inside her experience for what seems most fundamental and shared. Her common denominator is, in fact, an extrapolation of her most inner world. The ground on which she contemplates alternatives is her own, and she constructs descriptions of them with objects and concepts abstracted from her own arsenal of tools for knowing and being in the world. It is in this way that she extrapolates from her own assertion that relativism is true to the possibility that, in what she judges to be a different frame, something like truth may be a possible property and something like relativism may be a possible idea, but the former may not be a property of the latter. To say this, however, is merely to elaborate, not to refute, the very idea of relativism.

---

[67] Cf Michael N. Forster, "On the Very Idea of Denying the Existence of Radically Different Conceptual Schemes," *Inquiry* 41, no. 2 (1998): 133–85.

[68] See Chap. 1.

2.2.5.2 Relative Content

On an internal relativist account, alternative truths (values, etc.) do not pose a problem of logical incoherence. The same fact is not both true and false in the same frame, in the same way. And if we grant the role that I am suggesting for analogical thought, there is no problem of conceptual incoherence either. The relativist can acknowledge alternatives without leaving or negating her own frame of reference. Yet we might think that there remains a problem of conceptual incoherence, which, as we saw in Sect. 2.4, is in many ways captured by the UVNR: What do notions like truth and rightness mean if they are so bound to a frame of reference? In what sense are they world-determined? Are they held together by anything more than the mere internal coherence of a particular frame of reference? If so, are they not very weak and arbitrary? Is there anything more that the relativist can say of her truths and her actions than, "This is what I believe," and, "This is what I endorse"? Why should we even bother taking into account such notions as relative truths and relatively right actions? Do they amount to anything more than mere convention? Is relativism simply and necessarily a deflationary theory of key elements such as truth and rightness?

According to relativism, key elements are relative to and inevaluable independently of contingent or contextual factors such as perspective, conceptual scheme, culture, historical epoch, etc. This does not entail, however, that key elements are *reducible to* contingent and contextual factors. Perhaps the absolutist misses this insight because he is too much under the sway of a traditional absolutist picture, in which key elements not only transcend contingent and contextual factors, but enjoy an independent and paradigmatic existence beyond them. With transcendence, key elements rise above mere convention and show that they are in a greater sense world-determined. It is what, in the absolutist picture, marks them as interesting and as pieces of knowledge. The relativist, nevertheless, has a counterpart to such transcendence in her own picture. There is something more basic and less weighty which assures that her key elements are world-determined and amount to more than mere convention. It is, quite simply, the fact that the world *resists* and *responds* to her shapings of it.

When I was a little girl, I stared for hours at the vase on my mother's living room table trying to make it fly across the room. Of course, it never did, and I had to revise my ideas about matter and the power of my own willing, but this is a perfect example of resistance: the world sometimes accepting, sometimes refusing, but nevertheless responding to what we think and want it to do. For the relativist, the fact that the world resists her mere beliefs and whims of action, that something responds in counterpoint to her shapings of the world, causing both object and perspective to evolve, shows that her key elements capture more than mere convention and that the world makes its own contribution to her thought. Resistance and responsiveness can be delivered differently to different forms of subjectivity, and so they may be expressed relativistically as different truths and other key notions in varying contexts and contingencies. Yet, unlike the absolutist's transcendence, they need not have any frame-independent and/or ultimate manifestation. In other words, they need not undermine relativity in the way that absolutist transcendence does.[69] They allow the relativist to think of relative truth as world-determined without establishing common grounds and therefore evaluability across frames. In this way, they protect her from the charges of self-refutation and incoherence. While the relativist may have a general sense that she ultimately shares one world with alternative frames, and that it is this same world which informs her key elements as well as theirs, this need not imply that key elements have equivalent or comparable forms across frames.

Consider the difference between these two claims: (1) the world has resistance and makes its own contributions to my renderings of it; (2) the world is describable, accessible, evaluable in a way that transcends any particular renderings of it. The relativist can have world-determination by claiming (1) without (2). What makes resistance lighter and more basic than absolutist transcendence is its minimal metaphysical commitments. It is simply the fact of mind-independence, of a certain distance in the world from the conditions of subjectivity. In order to surmount the problem of arbitrariness, the relativist has no need to introduce things-in-themselves or even a fallibilistic sense that her understanding is reaching closer to the way the world ultimately is. She can allow resistance to give content to notions such as relative truth and rightness without hypostatizing this contribution into a thing in itself, or extrapolating into it the very terms of subjectivity. She might even say, in the spirit of Kant's First Critique, that to do so is to fall victim to a paradox much more worrisome than the one the anti-relativist has been trying to force upon her; it is to attempt, impossibly, to express the unconditioned in the very terms which condition our knowledge and experience of the world.

Structurally, the anti-relativist's charge of arbitrariness is the same in both the epistemic and the ethical case: Either the relativist must presuppose an absolutist picture, or she fails to give content to relative key elements that distinguishes them from mere convention. To a large extent, the relativist's response in both cases is also the same: The fact of resistance gives rich content to relative key elements without presupposing an absolutist picture. As long as there is room for the world to respond, room for the relativist to learn and to grow, her notions of truth, rightness, etc. are not in danger of collapse. Nevertheless, there is an important difference between the epistemic and ethical case which comes not from the structure of the anti-relativist's argument or of the relativist's response, but from the texture of the epistemic and the ethical themselves, and the way in which we relate to these domains in our own lives. Our claims to knowledge in the epistemic domain are directed toward a physical world which we experience as intersubjective, immediate, and shared. Our ethical claims, on the other hand, are directed toward a realm of right and ought which we experience much less immediately and obviously, even though it may in other ways be intersubjective and shared.

We have bodily senses and highly coordinated representations for intuiting the physical world, but not the ethical. If rightness were a color or values hit us like

---

[69] For more on this point, see Chap. 5.

apples falling to the ground, then perhaps resistance would strike us as equally appealing and intuitive in the ethical as in the epistemic case. Instead, the same types of considerations of relativity to contingent and contextual factors, which lead us in the epistemic domain to a theory of relativism, lead us in the ethical domain directly to a theory of arbitrariness. In the epistemic domain, we are generally convinced that there is something leftover, and consider relativism an inept theory if it is unable to account for whatever must transcend mere contingent and contextual factors. In the ethical domain, however, we are often quite convinced that there is no content beyond mere contingent and contextual factors, and conclude that relativism is a weak and unnecessary theory because there is simply no greater meaning for which to account. Ethical resistance in this case is superfluous; there is no more problem to solve.

I believe that this reduction of ethical relativism to a theory of ethical arbitrariness is the source of a great deal of the antagonism which relativism in general receives. Perhaps the realization that ethical and epistemic relativism are capable of supporting greater content without inconsistency will come as a relief to both sides of the argument – to the absolutist because he may engage the arguments for relativism without fear of losing the content to his own claims of truth and rightness, and to the relativist not only because the anti-relativist may in this respect lower his antagonism, but because she herself is free to search for and embrace content beyond mere contingency and contextuality.

Admittedly, resistance is much easier to grasp in the epistemic than in the ethical case. In the latter, we encounter resistance not in a shared physical world, but only in our hearts, in a deep but very inner feeling of how things should be. It is a feeling which we can nonetheless identify as beyond the mere contingency and contextuality of our frames because it is, like its physical counterpart, capable of overriding and reshaping our beliefs. I believe we see clearly this kind of ethical resistance at work in cases of moral objection and dissent.[70] It is, for example, what leads a group of individuals living in the grip of Nazism to shelter persecuted Jews. Yet we can, just as in the epistemic case, keep separate the claim that our reasons engage and respond to content beyond mere contingency and contextuality from the claim that such content has any frame-independent and/or ultimate manifestation. This means that resistance need not support the same right actions and ethical ideals in different frames. It also does not give us common standards for resolving conflict. But it does empower us as agents capable of assuming responsibility for our own contentful ethical ideas, and perhaps *that* is what is not only most possible, but most needed to adjudicate conflict in an age of as much diversity as our own.[71]

---

[70] I do not mean that it is only operational in such cases, but that it is easy to observe in them.

[71] For more on this point, see Chap. 6.

2.3 Conclusion

Looking back over our dance, we see that at a certain level the relativist and the anti-relativist are simply begging the question against each other. In the first and third moments, the anti-relativist insists on an absolutist picture of key elements such as truth and rightness by way of a dilemma: either the relativist asserts her claims on non-relative grounds and they are self-refuting, or she asserts them on relative grounds and they are incoherent. In the second and fourth moments, on the other hand, the relativist puts forth a relative picture of key elements such as truth and rightness. She clarifies that all her claims are asserted on relative grounds and goes on to show how such grounds can nevertheless be coherent. For the anti-relativist, the meaning of key elements must ultimately be grounded in a world external to frames of reference; for the relativist, key elements have no meaning external to frames of reference. The relativist develops a coherent position by insisting that the world at all levels refuses absolutes; it is captured in different ways by different frames, but never sorts out by key elements into a unified picture. The anti-relativist, on the other hand, pushes the relativist into incoherence by insisting that there is nothing for key elements to capture without the possibility of such a unified picture. Which picture is correct? Are key elements such as truth and rightness relative or absolute? What is the relationship between them and the world that is their object?

If the point in dispute between the two sides is metaphysical, then the question is difficult, if not impossible, to settle. The dialectic's pendulum of argument may swing back and forth indefinitely. In this case, we may at least find some illuminatory or hermeneutic value in the observation that behind the dispute over ethical and epistemic relativism lie unacknowledged and unqualified metaphysical assumptions. There is, however, an aspect of the anti-relativist's charges which does not rest on the truth of some form of absolutism or a game of question begging. It is the second horn of the dilemma, that relativism on its own relative grounds is incoherent. We perhaps will never determine whether the world adheres to some kind of absolutist picture in order to confirm the first horn of the dilemma, that relativism is self-refuting; yet we *can* evaluate the relativist on her own grounds to see whether her picture, metaphysics aside, is in fact coherent. Does the thesis of internality explain how the relativist can, without inconsistency, uphold the relativity of key elements to frames? Can she make sense of the idea that even relativism itself may be false in another frame? Does analogical thought allow her to grasp alternatives from a relativist point of view? Does resistance give meaningful content to relative key elements on relative grounds alone?

If the answer to these questions is affirmative, then I think we can at least say that the relativist's picture holds together; she does not fall on her own grounds. If she is not incoherent, then she escapes the second horn of the dilemma. In a sense, this clears her from the first horn as well. If her own view is a viable alternative, then there is no need to assume absolutism in the first place, and the self-refutation charge falls short. While this may show that the relativist can effectively escape the anti-relativist's charges, what it does not show is that she can convince the anti-relativist to embrace her view. After all, the relativist has only argued that her theory holds together, not that it is any better than alternative theories, and the anti-relativist may still be wedded to his absolutist picture of key elements. That, however, is an entirely different matter and at this point is of little consequence to the relativist. After all, a plurality of conflicting views, even about relativism itself, supports, rather than defeats, her theory.[72] For her, moreover, there are no neutral, non-relative grounds on which to defend her theory, and it would be disingenuous, if not self-contradictory, for her to act as though she expected to convince the anti-relativist in this way. It is much more consistent for her to build the case for her theory, as we saw in the previous chapter, through lived experience.

Relativism is a modest theory. We might say in the same vein that it is a Socratic theory; its primary claim to knowledge rests on limiting (the possibility of) knowledge itself. As we have seen, relativism's internal claims to knowledge in the epistemic and ethical domains are grounded in an equally modest metaphysical picture. Its metaphysical assumptions revolve around what the world cannot be for the human understanding, not what the world must be in itself. Yet relativism is not a purely skeptical or necessarily deflationary theory. It has positive content; the relativist can absorb and interact meaningfully with the world even though she refuses to give it an ultimate or best form.

In an age as aware of diversity and perspective as our own, I believe that both the widespread fear of relativism and the popularity of its vulgar forms are signs that it is a view of particular significance for us. It confronts us with a sense of unavoidability and inescapability. In the face of such imperativeness, our commonplace expressions of relativism strike us as platitudinous, if not foolish. As philosophers, the rush to charges of self-refutation and incoherence only betrays our fear. Yet it is not so much relativism that we fear as arbitrariness. We do not know how, within our awareness of diversity and perspective, of contingency and contextuality, to hold onto our own claims to key elements such as truth and rightness. In this respect, following the dance between the relativist and the anti-relativist is something like therapy. If we take up the analysis, confront our fear, and make our way through the arguments, then perhaps we will see that we are not so lost in relativism. We still have our own claims, our own truths at the end. Of course, the world that we get back after facing relativism is not as easy to grasp or to navigate as the absolutist one that we leave behind. But we may find ourselves better prepared to take on the complexities of relative truths. We may even find that they have become more meaningful for their very relativity to our lives, and for our own efforts to construct them.

[72] Krausz and Meiland, "Introduction to 'Fabrication of Facts,'" 16.

Chapter 3
Science, Success, and Alternatives

3.1 The Tension Between Science and Alternative Epistemic Practices

Our explorations of relativism so far have led us to the idea that our normative claims may be inextricably tied to a particular way of life.[1] Although there are different ways to formulate this insight, we have seen that some are more coherent than is commonly supposed.[2] This alone, however, may not be enough to persuade us that relativism is an attractive response to the diversity in practices and beliefs that we find across the anthropological and historical record. Relativism implies a sort of evaluative egalitarianism about our claims. It leaves us no way of upholding the claims that, "X is true," or, "It is right to Φ," without adding some such qualifier as, "relative to the context of such and such way of life." Surely, this restriction will strike some as unnecessarily cumbersome. They will ask why relativism insists on isolating our claims from each other on different islands called, "ways of life." They will point out that competing claims interact with and engage each other in the real world. At the end of the day, all claims seem to aim at disclosing and navigating the same world. Why, then, pretend that there is no non-relative way of arbitrating their conflicts? Isn't the best choice revealed in the world itself?

Although we sometimes encounter this sort of objection in the practical domain,[3] it is perhaps even more pervasive and persuasive in the theoretical domain. To us, the power of our own epistemic practices, as embodied in science, is awesome and undeniable. Science may rely on specific values (simplicity, generality, testability, etc.) and specific institutional contexts (the scientific community, research universities, government and corporate funding, etc.), but, at a certain level, we feel that its success speaks for itself. Airplanes fly through the sky, handheld devices play music,

---

[1] See Chap. 1.
[2] See Chap. 2.
[3] As regards the manifest superiority of our social institutions and mores.

© Springer Nature Switzerland AG 2020
A. Luboff, *Facing Relativism*, Synthese Library 425,
https://doi.org/10.1007/978-3-030-43341-3_3

and washing machines clean clothes. Anyone without prior knowledge of our way of life, it seems, should be able to appreciate such practical achievements with a simple demonstration. Over time, we imagine that she would come to recognize our more intricate successes – exploration of outer space, development of vaccines, manufacturing of microchips, in vitro fertilization, and so on. The list of achievements belonging to science and to no other epistemic practice is so long, so stunning that anyone who contemplates it must acknowledge, so the argument goes, that we have more and better knowledge of the world than all other ways of life to date. This suggests that the evaluative egalitarianism of relativism in the epistemic domain is not only unnecessary, but wrongheaded. We *can* compare the competing claims of different epistemic practices, and some are manifestly better than others.[4]

If this line of objection is right, the first problem that the success of science raises for relativism[5] is one of omission. Relativism seems simply to forget, and one wonders if it is even able to account for, the great success of science. The second, even deeper, problem is that the success of science seems to undermine the very case for relativism. In Chap. 1, we contrasted relativism with competing accounts of cultural diversity. We argued that specific features of the deep engagement with a radically different way of life at once complicate these competing accounts and make relativism a more compelling response to cultural diversity. Relativism argues against universalism, evolutionism, and absolutism that there are no neutral, highest, or absolute grounds on which to arbitrate conflicting claims across different ways of life. The success of science, however, suggests there may be powerful considerations that run the other way around, in favor of the non-relative accounts of cultural diversity:

(1) First of all, success seems to delineate the common evaluative framework supposed by *universalism.* We are all humans aiming to understand the same world. If the products of science are accessible and intersubjectively available such that any person from any way of life can see a helicopter hovering in the sky or watch a video recorder replay a recent scene, then there may be more space than relativism allows for *neutral grounds* of evaluation.

(2) Secondly, success seems to demonstrate the progress predicted by *evolutionism.* If our science has encountered more success than any other epistemic practice

---

[4]For an example of this kind of reasoning, see Ernest Gellner, "Relativism and Universals," in *Rationality and Relativism,* eds. Martin Hollis and Steven Lukes (Cambridge, MA: MIT Press, 1982), 181–200. For criticism of relativism as unable to account for the success of science, see, for example, Larry Laudan, "Explaining the Success of Science: Beyond Epistemic Realism and Relativism," in *Science and the Quest for Reality,* ed. Alfred I. Tauber (New York: New York University Press, 1997), Christopher Norris, *Against Relativism: Philosophy of Science, Deconstruction and Critical Theory* (Oxford and Malden, MA: Blackwell Publishers, 1997), and Paul Boghossian, *Fear of Knowledge: Against Relativism and Constructivism* (Oxford: Clarendon Press and New York: Oxford University Press, 2006).

[5]Throughout this chapter, I am concerned with epistemic relativism, or the epistemic dimension of a broader sort of relativism, like cultural relativism. For simplicity, however, I will hereafter refer to it as "relativism" *tout court.*

to date, it may offer a privileged, *highest ground* on which to arbitrate conflicting claims across different ways of life.

(3) Finally, success seems to point to the ultimate truths of *absolutism*. The depth and extent of science's success suggests that it effectively grasps the structure of a unitary world. If this is the case, science must be close to a comprehensive picture of the world, which could allow for mistaken and inadequate pretenders, but not for serious rivals. Science itself, then, would provide us with something close to an *absolute ground* on which to resolve conflicting claims across different ways of life.

For some, these considerations may be strong enough to unwind the case for relativism that flowed out of our exploration of deep engagement. After all, most of us have more direct experience with the fruits of science than with radically different cultures, and the former seem strongly to suggest that we can resolve conflicting claims across different ways of life on non-relative ground. Perhaps the difficulty of arbitrating conflicts is just a romantic exaggeration of the anthropologist and of other cultural interlopers. The perceived reasonableness of radically different claims, and the alleged effectiveness of the foreign practices in which they are embedded, could be due to a powerful delusion. The deeply engaged person may be more like a hostage who comes to sympathize with her captors than an investigator who uncovers alternative practices and truths that, in their own way, also hold of the world. It would not really be the case, then, that there are irresoluble conflicts across different ways of engaging and understanding the world. By considering the success of science, the person immersed in another way of life could come to her senses, put matters in proper perspective, and erase the mistaken validity of so-called alternatives. She might congratulate them on coming close to understanding certain aspects of how the world really is and how it really works – she might even incorporate a few of their insights and techniques into her own understanding – but, at the end of the day, she would return to the manifest superiority of Western epistemic practices, and of science, in particular.

Although I mean to reject this line of objections, I believe that it arises very naturally from within our science-dominated way of life and merits a careful response. I will begin in the present chapter by arguing that the awesome power and achievements of science constitute not a categorical, but a relative success, one dependent on the social, environmental, and conceptual context in which they are enacted. This context dependence of epistemic practice prevents science from constituting a *neutral ground* on which to arbitrate conflicting claims across different ways of life. In Chap. 4, I will argue that the very conceptual framework and standards of assessment that establish science as more successful than other epistemic practices are themselves internal to our way of life, and that we can recognize the shape and merits of competing conceptual frameworks and standards of assessment, by which science is not as successful. This conceptual dependence of measuring success prevents science from constituting a *highest ground* on which to arbitrate conflicting claims across different ways of life. Finally, in Chap. 5, I will argue that even within a view such as scientific realism, which takes the power and achievements of science as signs that our theory latches on very closely to the structure of a unitary world, we can identify a space that corresponds to alternative practices that navigate reality in a way that does not reduce neatly to the content and terms of our own science. This space within the comprehensiveness of science prevents it from constituting an *absolute* ground on which to arbitrate conflicting claims across different ways of life. In all, I aim to show that the success of science need not be anything mysterious or unaccountable to the relativist, and that she can acknowledge it without undermining her own view. Though in a general sense all epistemic practices may aim at disclosing and navigating the same world, this goal is too vague inasmuch as it is shared and too divergent inasmuch as it is specified to provide us with non-relative grounds for resolving conflict across different ways of life.

3.2   The Intuition of a 'Clear Winner' and a 'Clear Loser'

We have seen that the success of science opens the way for challenges to relativism at multiple levels. Yet, we still do not have an idea exactly in what the success of science is supposed to consist,[6] how it is measured, or how it connects to the arguments against relativism. Indeed, my strategy will be to show that relativism can defend itself by further analyzing and specifying these points. While there are many ways to characterize the success of science, we might begin by pointing roughly to two features.[7] The first has to do with the acuity of science in engaging the world.

---

[6] It is probably worth pointing out here that the question in what the success of science consists is distinct from, though not entirely unrelated to, the question of how to demarcate science from other practices that also aim to articulate, describe, and manipulate the world. My starting point is what I take to be the unreflective, received Western view: that science can be easily distinguished from other practices that aim to fix and justify belief, such as shamanism. I assume this starting point without any investigation into what the criteria of demarcation might be. However, if it turns out that the success of science is such a criterion, or even a tacit assumption behind at least some of the criteria, then my account of success (as inherently relative to the context of a particular way of life and to standards of assessment to which we can recognize meaningful alternatives) would tend to deflate the demarcation problem as well. At least part of the distinction between science and other practices would hinge on the context of a particular way of life and the adoption of a certain set of standards of assessment. Interestingly, though, a deflationary account of the demarcation problem does not necessarily diminish the idea that we should be able to appeal to the success of science to arbitrate conflicts between our claims and others'. In fact, dissolving the barriers between science and other epistemic practices might even encourage this idea. After all, if we can show that we are all engaged in the same enterprise, playing the same game with the same aims to satisfy the same needs, then why shouldn't we all be able to agree on the winners? Of course, this is precisely the question addressed in this chapter and the next.

[7] I do not mean to suggest that this is the only way to characterize the success of science, or that this first rough characterization is exhaustive. A critic might insist that my argument falls short because I fail to characterize the success of science adequately. I could only respond to such criticisms on a case-by-case basis. Nevertheless, I believe that the features which in my characterization make the success of science relative – context dependence, holism, and internality of standards of assessment – are quite general. So, the burden for a successful criticism would be to show that

Science allows us to describe, predict, alter, and control our environment at a level of detail far beyond that of our immediate reflection and analysis. It allows us to touch the moon, to open a blocked artery inside the heart, and to see a child before she is born. We can predict the weather, read the past from fossils and other markings on the earth, and map thoughts to regions of the brain. This is to name but a few of the seemingly uncountable superpowers that science has granted to us. The second feature of the success of science involves its adoption by others. Not only do we embrace our current science over the practices of other epochs in our own cultural history, but even people of very different places and ways of life seem to accept and endorse our science in place of their traditional practices. No one here cures by bloodletting anymore, and most parents across the globe would rather take their child to a Western surgeon to fix a cleft palate than to a traditional healer. Would the Chachi use cell phones or the North Koreans learn to build nuclear bombs if our science weren't clearly more successful?

It may be difficult, and contentious, to define the success of science, since many of our foundational ideas about knowledge, the world, and our relationship to it inevitably come into play in the attempt. And yet, at some level, the success of science seems simply manifest to us. We have a sense that we don't need to resolve on a theory of truth and knowledge in order to see that our practices are privileged. Within the glory and power of science lies an intuition that is difficult to pinpoint but goes something like this:

> *All humans have the same basic needs and aims; and, when we pit the methods used, knowledge gained, and technology produced by science against those of any other epistemic practice, science comes out the clear winner, and the alternative practice, the clear loser.*

While this intuition is quite seductive in the abstract, I will argue in the remainder of this chapter that it proves quite complicated on closer inspection and tends to come apart in concrete cases. The purpose of my argument will not be so much to depose a particular characterization of the success of science, or to prove that science is, in fact, unsuccessful, as to emphasize the context dependence of success, and to open our minds to the possibility that there may be alternative, conflicting accounts of success, a possibility which we will go on to explore more deeply in Chap. 4.

Let me start off, nevertheless, by pointing out that to assume that there could be a clear test by which science establishes itself as more successful than an alternative practice is to assume that the two practices are, so to speak, up to the same game. They fulfill the same functions in their respective ways of life, such as acquiring, refining, disseminating, and applying knowledge. They spring from the same motivation to understand the world around us and to negotiate our experience of it better – to improve our senses, such as what we see, hear, and feel in the world; to better satisfy our basic needs, such as what we eat, how we clothe ourselves, how

---

the success of science under some alternate characterization transcends these relativistic constraints. And, of course, in order to be an interesting criticism, this should be achieved in a way that is not merely stipulative.

we move ourselves around, and where we dwell; and to increase our vitality, such as how long we live and how we defend ourselves from illness. However, the reader would be right to note here that there is no uncontroversial way to characterize what it means for two practices to be up to the same game. Moreover, the degree to which they are homologous might vary greatly, and by description. I will return to these points in the following chapter, but for now, let us grant the universalist's assumption of comparability: science and alternative practices are enough alike, and the world that they aim to manipulate and understand is sufficiently manifest and shared, that we can simply test the one against the other.

Now, if we are going to make such a comparison, there seem to be at least two ways to go about it. We could compare the *fruits* of competing practices, such as the techniques and technologies they provide for meeting a shared goal, or satisfying a common need; or, we could compare the *inner workings* of their theories, such as what they are able to predict or explain. I will consider each case in turn.

3.3   Comparing the Fruits of Competing Practices

3.3.1   A Particular Example

Let us begin by considering a particular case of two competing technologies, the hand-powered oar versus the outboard motor. Both are methods of conveying a boat on the river. If the shared goal across diverse ways of life is simply to get from point A to point B as quickly as possible, and nothing else matters or is taken into account, then clearly the outboard motor is the winner. Yet no real comparison is so simple. For example, the Chachi who live on the Río Cayapas in Northwestern Ecuador traditionally traveled downriver for trade in dugout canoes that they rowed with tall oars. In the late 1960s and 1970s, American missionaries who went to live among the Chachi introduced outboard motors that they attached to canoes. The missionaries were thus able to travel from Loma Linda, their home among the Chachi, down to the mouth of the Río Cayapas in about 4 hours. The trip by hand-powered oars, in contrast, took at least 2 days, depending on the depth of the river, weather, and other traveling conditions. The missionaries hired a Chachi man to drive their canoe for them, who eventually bought his own outboard motor, as did many other local inhabitants of the river.

So far, this sounds like a clear case of success. Didn't even the Chachi endorse the superiority of outboard motors, and, concomitantly, the Western science that produced them, by purchasing some for themselves? What complicate the case are all the unanticipated consequences of the motors. Their noise scares away the animals that maintain the health of the forest and provide food for the Chachi. The gasoline from the motors kills the fish, shrimp, and turtles that keep the rivers vibrant and, again, provide food for the Chachi. The gasoline that powers the motors cannot be produced by the Chachi themselves in the forest, and so they are forced to participate more deeply in a cash economy. When they log trees for cash, the animals that they eat, the trees that provide materials for building and clothing, the plants that are sources of food and medicine, all disappear. When they find outside work for cash, they no longer have time to plant a variety of crops; their diet becomes poor and dependent on outside purchases. Those who have cash gain a sudden advantage over those who do not, creating marked social classes, and the communal work system erodes. The cash system also brings new outsiders into the Chachi world: intermediaries for logging companies who use bribes and death threats to enforce contracts, colonists who grab land and rape girls, even pirates who steal back the motors themselves. The Chachi, forced into another way of life, find for the first time that they are poor and uneducated. They come to despise themselves and their culture. Their language, their forest and their knowledge of it, disappear. In a broader context, the success of the outboard motor, and other related technologies, is no longer unequivocal.

3.3.2 Why the Intuition Fails

Our example, trite but true, tells the very familiar story of Westernization. On examining it closely, we can notice two related reasons why the outboard motor fails to be a clear success. The first is the *holism of culture*. As a student of mine once suggested, we can think of cultures as complex machines with many interdependent parts. The problem is that it turns out to be nearly impossible to swap out one part for a new one without unintended consequences to the rest. We cannot replace the hand-powered oar with the outboard motor without affecting the food people eat, the clothes they wear, the houses they live in, the work they do, or even how they envision themselves. Because of cultural holism, we cannot truly weigh one aspect in isolation (the hand-powered oar) against what seems like its counterpart in another way of life (the outboard motor).[8]

The second reason brought out in our example is *context dependence*. The success of an outboard motor does not lie in the motor alone. It depends on an amassing of wealth for the manufacturer to be able to produce the motor, on a division of labor for the assembly worker to make the motor, the shopkeeper to sell the motor, and the mechanic to fix it; on the large-scale mining of resources for the metal in the motor and the gasoline that powers it, and so on. Likewise, the success of the hand-powered oar lies in the ability of any Chachi to make and use one, in the low negative impact that it has on natural resources and communal structures, in the fact that when you

---

[8] It is important to distinguish this claim of cultural holism from a claim of cultural essentialism. While both claims are concerned with the interconnectedness of different facets of a given culture, the latter posits the good of a culture as it stands, statically and impermeably. The former, on the other hand, simply holds that the good of any particular aspect of a culture is not measurable in isolation. I hope it is clear that I do not at all endorse a view of cultural essentialism. I will return to this difference again in Chap. 6.

travel slowly downriver, you have time to cook your meals, chat with the people on the riverbank, even wash your clothes in the water as you float by. The success of the oar, like that of the outboard motor, depends as much on the context as on the object itself.[9]

3.3.3   A Bold Claim

Although oars and outboard motors are but one example, holism of culture and context dependence are, I submit, inescapable features of any way of life. For this reason, our ability to measure success will always tend to break down in concrete cases.[10] Now, against such a bold claim we instinctively (and rightfully, if it is to be well-tested) try to come up with any number of counterexamples. It is tempting, for instance, to think that matters affecting the body should offer clear and easy comparisons across different ways of life. What about life expectancy? It is true that Western medicine and sanitation have enabled us to live longer, on average, than almost any people of other times and places. Yet, this alone does not mean much without a picture of what makes life valuable, and what it means to have a flourishing life. Clearly, by certain measures of quality of life (such as suicide rates, cortisol levels, family stability), we are not simple winners. We should also consider length of life as compared to how time is perceived. Is living to 92 really quite the same thing in our fast-paced way of life as it is in another where time is savored?

---

[9]Lest the reader jump to the conclusion here that the oar is the clear winner over the outboard motor, let me remind her of the importance of context dependence, as well as of a factor that we will explore further in Chap. 4, standards of assessment. Relative to the context of traditional Chachi life and values, such as harmony with nature and union with the fruit of one's own labor, the oar may turn out to be a clear winner. However, there are still other contexts and standards of assessment relative to which it does not. Importantly, relative to the wider context of Western-style development and standards of assessment shaped by classical enlightenment values (favoring reason, autonomy, regulation of nature, etc.), the oar is not a clear winner. From this perspective, the impoverishment of Chachi life to which the adoption of the outboard motor is tied turns out to be but a minor, distasteful blip on the longer path to better understanding and improved conditions of life. By re-evaluating the oar versus the outboard motor from a different context and angle of assessment, I do not mean to suggest that we have the winners and losers the wrong way around, but rather that the very judgment of success cannot be separated from such a context and mode of assessment.

[10]Although I would like to encourage the reader to design and test counterexamples against this claim, I should also caution that hypothetical examples cannot constitute concrete cases. Such examples typically lack precisely what does the work in my claim – rich context, detail, and the interweaving of parts. It is also not clear that a concrete case can be drawn from a way of life that is newly thrown together, like a utopian colony. The idea that I am developing in this chapter and the next is that a way of life works out a relationship to the world, from a particular context and perspective, with its own set of advantages and limitations that cannot be grasped or weighed against each other in any neutral way. It is not clear that a very new or ad hoc "way of life" has had the opportunity to engage the world to such a degree.

We might think, again, that antibiotics are a good case of a clear success. If the shared goal is very narrowly to combat the greatest number of infections in the shortest time possible, then perhaps they are. Yet antibiotics are not successful on their own. They require a division of labor and amassing of wealth to be produced and distributed. They will cause even greater infection if not administered properly, so they demand the strict vigilance of professionals, and a concomitant loss of autonomy by those who are ill. Even under such vigilance, they lead to the evolution of superbugs, the weakening of collective immunity, and, in turn, an increased medicalization and loss of autonomy in our lives. Other cultural practices of treatment to which we might compare the use of antibiotics seek to cure not just the body, but the emotional and social causes of illness; they aim to cure not immediately, but in time, as, for example, a complex physical, emotional, and social process that unfolds in the context of a sickbed. In each case, it is the context as much as the technology that makes the treatment successful.

3.3.4 Success the Other Way Around

It is perhaps worth adding to these considerations the observation that Western knowledge and technology, when placed in a different context, often fail even to appear as clear winners. For example, a traditional Chachi hut, with its thatched palm leaf roof, widely slatted floors, and open sides, stays perfectly cool in the forest breeze. It is easy to keep clean, and the lack of enclosed cavities gives the abundant native cockroaches, rats, snakes, and venomous spiders few places to breed or hide. The smoke from the cooking fire and the breeze keep away the prolific mosquitoes and prevent the excessive humidity and molds from rotting the house or items within it. A Western, "modern" dwelling, on the other hand, rusts and rots in the rainforest, is excessively hot, and harbors tremendous vermin. Though perhaps a novelty, it is no clear winner. Without pesticides, protective resins, cooling systems, electricity, and massive clearing of the area around it, the house is uncomfortable, vulnerable, and even dangerous.

In effect, the Western dwelling, in order to be successful, *requires a shift in context*. It is not successful in the context of the Chachi way of life until that context itself changes. And, indeed, recent history has tended to produce exactly such a shift in context, with the destruction of natural habitats like the rainforest and the human ways of life that they sustained. Yet, we cannot leap from the fact of such a shift to its goodness or to the superiority of its forms, for they are only good in the context that the shift itself creates.

We imagine that the formulae of the physicist, the calculations of the computer, and the drugs of the doctor are clear winners in themselves. And we take the growing impotence of the Chachi's shamans, the malnutrition of their children, and the rupture of their families as evidence of the inferiority of their ways. Yet we forget in both cases how much knowledge and technologies depend on a wider context, a context that for people like the Chachi is rapidly being lost. We might ask ourselves what our own scientist, once removed from the context of contemporary Western life, would look like to an alien civilization. If sources of electric power were rare and she had no way to maintain her computer and other sophisticated instruments, if she no longer had access to much of the data and results of scientists before her, if she had no mentors and but a few distant colleagues with whom she could collaborate, if the aliens themselves had but a vague sense of the scientific method – its aim and how it works, then her ability to analyze and manipulate the world around her would be compromised. She would sometimes come through with interesting results, but they would be infrequent and unreliable. While some aliens might have a natural sympathy for her work, I have no doubt that she would, overall, seem as suspect to them as many a shaman or witchdoctor has seemed to us.

3.4   Comparing the Inner Theoretical Workings of Competing Practices

Let us turn now to the second proposed method for comparing the success of science and of competing practices: we could compare the *inner workings* of their theories, such as what they are able to predict or explain. The reader may notice that the complications we encounter with this method are not unrelated to those of underdetermination discussed by Duhem, Quine, and, later, Kuhn.[11] Yet, our comparison here is ultimately between competing epistemic practices embedded in different ways of life, not between competing theories within the same practice (science). I believe this difference of complexity and scale merits a careful discussion; hopefully, the reader will not feel that we are simply rehearsing old arguments.

In all of the examples that we have considered so far, the practices that we have contrasted with each other have answered to common aims and needs, such as traveling from point A to B, curing infection, and building shelter. In each case, I have challenged our intuition about the emergence of science as a clear winner. My point has not been to establish that the claims and technologies associated with an alternative practice are more successful than those of science, but rather to show that our intuition turns out to be much more complicated than it first seems. Though we may start at a general level from common aims and needs, the particular judgment of success depends deeply on the social and environmental context in which the technology is deployed.

One might object, however, that I have simply chosen the wrong sort of examples for establishing the success of science. By focusing on the technologies associated with different practices, I have myself imbedded the practices within particular

---

[11] See, for instance Pierre Maurice Marie Duhem, *La théorie physique: son objet et sa structure* (Paris: Chevalier & Rivière, 1906), W.V.O. Quine, "Two Dogmas of Empiricism," reprinted in *From a Logical Point of View: 9 Logico-Philosophical Essays* (Cambridge, MA: Harvard University Press, 1953), and Thomas S. Kuhn, *The Structure of Scientific Revolutions,* Second Edition, Enlarged (Chicago and London: The University of Chicago Press, 1970).

ways of life. The morass of cultural holism and context dependence thus only appears because I myself have invited it in. What I fail to see, the objection continues, is that there could be a simpler, direct test from which science emerges as the clear winner. At a certain level, we might take this as a proof of the claims of science and a refutation of those of its contenders.

What our hypothetical objector has in mind here is a special kind of explanation: the successful prediction. A garden-variety explanation aims at the present and is not very revealing; once the facts are before us, anyone can accommodate them with any sort of ad hoc explanation. The surprise of a successful prediction, however, is that it adds to our knowledge; it opens up facts that we had not yet seen.[12] What's more, it appeals to the rather common intuition that a practice like science gets things right because it latches onto the world with at least some degree of accuracy.[13] Although a surprise retrodiction might also add to our knowledge in this way, by pointing to facts in the past that we had not yet noticed, it is easier to imagine that different practices might disagree about how to interpret them. On the other hand, we could imagine a case where representatives of different ways of life agreed to test their respective practices against each other with respect to an event whose outcome both claimed to predict. They could agree on the rules ahead of time – the parameters of the test, the possible outcomes, and how they were to be measured. Then, they could experience the event together.

Of course, setting up the test would not be so easy. Representatives from the two ways of life would have to be located at the same place and time. A direct test of a Bronze Age Sanxingdui practice against contemporary Western science, for example, would be out of the question. The representatives would also have to be able to communicate with each other fairly well. They would need to have knowledge of a common language (though not necessarily a native language for either), which would already imply a certain degree of closeness and connection between the two ways of life.[14] The test, moreover, could not rely on theory-specific measurements, since this would beg the question of superiority of competing practices. The result could not be determined by a telescope or electromagnetic imaging; it would have to be measured by our senses and the basic equipment of the human body – something that we could easily see, for example. Also, the event predicted would have to meet needs and aims that both sides shared and to which they attributed more or less

---

[12] There is a whole literature on what (if anything) makes successful predictions important in evaluating scientific theories. I do not pretend to resolve that issue here; I am merely elaborating on the way in which the objector might take the direct test to work.

[13] Again, this is a weighted issue in the philosophy of science. I do not mean to recommend or defend the realist intuition here; I am only pointing out that it may add to the attractiveness of the direct test. Of course, we do not need to be realists to endorse the direct test. A pragmatist, for instance, could easily explain the import of the direct test as such: the winner's claim works, and the loser's does not; what else matters? For further discussion of the realist intuition, please see Chap. 5.

[14] Language, in fact, raises even deeper issues here, but let us ignore them for the time being out of charity to the example.

an equal degree of importance.[15] Otherwise, the test would again beg the question of which practice was superior, since certain successes or failures of prediction might not strike the people of a given way of life as particularly meaningful. Lastly,[16] the test would need to involve predictions that clearly contradicted each other. There could be many outcomes on which different practices concurred, though they might proffer very different explanations of them. The direct test could only work in cases where the predictions of competing practices clearly diverged.[17]

Our quick round-up of conditions for the direct test has already led to quite a list, but let us look past these difficulties and make a good effort, as the objector suggests, to find a simple test that neatly separates from the holism and context dependence of a given way of life. Evans-Pritchard recounts, for example, that the Azande observe the following rite for the purpose of delaying sunset:

> They place a stone in the fork of a tree and address it thus: "You, stone, may the sun not be quick to fall to-day. You, stone, retard the sun on high so that I can arrive first at that homestead to which I journey, then the sun may set." A man then proceeds on his journey and arrives at the homestead to which he was going.[18]

At first blush, it seems pretty obvious that we could design a simple test to show them that their practice gets the world wrong. Imagine an investigator like Evans-Pritchard living for a time among the Azande. Either he has a native translator who has learned English, or he himself has spent enough time in the land to communicate fairly well in their language. One day, the investigator is out on some business with a Zande companion when both realize that they need to make it to a particular homestead before sunset. They agree that the dense bush is dangerous and unnavigable after dark. The day is coming to a close and the Zande companion suggests

---

[15] I believe that this is a very important condition, and that recognizing when it is not met helps us to reconcile the contrasts/conflicts between different epistemic practices. We need not analyze this here, but see Chaps. 4 and 5 for further relevant discussion.

[16] This paragraph merely indicates some of the complexity in designing a direct test; it should not be read as a comprehensive list of conditions for carrying out such a test.

[17] I would be remiss if I did not mention that there is a very basic question here about whether other practices would grant the validity of a direct test. Evans-Pritchard, for example, claims that part of why the Azande do not realize the "futility" of their magic is that they "are not experimentally inclined." Edward Evans Evans-Pritchard, *Witchcraft, Oracles and Magic among the Azande* (Oxford: The Clarendon Press, 1937), 475, 477. Some might argue that the degree to which testing (and experimentation in general) inheres in a particular epistemic practice, namely our contemporary science, precludes its being used as a neutral arbiter of conflicting claims across different practices. However, I think we can grant that a certain aspect of human nature is simply inclined to experiment, whether or not in a given way of life this develops into the specific form of scientific experimentation. We see in early childhood and even in other intelligent animals an inclination to experiment. So, let us suppose that the direct test requires only this much of an opening to experimentation, and not a specific commitment to experiment in a strictly scientific manner, with the particular methods and context that it requires.

[18] Evans-Pritchard, *Witchcraft*, 468–469. According to Evans-Pritchard, the action of the stone, "is a simple expression of imitative symbolism: as the stone remains in the tree so may the sun remain on high in the heavens."

that they place a rock in the fork of a tree to assure that they make it to their destination in time.

So far, our example seems to fit all of the conditions enumerated above: we have two representatives of different ways of life at the same place and time, with a common language for communication, and a shared aim that both agree is of vital importance. According to the investigator, placing a rock in a tree can do nothing to affect the time of sunset. The spinning of the earth and its movement around the sun predetermine the time of sunset on any given day of the year for every location on our planet. There are no means by which a simple human rite could influence this process. The investigator bases his prediction on the time of sunset as determined by astronomical calculations, the distance from the homestead, and the speed at which he and his companion typically travel. The latter, on the other hand, bases his prediction on a rough sense of the journey and a belief in the effectiveness of his rite. Of course, there will be cases where both predict that they will arrive at the homestead in time (albeit for different reasons). In others, however, the investigator will disagree with his companion about the possibility of a timely arrival. It is these cases that seem quite ripe for a direct test of the Zande practice.

Now, both men, assuming that they stick together, can observe the event of whether and when they make it to the homestead, and they need no instrument beyond the naked human eye to determine whether they are in darkness, or the light of day remains with them. We should note, however, that whereas it is perfectly acceptable for the investigator to use a clock to make his *prediction* about whether they will arrive at the homestead in time, he and his companion cannot use a clock to determine the *outcome* of the test. Although their predictions should be based on their respective practices, the determination of the outcome must be theory-neutral. For all that it seems natural to us, a clock does not detach neatly from our ideas of mechanized time, the earth as a body moving around the sun, and so on. So, the outcome of the test must be determined by looking at the sky and finding oneself or not at the homestead, without consulting a timepiece.

Finally, our two representatives will have to agree as to what they mean by "sunset." For the investigator, "sunset" must be the moment at which the main body of the sun completely exits the observers' visual horizon. Given the context of the Zande rite, it seems more likely, on the other hand, that the companion has in mind by "sunset" something more like, "the moment at which no light from the sun remains in the observers' visual horizon."[19] Let us assume, though, that the two have clarified the term "sunset" with each other, and that they concur that there will be no moon or any other sources of light after the sun has departed. So, they both reflect on the situation. The investigator determines that they will not make it to the homestead in time, but his companion assures that they will. Although they both agree that under normal conditions they would not have enough time to make it to the homestead, the companion insists that the rite with the rock will make the difference.

---

[19] After all, what they need to arrive safely at the homestead is not to be able to see the sun, but to be able to see by the light of the sun. At least, this has been my own experience in living in an area without artificial lighting.

He has performed it many times on similar occasions and knows that it works. The investigator explains that it is impossible for the rock to alter the forces of nature. The two decide, then, to try their predictions against each other. What will the test show?

Of course, what we expect to happen is that the two do not make it to the homestead in time. For the investigator, this outcome indicates that Western science is the clear winner over Zande magic.[20] It is confirmation that science is more successful. For the Zande companion, however, the result is not necessarily the same.[21] He interprets the outcome as simply a single failure of his method, and he easily finds an explanation to accommodate it. A stronger magic, for example, must have interfered with the action of the stone.

Now, some might find this Zande reaction incredible. They might argue that either the Azande are very ignorant, or obstinate, or both, to fail to see that placing a stone in a tree has no effect on the time of sunset. Yet, consider how the reverse case would work. Let's say that the two travelers agree that they will not make it to the homestead in time under normal circumstances. The Zande man picks up a stone, places it in a tree, and recites the spell. Then the two continue on their way. At the end of their journey, the investigator is surprised to see that they have, in fact, arrived at the homestead before darkness. What will he conclude? He is not at all bound to conclude that Zande magic is successful – either that it somehow gets the world right, or that it is more successful than Western science. He can simply write off the test as a fluke. Something else must have happened that he failed to take into account. No major revision of his beliefs (as they constitute his practice or as they establish it as more successful than others) is necessary.

I think that we actually underestimate how often this second sort of case occurs, a matter to which I will return at the end of this sub-section. Let us assume for the moment, however, that the first case obtains: the two travelers fail to reach the homestead in time; the investigator takes this as a clear win for science, but his Zande companion dismisses it as an isolated failure. We may accept this resolution the first time around, but I think we expect not only that the Zande prediction will be wrong initially, but that it will be wrong over and again on similar occasions, and that, with enough repetition over time, our result will gain force. In other words, we expect that the Azande will eventually be forced to admit that magic is unsuccessful and science is the clear winner.[22] So, let's imagine for now that the Zande prediction

---

[20] At least for this test. For the sake of thoroughness, the investigator might wish to confirm his prediction against his companion's on repeated occasions. However, since the investigator already expected the success of his prediction, and this outcome coheres well with his other beliefs, which are themselves well tested, he may not see much need for further instances of the test.

[21] My claim here is not that the Zande representative will never concede the clear win of Western science over his magic. It is rather that he does not have to concede, and will in most cases resist so doing. I hope it is clear that I am saying nothing here about whether the Zande representative *should* or *is right to* concede.

[22] This argument assumes that all humans have a natural tendency to reason by induction, a point that some might wish to dispute. For example, Evans-Pritchard remarks that, "[the] Azande often observe that a medicine is unsuccessful, but they do not generalize their observations. Therefore

is repeatedly wrong. Whenever the investigator and his companion disagree about their arriving at a homestead in time and the latter performs his magic rite, it fails to produce the intended result. For the investigator, this is a clear demonstration of the inferiority of magic. For his Zande companion, however, there is still any number of other explanations available. Perhaps another, more powerful force of magic is interfering with his rite. Perhaps he has bad magic. Perhaps a change in the world itself has made the rite less potent. He need not infer that the problem lies at the level of his practice itself.[23]

Again, if the possibility of such an interpretation of the results seems astonishing, consider how the reverse case would work. Let's say that the Zande companion is repeatedly right. Every time the two men disagree about whether they will make it to the homestead in time, and the Zande man performs his magic rite, they do, in fact, arrive at the homestead before darkness falls. For the Azande, this is confirmation of the effectiveness of magic. Now, although the investigator can no longer write off the results of the tests as a simple fluke, he is certainly under no immediate pressure to abandon science. He may take the surprising success of the Zande predictions as a call for more investigation, for the precision, extension, or modification of existing theories, but there is nothing in the results themselves to derail science. In fact, he is most likely to interpret them from within the context of science itself: surely, there is just some sort of material force, mechanism, or effect that he has failed to take into account.[24]

---

the failure of a single medicine does not teach them that all medicines of this type are foolish. Far less does it teach them that all magic is useless." (Evans-Pritchard, *Witchcraft*, 475) Also, the validity of induction has been questioned from within our own philosophical tradition, notably by David Hume and his followers. Such factors might lead us to wonder whether the direct test can rely on inductive reasoning while remaining the sort of neutral measure that our objector hopes it will be. In his defense, at least at this point in the argument, I believe we can grant that induction is a thinking pattern that we share even with other intelligent animals. (My dog certainly believes that if one or two times he nods to the cookie jar and whines and I give him a cookie, then every time he repeats this behavior, it will produce the desired result.) The dispute, as I am about to argue, has to do more with which facts are salient and how we should reason by induction than whether or not we should reason by induction. Of course, to grant that we all do or, I suppose, must reason by induction is not to insist that it overcomes the limitations that those such as Hume have noted. In fact, these limitations, in light of the dispute about how and when to generalize, suggest why our conflicting claims might not be able to transcend relativistic constraints: if the world cannot be grasped, measured, or analyzed without our conceptual systems, if these systems vary by contingent factors such as culture and historical epoch, *and* if they necessarily underdetermine the world, then our claims might hold of the world and be responsive to it without there being any neutral, highest, or absolute measure to arbitrate their conflicts across different ways of life. This is a point that I will explore in more depth in Chap. 5.

[23] Of course, he *could* interpret the repeated failure of his predictions as a clear loss. I am merely pointing out that he is under no obligation to do so, and that, as I explain below, the case for conceding a clear loss need not be as compelling to him as we tend to assume. Let me also reiterate: this is only an assessment of how the Zande representative might interpret the results of the tests, not a claim about what they must mean.

[24] At a certain point, I do think the investigator may be inclined to make a further inference, leading to the adoption of relativism itself. If on repeated occasions he encounters the success of Zande

What we see here is related to Kuhn's point that scientists will tend not to abandon a paradigm in the face of anomalies.[25] They will simply reinterpret anomalies and make smaller adjustments or alterations to their existing framework in order to accommodate them. Yet what is at stake here is not competing paradigms within the same epistemic practice, science, but rather competing epistemic practices within the possible human modes of knowing and relating to the world. We are not deciding about a particular paradigm, but rather about the entire scientific enterprise itself. What sort of test could convince us to give up science as a whole? And from what sort of evaluative framework could we arrive at such a decision (given that the framework itself is part of what is in question)?

The believer in the direct test has, it seems to me, a ready answer to this question as well. He explains that the Zande representative will be wrong not only on repeat instances of the same test, but on multiple kinds of tests, as regards different aspects of his practice, and on various fronts. Eventually, then, he will be forced to acknowledge the inefficacy of magic and the superiority of science. Indeed, this sort of cumulative pressure is part of what Kuhn describes as leading to the abandonment of an old paradigm and the adoption of a new one.[26] So, why not think that the same thing happens at a larger scale as regards the adoption and abandonment of entire practices themselves?

Now, contemporary history does bear out these sorts of shifts from traditional practices to science, but I would like to caution against reading them as the clear triumph of science over other epistemic practices.[27] There are at least three important points to keep in mind here. First of all, it is a rather naïve assumption that other practices so clearly fail. They are not inept at navigating the world, and the evidence

---

practices, then he may look for a way to acknowledge that they, too, in their own way, hold of the world. I believe this is often the reasoning of the investigator who, for example, becomes deeply engaged in another way of life (see Chap. 1). Moreover, I believe that this stance is compatible with the acknowledgement of the (relative) success of our own science, which is, of course, the point of the present chapter (and the next two). Let me also concede here that it is possible for the investigator to respond to the repeated success of Zande practices by adopting them himself. In order to reject science, however, he would have to have other sources of dissatisfaction with it, a matter that I discuss below as regards the reverse situation, where the Zande converts to science (and a Western way of life).

[25] Kuhn, *Structure.* Kuhn, of course, would not be happy to be called a relativist. Yet I do not deny what was important to him: that given a particular context and standards, our current science is more successful than our previous science and than other epistemic practices. What I question is the ultimacy and priority of such a context and standards. I develop this argument further in Chap. 4. Moreover, my discussion of the dynamic of resonance and loss (especially of *loss*) in that chapter develops two related insights that Kuhn seems to share: that competing practices make incommensurable trade-offs in what they know of and how they relate to the world around them, and that they are not easily combined. So, while Kuhn adamantly disavowed being a relativist in the radical, Feyerabendian sense, I am not convinced that being a relativist in my sense – acknowledging, yet qualifying the success of science to allow a space for competing practices on divergent grounds – would be so offensive to him.

[26] Kuhn, *Structure.*

[27] For a very clear example of this sort of reading, see Gellner, "Relativism."

against them is not typically as obvious or as overwhelming as we assume. If my own experiences seem too partial here to be summoned as support, let me defer to the words of Evans-Pritchard, who was so determined to give a neutral portrayal of the Azande:

> The results which magic is supposed to produce actually happen after rites are performed. Vengeance-magic is made and a man dies. Hunting-magic is made and animals are speared.[28]

Evans-Pritchard also admitted that he found using the poison oracle to be a perfectly efficient way of managing his home.[29] He noted that his observation of a strange light coincided perfectly with the Azande's independent report of a witch's activity in the area on the same night.[30] He even reported that when he saw a Zande man use a rain whistle to shoo away the impending rain, it, in fact, did not rain.[31] We like to believe that native practices are nothing but superstition grounded in infantile patterns of belief. We tell ourselves that humankind lived in utter folly for tens of thousands of years before the advent of Western science (and civilization). Yet, when one actually experiences a non-Western way of life from the inside and contemplates the long history of humankind without Western science, it is this belief itself that can seem more like folly.

Second, and this is Kuhn's point, a shift does not happen because practitioners step back and consider alternatives from a place of neutral evaluation, but rather because they undergo a conversion whereby the context itself that they occupy changes.[32] We saw this in the previous section as regards a Western style dwelling and the success of the science that designs it. The failure of the Zande prediction, if indeed it fails, does not become a clear loss until it is experienced through another perspective. It is such Western concepts as the disenchantment of Nature, the mechanization of time, and the Copernican solar system that make the Zande prediction a clear loss, not the event in itself.

Finally, the context dependence of this shift might not be a source of much concern if we could establish that our standards and context were themselves superior to others. After all, one might assume that the best concepts lead, overall, to the most accurate beliefs. Of course, then, the Azande could not properly assess the direct test until they shared the context of our science. I will argue in the following chapter, however, that we can appreciate the grounds of legitimacy of other standards and contexts, and that we have no way outside of such standards and contexts to judge one set superior to another. So, while we may note that a majority of ways

---

[28] Evans-Pritchard, *Witchcraft,* 475. Interestingly, Evans-Pritchard offered this observation as part of an explanation of why the Azande failed to recognize the erroneousness of their magic. He argued that its apparent efficacy got in the way of understanding its actual falsity. Of course, it is precisely such an attitude toward the superiority of science that I am calling into question.

[29] *Ibid.,* 270.

[30] *Ibid.,* 34.

[31] *Ibid.,* 472–473.

[32] Kuhn, *Structure.*

of life that have come into contact with ours have gone on to adopt, for the most part, our science, and increasingly, our context and way of life, this fact does not demonstrate the superiority of science or provide us with neutral grounds on which to resolve conflicting claims across different ways of life. It merely points out that we find ourselves, increasingly, on something like a cobbled same ground of evaluation, or on a ground that renders the conflict obsolete. Yet we have no way of attributing this contingent fact to the greater truthfulness of our practices, or to their superiority in articulating, manipulating, and describing the world as a whole. Why attribute it to truth and rightness, if there are so many other factors that have led to a situation where alternative contexts are simply no longer available? We have already mentioned some recent factors in the case of the boat motor that have destroyed a native context.[33] But we might remind ourselves of just a few of the factors that, at a general level, have made non-Western contexts increasingly unavailable since the Age of Exploration – virulent communicable diseases that wiped out entire populations of natives, gunpowder that made rapid mass destruction possible, dumb luck, like the timing of the Spanish Conquest in Ecuador, which was able to turn the recent Incan Conquest of the land to its advantage, lust that made Westerners so eager to invade other lands, ruthlessness that made us take others as slaves, zealousness that prevented us from leaving others and their beliefs alone...given that there are so many other, contingent factors involved in the dominance of Western ways, why must we attribute the adoption of our science to greater truthfulness, or more generally, to the superiority of our knowledge?[34]

3.5 Reassessing the Intuition of Success

We began this chapter by considering the objection that the success of our way of life and of our science, in particular, seems to undermine the evaluative egalitarianism of relativism. It suggests that relativism cannot account for the manifest success of our practices and that we *do,* in fact, have non-relative ground on which to arbitrate conflicts across different ways of life. We saw, however, that whether we

---

[33] See Sect. 3 above.

[34] Cf Jared Diamond, *Guns, Germs, and Steel: The Fates of Human Societies* (New York and London: W.W. Norton & Company, 1999), in particular, Chap. 3, "Collision at Cajamarca." If the Spanish conquered the Incas in part because Atahualpa expected Pizarro to be a man of greater honor, who knew how to receive a foreign leader, kept his word, and was not up to bloodthirsty deceit, where did the superiority lie? If native peoples did not have resistance to diseases like smallpox because their ancestors never had to survive the filth and poverty of medieval cities, what sort of lack of development was that? If only Westerners were willing to dominate the world by means such as a massive human slave trade, the wholesale extraction of non-renewable resources from the Earth, and unprecedented rates of genocide, again, did their eventual victory owe itself to epistemic superiority, or to what on closer examination, and by Western standards themselves, might look like moral failure? For further discussion related to these points, see the beginning of Chap. 5.

compare the success of competing practices by their fruits or by the inner workings of their theories, the determination of success does not separate neatly from the social, environmental, and conceptual context in which the practice is enacted. Because of this context dependence, the success of science does not constitute a neutral ground on which to arbitrate conflicting claims across different ways of life. The ground on which we discover success is itself deeply shaped by context. Yet, we still have not seen whether the success of science leads to a highest or absolute ground on which to evaluate conflicting claims, matters that we will go on to explore in Chaps. 4 and 5, respectively.

Chapter 4
The Dynamic of Resonance and Loss

4.1 Introduction

In the previous chapter, we raised the concern that the success of science seems at some level to undermine the very possibility of relativism. Though this concern arises rather naturally within our science-dominated way of life, it is not immediately clear how to formulate it into a specific objection. How exactly does science establish its claims over those of other epistemic practices? We started off by assuming that other epistemic practices are mostly homologous to science. They play, in their respective societies, the same game as science of understanding and navigating the physical world around us. Under this assumption, we might formulate the argument from the success of science against relativism as follows:

> Other epistemic practices perhaps at times have a few things to add to science. They may do science primitively (proto-science), they may do science mixed up with some nonsense (superstition), or with something else (like psychotherapy); but, for the most part, the knowledge that they extract of the world either easily reduces to or complements that of science, because we share a single, unitary world that can best be understood in one way. Given our common aims and our common world, we can easily compare other epistemic practices to science, and it is at this level that the success of science dissolves the incommensurable alternatives required for relativism.

We started to see, however, that a determination of "success" is not as easy to make as it first seems. When we compare the success of our respective technologies in completing the same task, for example, the judgment of success does not separate neatly from the social and environmental context in which the technology is used.[1] We also find that we cannot measure particular technologies and single tasks against each other in any straightforward way, because a society is a complex, interwoven whole, and changing one part can produce unintended, often deleterious

---

[1] Chapter 3, Sect. 3.2.

© Springer Nature Switzerland AG 2020
A. Luboff, *Facing Relativism*, Synthese Library 425,
https://doi.org/10.1007/978-3-030-43341-3_4

consequences to the rest.[2] On the other hand, when we compare the success of our respective theoretical understandings against each other, for example, in making a prediction regarding the same event, we run into problems of underdetermination.[3] The only way to read such a test as a clear success for science over other epistemic practices is to assume the priority of our own conceptual background, and often that of our own social and environmental context, as well. This, of course, raises the question whether our own way of engaging with the world deserves such priority.

I would like to suggest that perhaps it does not. Perhaps science's greatest priority simply stems from the fact that it is our own epistemic practice. In this chapter, I will show how the relativist can reserve a space for the recognition of alternative standards of assessment, fundamental concepts, and social-environmental contexts so that the success of science can coexist alongside that of other epistemic practices. In simplest terms, the relativist can relativize the success both of science and of alternative practices by recognizing a plurality of ways of understanding the world and an incommensurability among them. In raising this possibility, we are moving away from the aforementioned assumption of the previous chapter. The more deeply we delve into the contrast between science and other epistemic practices, the less they appear homologous. Their differences become more prominent; their ways of understanding and navigating the world no longer seem to reduce neatly to each other. This stricter demarcation between science and other practices, however, introduces a new problem: why should we even think of these other practices as epistemic? Why should we recognize what they capture of the world as any species of theoretical knowledge? The answer, as I hope will become apparent, is that the content and aim of alternative practices, while not identical to those of science, overlap significantly with them. Because they rely on somewhat different fundamental concepts, standards of assessment, and social-environmental contexts, the range of their knowledge is oblique to and entangled with that of science. Yet we cannot make the argument that there is one best form of knowledge, or one best practice for accessing it, without, in fact, occupying the standpoint of science and presupposing its primacy.

4.2   Relativism and Ambivalence

We often think of relativism as a view grounded on the mutual incomprehensibility of radically different conceptual schemes.[4] Although this might describe some relativisms at their greatest height of zealousness, it is, as we have discussed, in tension

---

[2] Chapter 3, Sect. 3.2.

[3] Chapter 3, Sect. 3.3.

[4] For what is perhaps the canonical formulation of such a relativism, see Donald Davidson's seething anti-relativist attack, Donald Davidson, "On the Very Idea of a Conceptual Scheme." In *Relativism: Cognitive and Moral*, edited by Michael Krausz and Jack W. Meiland, 66–80 (Notre Dame: University of Notre Dame Press, 1982). Reprinted from Proceedings of the American

with the very possibility of anthropological work and not representative of the experience of deep engagement.[5] Throughout this work, I have been careful to characterize relativism not by radical untranslatability, but by the complex differences in the ways that our claims about the world are formulated and grounded. In the epistemic domain, such a view distinguishes itself from a mere alethic relativism, which claims that what is true and what is false is relative to a cultural context, or way of life. Truth is not the only concept we use to evaluate knowledge claims, and a richer version of relativism allows for the possibility that the same concept of truth may not itself be shared across all cultures.[6] It also contrasts with a strawman relativism that is defined paradoxically, as the claim that both P and not-P are true relative to different cultural contexts. If distinct cultural contexts grasp the world in different ways, then relativism must allow for the possibility that the very same claim, P, might not even be formulable in both contexts. In the epistemic domain, a rich relativism is characterized not by the diametrical opposition of knowledge claims, but by their incommensurability. The conflict that emerges is rarely between P and not-P, but is more generally between P and א, where it appears that there is no straightforward way of endorsing both claims together,[7] but we take them, nevertheless, to refer to the same, or at least to overlapping, phenomena. This is what I call, "entrenched conflict." As we have seen, the claim that defines relativism in this case is mostly negative: we have no absolute, highest, or neutral ground on which to arbitrate the conflict between P and א.[8] We may find that P holds relative to the one cultural context and that א holds relative to the other, but we have no non-relative means of asserting that either grasps the world more accurately or effectively than the other. In terms of this definition, then, the present chapter argues that science fails to undermine relativism by providing a highest ground for arbitrating entrenched conflict.[9]

David Wong, in his essay, "Three Kinds of Incommensurability," takes a similar approach to defining relativism. He argues that what grounds the view is not the mutual incomprehensibility of different ways of life, but the fact that we *can* make another, "[culture] intelligible enough to realize that their fundamental concepts, beliefs, and modes of justification are different from ours."[10] In his more recent

---

Philosophical Association 47 (1973–74): 5–20. I hope it is clear that this is not my version of relativism. For more on this difference, see Chap. 6.

[5] See Chaps. 1 and 2.

[6] In other words, it emphasizes that our particular concept of truth has a distinct history, one that is not necessarily shared across different ways of life. For more on this point, and on relativism defined by entrenched conflict, see Chap. 6.

[7] That is, as long as we understand each claim to be non-relative.

[8] This definition of relativism should be familiar from Chap. 2.

[9] Similarly, Chap. 3 argues that science fails to undermine relativism by providing *neutral* grounds of arbitration, and Chap. 5 argues that science fails to undermine relativism by providing *absolute* grounds of arbitration.

[10] David B. Wong, "Three Kinds of Incommensurability," in *Relativism, Interpretation and Confrontation,* ed. Michael Krausz (Notre Dame, Indiana: University of Notre Dame Press, 1989), 142.

work, Wong describes our ability to conceive of a way of life at odds with our own as a sort of *ambivalence*.[11] It is because of the diversity and complexity within our own experience that we are able to extrapolate to an appreciation of practices and beliefs that are quite different from and often in strong tension with our own.

Such an appreciation of alternatives comes not so much from an explicit argument or demonstration as from an exercise of analogy that builds on our own experience and self-reflection. In Chap. 1, I described how the anthropological investigator can use the return to a childlike state to build an appreciation of new concepts, of the cultural context that they inhabit, and of the claims that distinguish that context. In Chap. 2, I argued that the relativist does not jump out of her skin to inhabit another way of life, but rather develops an understanding of what that way of life must be like through an exercise of analogical thought. In the present chapter, I will continue to develop these themes by exploring ambivalence in greater detail, or what I will refer to as, "the dynamic of resonance and loss." This dynamic, I contend, prevents us from recognizing our own standards of assessment as highest or absolute, and so leaves open a space for asserting relativism alongside the (relative) achievements of science.

4.3   Introduction to the Dynamic of Resonance and Loss

Although Wong's treatment of ambivalence is mostly concerned with moral relativism, he discusses an example from Charles Taylor of particular importance for the epistemic domain. This is our stance toward knowing the world.[12] In an essay entitled, "Rationality," Taylor attempts to make sense of magic rites, such as the Azande's, and their relation to Western science. He believes that in order to do so, we must appreciate a contrast between two possible modes of engaging the world. One mode takes the world as an inanimate object of understanding, distanced from ourselves. The other mode seeks attunement with the world – loving, following, merging with it.[13] Taylor notes that the great achievements of Western science owe themselves in large part to the distinction we place between these two modes and to the strong preference that we give to the first. And yet, he explains, magic rites become more reasonable to us when we can at least see that they are undertaken from a perspective in which our distinct concepts of understanding and attunement are fused together.[14]

---

[11] David B. Wong, *Natural Moralities, a Defense of Pluralistic Relativism* (Oxford and New York: Oxford University Press, 2006), 6–28.

[12] Wong, *Natural Moralities, op. cit.,* and Charles Taylor, "Rationality," in *Rationality and Relativism,* ed. Martin Hollis and Steven Lukes (Oxford: Basil Blackwell Publisher Limited, 1982), 87–105.

[13] Wong, *Natural Moralities, op. cit.,* and Taylor, *op. cit.*

[14] Taylor, *op. cit.*

This ability to locate some small piece within our own perspective, a sort of miniature analogue, which we can then use to develop an appreciation of a very different way of relating to the world, is exactly what Wong has in mind by ambivalence. Interestingly, though, Taylor draws the contrast between the two modes of engagement in rather ethnocentric language. He refers to the mode of our own practice, science, simply as "understanding," whereas he describes the mode of the foreign practice, magic, as understanding mixed up with something else that is supposed to be less important or less relevant. We can, however, frame the contrast in more neutral terms. We can say that science and magic both aim to *understand* the world, inasmuch as this means that they are both practices aimed at describing, articulating, and manipulating the world. The greatest difference between the two, then, lies not in their general aim,[15] but in how they relate to an object of understanding. Science takes its object of understanding as fundamentally and necessarily detached or removed from itself. Practices such as magic, on the other hand, take their object of understanding as essentially related to, or connected with themselves.

Taylor's essay is part of the Rationality Debates of the 1970s and 1980s, where social scientists and philosophers were working to understand the relationship between science and the practices of non-Western societies. Their discussions drew on the ethnographies of Evans-Pritchard and Malinowski, among others, as well as on the work of earlier cultural thinkers, such as E.B. Tylor, James Frazer, and Lucien Lévi-Bruhl.[16] In what follows, I develop a more detailed account of the contrast between the two modes of knowing the world that Taylor seems to have in mind. My analysis draws from my own experience with alternative epistemic practices, as well as from the general spirit of recent work in environmental philosophy, particularly ecofeminism, and in feminist epistemology and philosophy of science. My point, however, is not to provide a better etiology of practices such as magic, or a more comprehensive account of the distinctiveness of science. I also do not mean to argue for the superiority of alternative epistemic practices over science, or to correct our practice of science and use of technology for what we might come to understand as patriarchal and anthropocentric bias. Rather, my point here lies in our *relationship to* the contrast between science and alternative practices; our ambivalence, I argue, creates a space for relativism, and for acknowledging the success of science alongside that of incommensurable alternatives.

I examine the dynamic of resonance and loss in several stages. I begin by characterizing the way of knowing the world, or epistemic stance, associated with the two sides in Taylor's distinction: the impartial stance of science, and the relational stance of alternative practices such as magic (Sects. 4.4–4.7). I then show that a relational stance, while not dominant in our way of life, resonates with us; it stirs familiarity within us, and elicits from us what I call "constructivity," the ability to

---

[15] Of course, they may still have great differences in their *specific* aims.

[16] Much of these debates is captured in the following three collections: Bryan R. Wilson, ed., *Rationality,* (Oxford: Basil Blackwell, 1970, 1974, 1977), Robin Horton and Ruth Finnegan, eds., *Modes of Thought* (London: Faber & Faber, 1973), and Martin Hollis and Steven Lukes, eds., *Rationality and Relativism* (Oxford: Basil Blackwell, 1982).

grow small seeds from our own experience into a deep appreciation of the very different practices and beliefs of another way of life (Sect. 4.8). In appreciating the understanding captured by a relational stance, we also recognize what is lost to an impartial stance (Sect. 4.9). We sense this in our own way of life as alienation (Sect. 4.9.1). In comparing the two stances, we come to see that some loss is inevitable; they pull in different directions and cannot be combined fully into a single way of knowing the world that maintains all of their individual advantages (Sect. 4.9.2). And yet, the very judgment that one set of trade-offs is better than another – that one way of knowing the world comes closest to getting it – itself depends on the context of a particular way of life (Sect. 4.10). This deep ambivalence at the level not only of practices and beliefs, but of standards and contexts of assessment, relativizes the success of science and so neutralizes the objection that the manifest superiority of our science leaves no incommensurable alternatives to our way of life for relativism ever to get started in the first place (Sect. 4.11).

4.4   Two Contrasting Epistemic Stances

Let me start with a few caveats. First of all, our exposition here of the Dynamic of Resonance and Loss will share some non-standard qualities with that of Deep Engagement in Chap. 1. The well-seasoned analytic philosopher might wonder why in both cases I use more descriptive, or, he might complain, "poetic" language. The reason is that in each case I am aiming to explain particular kinds of experience and the possibilities of knowledge that they open to us. In Chap. 1, I described specific features of the experience of deep engagement with another way of life to show how they suggest that our own way of articulating, ordering, manipulating, and valuing the world is not absolute. In this chapter, I will describe specific features of the experience of ambivalence about our way of knowing the world to show how they suggest grounds of legitimacy for epistemic practices other than science. While both arguments are systematically rigorous, their content, and the language needed to refer to features of that content, may be unfamiliar and even uncomfortable for the more traditional analytic philosopher. I hope that these arguments, indeed this book itself, may shed some light on that discomfort – of facing relativism, of facing the other, of facing ourselves. I hope that they help to elucidate, as much new feminist and critical philosophy has, the relationship between experience[17] and truth. I take this work to be within but also about the limits of analytic philosophy. I believe, moreover, that our discipline's Socratic routes can teach us to hold steady and to look deeply in the face of such discomfort. It is in that spirit that I offer an account of the dynamic of resonance and loss and hope that my more analytic readers at least

---

[17] The access we have to it, the ways that we manage it, what we acknowledge within it…

come along for the ride. I don't believe, however, that the coherence of my argument requires their assent.[18]

Now, as we get into the work of describing the two contrasting stances, we must remember that demarcating a way of life is itself a relative act. It depends not only on the perspectives of those involved, but on the discussion at hand. When debating whether the success of science leaves any room for the incommensurability of alternative epistemic practices, we are working at a very high level of abstraction, and so our demarcation of different ways of life is very broad. We can speak, however, of a way of life dominated by the practices of Western science without denying the heterogeneity, fluidity, and dynamic nature both of science and of the way of life that it permeates. That is, we can work with abstractions without giving in to reifications. We can acknowledge that there is no single, unified practice, "Science," and no neatly demarcated, uniform, static entity, "Western society," yet still recognize the insights that arise when we consider as a whole the collection of practices typically called "science" and their relationship to the organization, values, and self-understanding of the people who participate in them, whether directly or indirectly.

If there is no monolithic Western scientific (or perhaps, "scientistic") culture, there certainly is no such "non-Western" culture of contrasting epistemic practices. In drawing the distinction between an impartial and a relational epistemic stance, which pits Western science on one side of a divide and virtually all[19] other epistemic practices on the other, I do not mean to assimilate these diverse non-scientific practices, to deny their richness and individuality, or to entrap our analysis in the Orientalizing dichotomy of self/other. I do want to suggest, however, that there is something very important that we (those of a science-dominated way of life) can learn about ourselves through the analysis of the contrast between an impartial and a relational stance, and that this greater self-understanding is, at the same time, a means for a better understanding of others.

Finally, and this is perhaps the most important point, let me caution that we do not experience the contrast between the two stances as a perfect dichotomy. We do not ourselves perfectly inhabit an impartial stance, and the features of a relational stance are not entirely foreign to us.[20] In fact, if this were the case, we could not feel ambivalence, and the dynamic of resonance and loss could never take hold. I would like to argue that the distinctiveness of our way of knowing is not its identity with an impartial stance along any particular axis, but the degree to which we favor it across a collection of features as a whole. Yet, as we will see, it is our ability to grasp a different weighting or prioritization of these features that lends plausibility to the methods and claims of contrasting epistemic practices.

With these caveats in mind, let's sketch some distinguishing features of the two stances, the impartial stance that dominates science, and the relational stance that

---

[18] See Chap. 2 and the end of the current chapter.

[19] Virtually, but not necessarily, all.

[20] Conversely, the features of an impartial stance are not entirely foreign to practitioners of contrasting epistemic practices, either.

dominates contrasting epistemic practices such as magic. We will begin by examining the relationship between the subject and object of understanding in both stances (Sect. 4.5). We will then consider how this relationship affects the way each stance captures information (Sect. 4.6) and calibrates understanding about the world (Sect. 4.7).

4.5   Relation between Subject and Object

This first axis looks at the way subject and object relate to each other in each stance. A subject is that which knows, that which gathers information and shapes it into knowledge. An object is simply that which the subject aims to know. In the names of our two stances, we already capture quite a bit about how each conceives of the relationship between subject and object. In the impartial stance of science, a subject is just that, "im-part-ial," or, "not-a part-of,"' its object. The two are separate; the relation between them is merely epistemic in the narrowest sense: one is the knower, and the other is what is known. In the relational stance of magic, on the other hand, a subject is always recognized as *in relation with* its object. The connections between the two are rich and play an important role in conveying information.

The distinguishing features along this axis perhaps capture best the contrast that Taylor had in mind. In the impartial stance that characterizes science, we find a relationship of *detached understanding* between subject and object; and in the relational stance that characterizes magic, we find a relationship of *loving attunement* between subject and object. In an impartial stance, knowledge results from distancing subject and object. In a relational stance, on the other hand, knowledge results from bringing the two closer together, from mingling, and sometimes even merging, subject and object. Below, we will examine the relationship between subject and object in each stance more carefully by looking at three aspects: (1) the proximity of subject and object, (2) the likeness between subject and object, and (3) the struggle between subject and object. As we develop a picture of each, it will become apparent that stances are both descriptive and normative. An impartial stance not only conceives of subject and object as separate, but facilitates and endorses their separation. Similarly, a relational stance not only conceives of subject and object as richly related, but facilitates and endorses their mingling.

4.5.1   Proximity of Subject and Object

In an impartial stance, subject and object stand far away from each other. In a relational stance, they intermingle. This means that each stance gathers information and, in turn, constructs knowledge about the world at a different distance between subject and object. We might say that each stance has a different *ideal epistemic proximity*, or distance between subject and object at which information is most reliably sourced. For an impartial stance, the ideal proximity is found as subject and object are increasingly separated from each other. Science traditionally prizes "objective" knowledge, knowledge in which the subject and object are so separate that none of the subject's influence is detected in reports about the object. In fact, science even makes use of a pejorative concept to identify and root out insufficient separation between subject and object: *bias*. For a relational stance, on the other hand, knowing the world occurs as subject and object come into relation with each other; they realize themselves through each other. To borrow a phrase from nondual philosophy, subject and object are, "not one and not two." We might understand the subject-object dynamic of a relational stance in terms of a child in the womb.[21] They form a system together. They influence each other and work together. They are distinct, but not separate. For a relational stance, the ideal epistemic proximity is not as wide, but as narrow as possible. Knowledge results not from the separation, but from the rich interplay of subject and object.

Compare for a moment a shaman and a scientist gathering knowledge. Imagine each with some of their tools – the shaman with his magic stones, a bottle of rum, and a candle; the scientist with her microscope, petri dishes, and slides. As the scientist peers through her microscope, the extra *distance* it creates between subject and object functions to improve her vision. The clean white coat that she wears protects her from her object and attests to their separation, as it would clearly show if any piece of the object tainted her. The shaman, on the other hand, drinks the rum, sings to his magic stones, and looks at the wick of the burning candle for a vision. He knows his object through the image that comes to his mind's eye. There is nothing to attest to the separation between subject and object. He ingests his tools, collaborates with his objects of study, and collects information through his own experience. Just as distance facilitates knowledge from an impartial stance, *intimacy* facilitates knowledge from a relational stance.

4.5.2   Likeness between Subject and Object

When two things are in relation with each other, they cannot be completely unalike. If they were unalike, there would be no means to establish a relation between them. And, of course, if there is a relation between them, the two things must at least have the relation itself in common. Conversely, if two things are completely separate from each other, they cannot be alike. Any sameness between them is grounds for a relation, for bringing them closer together. This helps us to understand, then, why an impartial stance takes subject and object as very much unlike each other, and why a relational stance takes them as resembling each other in important ways. Difference preserves distance; likeness preserves intimacy. *Subject-object likeness* is small for an impartial stance, and great for a relational stance.

---

[21] Morris Berman develops this image beautifully in his work, *The Reenchantment of the World* (Ithaca: Cornell University Press, 1981).

According to an impartial stance, only subjects possess agency and reason. They are the ones who identify, collect, and control information. Objects, on the other hand, lack agency and play no role in shaping knowledge beyond being themselves revealed. The impartial stance of science typically grants resemblance only where necessary. If the objects of study are themselves human, they may be recognized to possess reason and agency, but not in the particular area of the study.[22] If the objects are closely associated non-human animals, they may be recognized to possess feelings and some cognitive abilities, but not full agency. Other less associated animals may be recognized to possess only perceptive abilities, if anything at all. Typically, non-animal life forms are attributed no such abilities, and matter itself, according to science, is not even living. It is inert, completely disenchanted. It has no telos. It composes the unthinking, unfeeling world of Darwin, mindlessly playing itself out.[23] It follows laws, which may be discerned by the subject, but have no reason of their own. Its parts move with the cold regularity of a machine. Change is simply the succession of one process determining another. In such a world, the only force is survival, the struggle of power itself; it is void of reason and emotion, of wisdom and compassion.

For the same reason that an impartial stance takes objects as lacking the hallmarks of subjectivity, a relational stance takes objects as possessing them. For subject and object to stand in relation to each other, they must have some means of coming together, of communing and sharing. A relational stance takes subjects and objects alike as minded and animate. Agency is not limited to subjects; objects, too, have reason, emotion, and will. Knowing is a relation between subjects and objects. Objects themselves possess understanding and purpose. A plant, for instance, may call a shaman's attention as he is walking through the forest and cause to arise in his mind the understanding of what illnesses it cures, along with how it should be prepared and administered to a patient.[24] Or, a mineral may reveal its location to a shaman in a dream, making itself available for the people's use. In that case, they

---

[22] This closeness may shed light on why sciences that study humans, such as psychology and sociology, are often referred to as, '*soft* sciences.' When human objects of study do possess the same abilities and training as the researchers (e.g. when they are themselves scientists), they are often excluded from participating in studies, or, extra steps are taken to assure their distance (lack of bias) in collecting and analyzing data.

[23] I have in mind here Michael Ruse, *The Darwinian Revolution: Science Red in Tooth and Claw*, second edition (Chicago and London: The University of Chicago Press, 1999).

[24] In other words, the thoughts associated with this understanding will appear in the shaman's mind when he takes notice of the plant. "Taking notice" here is the simple act of opening a line of communication, like when we notice someone in the street and say, "Hello." The difference is that the exchange happens at a level that is not primarily linguistic. Although the shaman can later express his understanding in words, the information will first come to him primarily as pictures, as other sensory impressions, or as a simple feeling of knowing. If the reader finds such an exchange impossible to imagine, it may help to recall that the activity associated with most regions and processes of the brain is also not linguistic. If this does not help, the reader still need not be alarmed. The point of this section is only to characterize, not to endorse or to fully understand, a relational stance.

may ask permission[25] to extract the mineral and offer a gift of appreciation in exchange. In a relational stance, what objects know is not only received, but deeply respected by subjects.[26]

Consider again the contrast between our shaman and our scientist. The latter collects information from her object and analyzes it. What she knows of a plant's properties or a mineral's location is extracted only from her observation and analysis. In this process, she is solely and fully active; she alone must *make sense of* her object. The object has no consent to give for the information she takes and no wisdom of its own to impart to her. The shaman, on the other hand, *reasons with* the elements of Nature. He receives information from his objects of study and honors them. Knowledge is a collaborative work and exchange.

4.5.3 Power between Subject and Object

From an impartial stance, the world and all that it contains is here for us to use and control. We farm, harvest, hunt, poison, and alter its life forms as we like, down to their genetic code. We drill and mine its resources to satisfy our own needs. We move, destroy, and reshape its landscape to suit our own designs. And we use science as a tool to serve these ends. The purpose of our understanding is to gain greater control.[27] A relational stance, on the other hand, seeks not so much to *dominate* the world as to *influence* it. It uncovers the ways of the world in order to capture what the world itself wants, not to mold the world to its own design. The purpose of understanding is greater harmony. What we see is a difference of power in the relation between subject and object when we look at the two stances. In an impartial stance, the subject holds a relation of *power over* its object; in a relational stance,

---

[25] For example, from the mineral itself or from the formation of earth that contains it.

[26] For more on this relationship with the natural world, see Lynn White Jr.'s seminal essay, "The Historical Roots of Our Ecological Crisis," *Science* 155 (1967): 1203–07.

[27] There may seem to be an inconsistency here between the claim that in an impartial stance the subject aims to have power over his object and the earlier claim that in an impartial stance the distance between subject and object is much farther than in a relational stance, where the subject and object are intermingled (Sect. 4.5.1). If a subject is far away from his object, how can the former control the latter? The object is not so far away that it ceases to be the subject's object of inquiry, yet it is far enough away that the two are different and separate. Distance is a key to othering and to gaining control. It allows the subject to treat the object in a way other than he treats himself or allows himself to be treated; the object is excluded from the subject's same code of ethics and from his entitled rights. Denying the same treatment and rights is how, for instance, we can raze a forest to make a palm oil plantation without regard for the plants and animals losing their home, or how we can extract massive amounts of gold without regard for the river that is poisoned. We find the particular strategy of distance at play on a plantation, for example, where the slaveowner, who takes his slaves as objects, or property, boards them on the plantation, but not where he lives, in the same space, or in the same conditions. That separation helps him to deny their likeness, and so the horror of enslaving people who have equal agency and deserve equal rights.

the subject holds a relation of *power with* its object. The scientist studies and manipulates her object, while the shaman communes and negotiates with his.[28]

One way to locate the contrast in subject-object power relations between the two stances is to consider the difference between a weather forecast and a rain dance. The matter is not so much their comparative effectiveness as their *aim*. The weather forecast names and studies every aspect of the climate in order to predict and control, to the best of our abilities, the waters, land, wind, and air, so that they promote, and do not get in the way of, our activities and plans. The rain dance, on the other hand, sings and makes offerings to the sky, *asking* the sky to rain. It neither predicts nor demands results. It simply aims to assist them, to urge them on.

4.6   Capturing Knowledge

Along the first axis of comparison, we saw that the engagement between subject and object in an impartial stance is characterized by distance, difference, and control. In a relational stance, on the other hand, their engagement is characterized by intimacy, likeness, and collaboration. These observations will help us in our examination of the second axis of comparison, which looks at how each stance captures knowledge. The primary contrast along this axis is that of *revealing an object* versus *relating to it*. If we consider again our laboratory scientist and our shaman, we find that the former aims to unmask the world, to discover what it is made of and how it works. The latter, on the other hand, seeks to develop a particular connection or relationship with the world.

4.6.1   Process of Gathering Information

Because the likeness between subject and object is so minimal in an impartial stance, the process of gathering information from an object disconnects neatly from the particular experiences of the subject.[29] The subject's experiences are not a critical part of the process. They are replicable by anyone in the same circumstances, and so leave no particular mark. In other words, the process of gathering information in an impartial stance is *object-ive*. It is tightly and almost uniquely focused on the object. The subject strives to know the object in as pure and unadulterated of a manner as possible. In a relational stance, on the other hand, the subject gathers

---

[28] This contrast has been articulated beautifully in recent work by ecofeminists, which, unfortunately, I cannot index here. For one of the earliest discussions of "power over/power with" in ecological thought, see Lynn White Jr.'s, *op. cit.* For the struggle to dominate and control nature as an expression of patriarchy, see Karen Warren, "The Power and Promise of Ecological Feminism," *Environmental Ethics* 12 (1990): 125–46.

[29] We might argue that this breaks down in quantum mechanics. Indeed, that is what makes the field so fascinating; at some level, it seems to challenge science's entrenchment in an impartial stance.

information about the object by experiencing it in a certain way. Information does not separate neatly from the particular experiences that bring it to light. What becomes known bears the indelible mark of the subject. In other words, the process of gathering information in a relational stance is *subject-ive.*

When I lived with the Chachi, they liked to tell this story. There was a foreigner who sometimes brought groups of tourists up the river to visit their village. The guests would hike in the forest, visit the shaman, and spend the night. On one of their trips, the tour leader lost his watch. He was very upset that it was missing and a bit suspicious that it might have been stolen, so he asked the shaman, whom he trusted deeply, if he could help. The shaman performed his ritual, singing to his special stones, ingesting his drugs, and looking deeply into the wick of a burning candle. He received a vision and then explained to the tour leader that his watch had fallen off while he was taking a bath in the river. He described the exact location where the watch was located, under a rock. They then went there and found it.[30]

It is easy for our Western, scientific minds to get caught up in questions like, "How did he do that?" "Did it really happen?" "Was it some kind of set-up or hoax?" We can, however, set aside these questions to appreciate the story in its native context. Knowledge in a relational stance is captured through the subject's connections. The shaman discovers the location of the watch through his attunement with the world around him. He is connected with a network of living forces that he can ask for information. He speaks through his art with the stones, the river, and the land. It is through them that he receives his answer, one that appears to him in his mind's eye. Knowledge in a relational stance is a relation shared with the world and is experienced directly through the subject.

The questions that come to mind when we consider the example of the Chachi shaman alert us to the fact that our impartial stance conceives of the entire situation in a different way. In fact, not only does information in an impartial stance appear with different qualities and through a different process, but it is also harvested and processed with different tools. Instead of drugs, candles, and stones, a scientist may use a metal detector to scan the area for the tour leader's watch. There is no intimate connection between the subject and the world around her. Knowledge is simply an extraction and analysis of information from the object. The scientist needs only to *reveal* the underlying structure, not to *relate* to it. Anyone trained in the procedure under similar conditions will collect exactly the same results in exactly the same way.

4.6.2 Form of Information

Consider the form of information collected by the scientist using a metal detector versus the shaman performing a contemplative ritual. The beeping of the detector indicates metal underneath. A simple visual inspection reveals whether the metal

---

[30]This is but one of many examples. I heard this particular story not only from several Chachi people, but also from an ex-U.S. Peace Corps volunteer who knew the shaman at the time.

corresponds to the watch or not. The information is clear and present to any trained observer. On the other hand, the shaman receives information through his mind's eye. It is initially present only to him. No one else shares the experience of his vision, and he must interpret it before it has meaning. From an impartial stance, the form of information is *literal and concrete*. Information shares the rigidity and givenness of the object itself. Its meaning is direct and unchanging.[31] From a relational stance, on the other hand, the form of information is interpretive and personal. It captures the object through its relation with the subject. Its meaning is *metaphorical and dynamic*. A scientific procedure has the same meaning and yields the same results for every qualified observer (or subject). A shamanic vision, on the other hand, must be interpreted in the context of a particular subject and experienced in order to have meaning.

4.6.3 Primary Mode of Constituting Knowledge

We have seen that, within an impartial stance, information is gathered through an object-ive process, in a form that is literal and concrete. Within a relational stance, information is gathered through a subject-ive process, in a form that is metaphorical and dynamic. We find that not only does each stance gather information through a different process and in a different form, but each constitutes knowledge using a different primary mode.[32] Within an impartial stance, knowledge is acquired primarily by *observation and reasoning*. The subject abstracts knowledge by collecting and analyzing information from the object. Within a relational stance, on the other hand, knowledge is acquired primarily by *intuition or revelation*. Subjects both receive and process information by placing themselves in a certain relation of openness to the object. The fabrication and use of a metal detector is not a piece of understanding received by a great scientist through her vision and then passed down to generation and generation of scientists through a process of initiation. It is a tool developed and then used, through the method of observation, reasoning, and testing, in order to derive an understanding of the properties of matter and the laws that describe its behavior. A shamanic vision, on the other hand, is learned by positioning and developing a particular relationship to the world. It is, moreover, through the shaman's own personal connection – namely, the vision that appears in his mind's eye – that he accesses the information. It is not about collecting information

---

[31] As Thomas Kuhn has brilliantly argued, meaning *does* change when scientific theories change. However, I am assuming here that the background scientific theory for processing information is not at stake. *The Structure of Scientific Revolutions,* Second Edition, Enlarged (Chicago and London: The University of Chicago Press: 1970).

[32] What constitutes information? What constitutes knowledge? Is all information knowledge? Is all knowledge information? – The careful philosopher might worry that I have neglected or elided these important questions. However, the point of the argument being developed in this chapter is that these questions themselves are at stake, they will be answered differently across different ways of life, and we can recognize significant ambivalence across the differences. Instead of parsing and answering these questions, I have tried to describe the elements and process of knowing in as general of terms as possible.

from the object, or figuring out the laws that describe its behavior; it is about very fully opening himself to the object, with his most subtle senses, and knowing it through the impression that it makes on him.[33]

4.7 Calibration of Knowledge

The first two axes of differentiation between an impartial and a relation stance concern the interaction of subject and object – how they relate and are known to each other. The third axis of differentiation that we will consider here is a bit different. It looks at how knowledge is calibrated – how the amount of knowledge is measured, how it is dispersed in a society, and how it is valued. The primary contrast along this axis, as we will soon see, involves the *location of knowledge* – whether it is dispersed across society as a whole, or held primarily within individual lives. The difference here lies between a highly diversified society, where there are many kinds of specialists, each with their separate knowledge and function, and a more "traditional" society, where there are fairly autonomous individuals, each with the knowledge and resources to make a life on their own.

4.7.1 Measurement of Knowledge

Because an impartial and a relational stance have different underlying pictures of the organization of society, they measure knowledge in a different place. Given the complex, diversified picture of society associated with an impartial stance, it measures knowledge *dispersed across society as a whole*. It measures the quantity of knowledge contained in a practice, such as science, across the various resources and components of society – books, databases, universities, think tanks, corporations, etc. Everything that is somehow, somewhere noted or known counts as knowledge.

---

[33] A good philosopher of science might ask here whether shamanic intuition is as reliable as scientific observation and reasoning. First of all, it is important to remember that, just as the scientist goes through years of training to develop her skills, so does the shaman. And, just as there are levels of scientific practice, so there are levels and progressions of skill and knowledge in shamanic practice. The shaman learns how to receive and process information with greater range, depth, acuity, and skill. Interestingly, although his mind and body are intimate tools of his craft, he also learns (in a way that may resonate with, or evoke some attributive symmetry for, those of us viewing shamanism from an impartial stance) how to untangle his own feelings and responses within the information he receives. It would be unfair to compare the reliability of our common, untrained intuition with that of a well-seasoned shaman. To do so would be like confusing the reliability of children using a toy chemistry set with that of university researchers at our best institutions. As I argued in Chap. 3, a scientific value like reliability also may not separate neatly from the context of a particular way of life – in terms of what it means, how it is measured, and the importance it carries. Finally, in this section our aim is simply to characterize a relational stance, not to weigh it against an impartial stance, although contrasts between the two can help us to understand each better in turn.

Society itself is the receptacle of knowledge. On the other hand, given the simple, autonomous picture of individuals in society associated with a relational stance, it measures knowledge *actuated within a single life*. The individual herself is the primary receptacle of knowledge, not society at large. A relational stance measures the quantity of knowledge contained in a practice at the level of the individual in action. Only what is lived in the context of an individual life counts.

One way to think about this contrast between the two stances is to note the difference between the pill that I buy at the pharmacy for stomachache and the herb that the Chachi woman picks in the forest to make her medicinal tea. The knowledge used to produce and distribute the pill is extremely complex and precise, but it is dispersed across society and resides in no one in particular. The specific formulation of the drug may be the intellectual property of a particular pharmaceutical company, but the math and science used to formulate it, the supply chains and communications responsible for producing it, and the extensive infrastructure that makes it all possible – from educating workers to shipping freight – reside in the collective ether, dispersed across massive systems of knowledge and action. In contrast, the knowledge used to make the tea resides in the woman herself, and is actuated directly by her picking the herb and preparing and drinking the tea. The process involves no specialized knowledge or function beyond that which she directly possesses herself. If a disaster shut down the pharmacy, or any key piece of infrastructure, I would have no access to the pill, and no idea or means to reproduce it. On the other hand, if a disaster shut down any feature of the Chachi woman's society, if it cut her off from their collective systems, she would still be able to walk into the forest, pick the herb, and make her tea.

4.7.2   Aim of Collecting Knowledge

Not only do the two stances look to different locations in society to measure knowledge, they also measure the collection of knowledge in different ways. An impartial stance aims at an *extensive collection* of knowledge. The greatest knowledge covers the widest range, from the very small to the very large, across every imaginable discipline and aspect of life. A relational stance, on the other hand, aims at an *intensive collection* of knowledge. The greatest knowledge brings those who possess it deeply into contact with the world around them. Given the different underlying social pictures of the two stances, this should come as no surprise. What it means for an individual to excel at knowledge, or to be wise, can be very different than what it means for a society. Consider the difference between the physicist, who can explain the behavior of the smallest particle to that of bodies in faraway galaxies, and the traditional Chachi, who understands and interacts with every aspect of the world around him, from the trees that give him food, clothing, shelter, tools, transport, and musical instruments, to the water that carries, cleans, nourishes, conveys, and feeds him. A society that can produce a physicist has – quite literally – extensive knowledge about the nature of the universe. And such a specialist, the physicist herself, may be very intimately involved with her work. However, she is not as intimately involved with the world around her. Moreover, as we will see in more detail below,[34] the very fact of her being a specialist prevents her from having the time and attention to know her personal world – the place of her food, shelter, clothing, etc. – as intimately as the traditional Chachi knows his.

4.7.3 Value of Knowledge

We have seen that an impartial stance locates knowledge across society as a whole, and aims for an extensive collection of knowledge about all there is, from the nano to the galactic. A relational stance, on the other hand, locates knowledge within the individual, and aims for an intensive collection of knowledge about all that connects with the knower in his daily life. Another way to conceive of the difference in how each stance calibrates knowledge is to compare how they value what is known. An impartial stance values *knowledge in itself*; there is good simply in acquiring knowledge and storing it away. We may develop useful technology that depends on knowledge of the structure of the hydrogen atom, but there is good just in the knowledge itself of what the hydrogen atom is like.[35, 36] A relational stance, on the other hand, measures the quantity of knowledge contained in a practice at the level of the individual in action. Only what is lived, what is actuated in the context of an individual life, counts. Knowledge is good inasmuch as it is *lived*.[37]

We can think of the contrast here as the difference between the information stored in a university library and the information actuated as a Chachi hunter scans the forest. Clearly, the tower of knowledge held in the library stacks greatly surpasses what any individual could know. And yet, that is precisely the point of the contrast. Most of the library knowledge is not lived or known. It is disembodied. It simply sits there, recorded. On the other hand, as the hunter feels the mud beneath his feet, notices the plants nearby, sees the tracks, smells the air, hears movement…his knowledge is alive and actuated. It vividly connects him with everything in his world.

---

[34] See Sect. 4.9.

[35] Of course, this example might immediately bring the hydrogen bomb to mind, tempting the reader to add that, not only does knowledge yield utility, but it also wields power. I argued in Chap. 3 that utility is context dependent, and I have suggested that power is as well. This observation, then, does not seem to undermine my account by elucidating any sort of non-relative standard. Rather, context dependence helps to explain why the conquistador (colonist, missionary, global aid director, etc.) is so eager to change the natives' context and convert ("enlighten") them. As the native way of life is engulfed by the outsider's, truth, knowledge, utility, and power shift as a package. They do not hold outside of a particular way of life, but rather are realized by the conversion itself.

[36] Others might think from this example that they are not inclined to call some science, like that used to produce weapons of mass destruction, "successful" in the first place.

[37] I have been asked if the distinction between a relational and an impartial stance here corresponds to the difference between knowing how and knowing that. The point is not that relational knowledge is "knowing how," and impartial knowledge is "knowing that." Rather, the point is that from a relational stance, the two concepts of knowing how and knowing that simply do not come apart.

4.8 Resonance

We have now examined the contrast between an impartial and a relational stance along three axes: the relation between subject and object, the capture of knowledge, and the calibration of knowledge. At this point, the characteristics of each stance, as well as the differences between them, should be a little clearer to us. We must also begin to realize that, although the impartial stance of science dominates our contemporary Western lives, a relational stance is not entirely foreign to us. Taylor and Wong suggest, for example, that we can appreciate attunement because it was much more closely tied to understanding in Ancient Greek thought, and the two modes of engagement (the loving attunement of a relational stance and the detached understanding of an impartial stance) remained closely linked in Western history through the Renaissance. Our canonical texts are full of references to attunement, and even today, such intimacy with the world – loving it, believing in its goodness, being one with it – continues to be valued by many.[38]

Often, a relational stance exists minimally in our own way of life.[39] We can find in our own experience little pieces, little marks and clues of it. For example, our language harbors vestiges of it in old aphorisms and turns of phrase. The saying, "Beauty is in the eye of the beholder," encodes knowledge in relational terms; it characterizes understanding as dependent on subjective experience and interpretation. Similarly, the saying, "You look so good I could eat you up," locates knowledge in relational terms, in a certain intimacy with the object; knowing its goodness is not distinct from being a part of the object, from consuming it. The common phrase, "Mother Nature," identifies a deep relation with an object of the same kind, one that is animate and minded, like the knowing subject herself. Also, the phrase, "Know by heart," refers to knowledge that is stored and valued in the individual, and that exists as it is actuated in her life.

We find pieces of a relational stance not only in our language, but speckled throughout our ideas, customs, and practices. Some are carryovers from other times in our cultural history when this stance was more dominant; others have been recovered from the past, or were never entirely lost to modernity. The pedagogy of experiential learning, for instance, recovers the idea that knowledge is located in a certain intimacy, or relation, with its object. The custom of using animate language to refer not only to Nature, but also to technology (e.g., "My car doesn't want to start," or, "The GPS says you should turn here.") retains the identification of objects as minded like us. Love and spiritual practices such as meditation carry on the idea that the proper attitude toward an object is surrender, not control. The metaphorical and

---

[38] Wong, *Natural Moralities,* 8–9, and Taylor, "Rationality."

[39] I do not mean, however, that alternative practices are easy for us to understand, that they are very much like our own, or that all of their features resonate with us. I only mean that this positive aspect of ambivalence, what I call "resonance," can be a means for us to come to terms with an alternative practice. Ultimately, when we consider the negative aspects of ambivalence, or what I call, "loss," it is also a means for us to come to terms with the incommensurability of such a practice and our own (See Sect. 4.9).

figurative language of poetry, literature, music, and other fine arts encodes knowledge not as invariant, but as subjective and dependent on interpretation. Certain hobbies, such as cooking, fishing, sewing, and woodworking continue to value knowledge not in itself, but as it is stored and actuated in the individual.[40]

We may notice that these examples of resonance correspond to all three axes of a relational stance from Sects. 4.4–4.7: the relation between subject and object, the capture of knowledge, and the calibration of knowledge.[41] The small pieces of a relational stance that we find in our own way of life give us access to alternative practices that do not rely on the impartial stance of science. We can use them as building blocks for growing new concepts and appreciating other ways of engaging the world.[42] This may be the case for the anthropologist or other such visitors who become immersed in a very different way of life. For instance, while living with the Chachi, I may first learn to wash my clothes in the river as they do because it strikes me as a quaint hobby. This will give me enough interest to acquire my own washbasin and enough patience to learn to make the right sort of squeaky sounds as I twist my clothes and the respectable smack that reverberates across the river as I hit my clothes on it to rinse them. But somewhere in the process of sitting in the river working on a small stain as the children splash around me, of hanging clothes on the line while the chickens peck at the cacao drying in the sun, of running to grab my favorite shirt before the little drops of water falling from the sky turn to bubbling mud dancing between my toes, I start to appreciate that the Chachi have a very different mode of knowing and relating to the world. Of course, this does not all come from one single hobby, but from a collection of similar experiences, walking with the Chachi to the fields, rowing in a canoe, accompanying the women at a dance, sitting with the shaman through his séance, etc. I marvel at how the Chachi themselves provide for every aspect of their lives, from their food and clothing to their homes, transportation, and medicine. I admire how seamlessly they fit into the fabric of the forest, aware of every detail without causing great disturbance to any. The little pieces of a relational stance once known to me have grown into a much fuller appreciation of the Chachi way of life. Theirs is not the detached knowledge of science

---

[40] We might add that, in many cases, innovators, including philosophers, have worked to resuscitate aspects of a relational stance that are faded and live dormant within our own way of life. It seems to me that systems theory could be interpreted in this way, particularly its examination of the efficiency of interdependent networks and feedback loops [power with] versus that of systems with monodirectional control [power over]. In philosophy, Foucault's late work on parrhesia aimed to recover from the ancients the idea of truth embodied in a life [knowledge as it is actuated]. See, for example, Michel Foucault, *Le gouvernement de soi et des autres. II, Le courage de la vérité: cours au collège de France, 1983–1984*, ed. Frédéric Gros, under the direction of François Ewald and Alessandro Fontana (Paris: Gallimard/Seuil, 2009). Similarly, Pierre Hadot's work on philosophy as a way of life revived from ancient philosophy the idea that knowledge comes from intimacy with its object. See, for instance, Pierre Hadot, *Exercices spirituels et philosophie antique* (Paris: Éditions Albin Michel/Bibliothèque de «L'Évolution de l'Humanité», 2002). For more on a relativist perspective and the capacity for self-critique/transformation, see Chap. 6, esp. Sect. 6.3.

[41] The reader may find it helpful to refer to Table 4.1, which is discussed below in Sect. 4.11.

[42] See Chap. 1, esp. Sects. 1.2.2 and 1.2.6.

that stands apart from man, growing and progressing as if it had a life of its own. It is the traditional knowledge[43] that connects the individual to the world around her, knowledge that does not progress across time, but only intensifies within a particular life, and is passed on directly from one to another through experience.

A relational stance has a foothold in our own experience and the capacity to grow into something much more. We can see from this resonance that a relational stance is a part of the human experience, but not one that is accentuated in our own. Resonance gives us reason to consider practices that rely much more deeply on a relational stance and helps us to understand them. At the very least, once we find resonance, we cannot simply write off alternative practices as unrecognizable or unfathomable. Of course, once we take note of them, it is another question what we should make of them. We will discuss this further below.[44] Here we must note, however, that the little pieces, the miniature analogues that we find in our own experience to develop into an appreciation of a relational stance, are not equivalents between different practices, or between the different ways of life in which they are embedded. They are more like little bridges, or even less, like the markings of a small ford where we could begin to wade across the river that separates us. And when we get to the other side, the other way of life, its practices and concepts are not all there in themselves, ready for us to understand. We must build our appreciation of them, through analogy and experience, piece by piece.[45] What resonance offers us is not ready-made equivalences, but *constructivity*, the possibility of growing an understanding. This possibility of growth is both what allows us to appreciate alternatives and to measure their distance. The distance between practices that rely deeply on a relational stance from those, such as science, that rely deeply on an impartial stance should become clearer in Sects. 4.9 and 4.10 below.

---

[43] There is a question here as to what, if anything, we might recognize in the Chachi way of life as a counterpart to science. In Sect. 4.10 below, I respond to the suggestion that the Chachi may have no epistemic practice at all. Leaving that worry aside, the reader might still wonder here why I contrast science with "traditional knowledge" more globally, instead of with shamanism, specifically. Indeed, earlier on I seem to have implicitly accepted that the equivalent of science in a traditional way of life would be something like magic or shamanism, so why would I state it differently here? While it is true that we Westerners have our own traditional knowledge and that the Chachi have their own specialists (shamans), the difference between traditional knowledge/specialized knowledge and between the general people/scientists is more pronounced for us than for them. It is from an impartial stance that these two poles tend to come apart, because such a stance construes knowledge as something that stands on its own, separate from the act of living in a certain relation to the world. However, when we view the question of counterparts the other way around, from a relational stance toward an impartial one (as I am doing at this **very** point), the answer changes. Knowing, in this case, cannot be separated from standing in a certain relation to the object, or from the subject that occupies such a relation. At this point, at least potentially, the practitioner becomes every individual and the practice, the act of living itself.

[44] For more on intolerance and disagreement, see also Chap. 6.

[45] And even then, it is not clear that we have appreciated another way of life as from the inside. For more on this process, see Chap. 1.

4.9 Loss

Resonance is the aspect of ambivalence that brings alternatives into view. It lights up little unaccented pieces of a relational stance within our own experience, which we can then use to build an appreciation of alternative practices that do not rely deeply on an impartial stance. Loss, on the other hand, is the aspect of ambivalence that forms a counterweight to resonance. As we will see, it at once reinforces the possibility of alternatives and restricts their resonance. This happens in two distinct moments, which I will refer to as, "estrangement" (Sect. 4.9.1), and "pull" (Sect. 4.9.2).

4.9.1 The First Moment: Estrangement

One way to appreciate the first moment of loss is as the negative of resonance. We detect in our own experience not the minimal presence of something shared with alternative practices, but the distinct absence of something meaningful. It is a sort of emptiness or longing that gives value to what is not there. Taylor and Wong note that our knowledge has flourished because we embrace detached understanding over loving attunement with the world; however, what gets in the way of claiming the absolute superiority of our science is not only that we can grasp what attunement is, but that we also sense the cost of our failure to embrace it.[46] To quote Taylor, "there is no such thing as a single argument proving *global* superiority. The dissociation of [impartial] understanding of nature and attunement to the world has been very good for the former. Arguably it has been disastrous for the latter goal. Perhaps the critics are right who hold that we have been made progressively more estranged from ourselves and our world in technological civilization."[47]

What is this estrangement? And how can we identify it? It may be hard for the analytic philosopher to accept a gesture that is the pointing to the absence of something hardly known, of something that registers only in our periphery. We can only with difficulty locate the phenomena in question. We have few, if any, concrete descriptions to offer or direct causal links to point out. More often, we have only

---

[46] Taylor, "Rationality," and Wong, *Natural Moralities*.

[47] Taylor, "Rationality," 103. Taylor does believe, however, that Western science provides a better understanding of "inanimate nature," and that our technological superiority is unequivocal. In Chap. 3, I argued that the success of our technology is not unequivocal, but dependent upon the context of our way of life. I am more willing, nonetheless, to concede the first part of Taylor's claim. Our science may offer the most complete understanding of inanimate nature. After all, it is through an impartial stance that nature is constituted *as* inanimate, so our science should describe this better than other practices. The real question is, what makes the mode of impartial understanding canonical and superior? The point of ambivalence – or, more specifically, of the dynamic of resonance and loss – is that we can appreciate alternate modes of understanding, the trade-offs made between them, and the lack of an absolute standard to arbitrate their differences.

vague associations, or a few tenuous correlations. And yet, I believe that when we reflect deeply and openly on our own experience, we can, in many cases, sense these absences, or negatives. It takes a brief suspension of judgment and a certain honesty with ourselves about how it feels to inhabit our way of life. In this spirit, I ask the reader to consider for a moment with me what might be the corresponding negatives for each feature of an impartial stance. Let us review them in the same order as they were presented in Sects. 4.4–4.7:[48]

4.9.1.1   Relation Between Subject and Object: Detached Understanding vs. Loving Attunement

In an Impartial Stance, the Ideal Epistemic Proximity Is Large; It Locates Reliable Information in the Separation Between Subject and Object

Within a stance that locates knowledge in distance, we may feel the negative resonance of loss, or estrangement, as alienation from the objects around us. They may be so far removed from us that they seem empty and purposeless. We find no connection with them at all. They have as much meaning for us as the chicken leg placed on Styrofoam and wrapped in cellophane that we pick up at the supermarket – the part severed from its main body, feathers plucked, lifeblood washed away. No deeper connection with sentient, feeling life remains for us to sense.

When we relate to ourselves in this way, as distanced objects, we may feel estrangement as the emptiness and purposelessness of self. We lose track of who we are, and why we are here. We feel great confusion and loneliness. We sense no deeper connection or purpose. This is the estrangement of the face in the mirror plastered with make-up. It is the emptiness of the body filled with doctor's pills and self-inflicted remedies. Our own separateness becomes so pronounced that we feel hollow.

In an Impartial Stance, Subject-Object Likeness Is Minimal; It Construes Objects as Inanimate and Mindless

Within a stance that takes objects as radically different than subjects, as lacking reason and purpose, we may feel estrangement as alienation from Nature. This manifests in our physical world as the destruction of the environment. It is the rainforest stripped into desert, as if the ecosystem had no meaning and purpose in itself. It is the endless stream of waste piled into our garbage cans, as if objects, once we are done with them, ceased to exist. The trash no longer matters, completely vanishes, once it is out of sight.

---

[48] It may also help the reader here to refer to Table 4.1, which appears at the end of the chapter.

When we relate to our own bodies in this way, as lacking reason and purpose, we may feel estrangement as the disruption of our natural regulatory systems. The loss lies in our inability to thrive at the basic human functions. We see it in the high rate of illness caused by stress and contamination in our society. We find that we cannot work, rest, feed, play, or even procreate in a balanced way, at the appropriate times. It is the blaring light above our heads in the middle of the night. It is our eyes and fingers glued to the screen of the newest electronic device.

In an Impartial Stance, the Subject Seeks to Dominate Its Object; Knowledge Is a Relation of Power over Objects

Within a stance that is focused on control, we may feel estrangement as anxiety. No matter how much we predict and command the actions of the objects around us, it does not satisfy. The feelings of order, safety, and achievement quickly fade away, as we focus on what we still do not know and still cannot do. We race toward the next big cure, the next great discovery, the faster computer, the smarter phone. Our world propels forward faster than we can connect with it, than we can make sense of it, or even than we can make choices about it.

In our personal lives, the constant struggle to control can lead not only to generalized anxiety, but to feelings of powerlessness as well. It is the fear that the world will slip away from us. It is the constant restlessness that keeps us from sleeping at night and fuels us with coffee in the morning, as we look for that ineffable more. It is the endless planning and worry that takes us out of the moment and leaves us in a space of dysregulation and confusion. It is the sense that nothing is really real and nothing really matters. We stop speaking up. We stop reaching out. We stop voting or participating in civic life.

4.9.1.2   Capturing Knowledge: Revealing the Object vs. Relating to the Object

In an Impartial Stance, the Process of Capturing Information Is Object-ive; It Is Tightly and Almost Uniquely Focused on the Object

Within a stance where the subject's experiences are not a critical part of the process of knowing, we may feel the negative resonance of loss, or estrangement, as confusion about the first person and about subjective experience in general. The subject stands almost outside the act of knowing, and outside the world that is known. This gives subjectivity an inexplicable and extraneous quality. Consciousness appears as a mysterious extra layer on top of physical reality.

At a personal level, we may feel this estrangement as the superfluity of our own experience. This leads to dissociative states and depression. It is our inability to explain what it means to experience the world as "I," or why we matter. It is our failure to recognize our own feelings or their significance. Our intuitions appear like chaff to be cleared and discarded. Soon the world, like us, feels faraway and unreal.

In an Impartial Stance, the Form of Information Is Literal and Concrete; Information Shares the Rigidity and Givenness of the Object Itself

Within a stance where information bears no mark or relation with the perceiving subject, we may feel estrangement as inexplicable puzzles. We cannot see how the experience of being and acting in the world relates to the world itself. As we saw above, it becomes difficult in an impartial stance to explain how consciousness arises from the physical world. We may also find it puzzling how the will relates to action, and how action relates to manifest reality.

At a collective level, these may be theoretical puzzles for disciplines such as philosophy, psychology, neuroscience, and physics to debate. However, we also sense them at a personal level. As with the other features along this axis, we may sense the estrangement of living in a rigid, concrete world through feelings of disassociation. It is our inability to see how what we know, what we choose, what we feel, and what we do relate to the state of the world. We feel apathetic, disengaged, and powerless.

In an Impartial Stance, Knowledge Is Acquired Primarily by Observation and Reasoning; The Subject Abstracts Knowledge by Collecting and Analyzing Information from the Object

Within a stance where intuition, or the act of receiving information, does not play a significant role in acquiring knowledge, we may feel estrangement as incompleteness. There is nothing to certify knowledge, nothing to let us know that we have reached a satisfying answer. Our path becomes an infinite regress, as we constantly look for more. There is never an ultimate cause, a final answer.

At a collective level, the endless searching leads to a confusion of priorities. We keep searching without realizing what we have found. It is the race to get our children to earn higher test scores instead of nurturing them as people. It is the money poured into high-tech research to cure illnesses caused by stress instead of building a society where people lead less stressful lives. At a personal level, the endless searching leaves us feeling lost in a sea of information. It is the inability to keep track of answers and to keep track of ourselves. It is the feeling that everything we know and everything we do is meaningless.

4.9.1.3   Calibration of Knowledge: In Society as a Whole vs. In an Individual Life

An Impartial Stance Measures Knowledge Dispersed Across Society as a Whole; Society Itself Is the Receptacle of Knowledge

Within a stance that does not measure knowledge as it is actuated within the individual's life, we may feel the negative resonance of loss, or estrangement, as alienation from our primary life functions.[49] Our own actions and the basic elements of living a life seem not to connect with each other.[50] It is our inability to feed, to clothe, to house, to educate, or to cure ourselves on our own or in our own family units. Our food fails to nourish our bodies and our connections fail to nourish our souls because they are packaged and served as if from outside of us. It is our increasing dependence on technology and consumerism to satisfy all of our needs: the clothes thrown in the washing machine, the packaged food popped in the microwave, the kids being babysat on their parents' phones. It is our intimate conversations managed by social media, our emotions transmuted into emojis. We feel mechanical, dissatisfied, and unreal.

An Impartial Stance Aims for an Extensive Collection of Knowledge

Within a stance that does not measure knowledge intensively, as it is actuated in an individual life, we may feel loss as the inability to understand or synthesize information. We *use* our best physical theories, such as quantum theory and relativity theory, but we cannot make out what they *mean* or how they fit together. At the theoretical level, this manifests as puzzles for scientists about how to interpret, unify, and complete our most advanced theories. At the practical level, on the other hand,

---

[49] As Marx describes, "…the relation of the worker to his own activity as an alien activity not belonging to him; it is activity as suffering, strength as weakness, begetting as emasculating, the worker's *own* physical and mental energy, his personal life or what is life other than activity – as an activity which is turned against him, neither depends on nor belongs to him." The result of estranged labor, according to Marx, is estrangement of man from nature, from himself, from his species, and from fellow man. Karl Marx, "Estranged Labour (Economic and Philosophic Manuscripts of 1844)," in *The Karl Marx Reader,* Second Edition, ed. Robert C. Tucker (New York and London: W.W. Norton & Company, 1978) 74–75 and 70–81.

[50] As Hegel describes, "every individual, losing his independence, is tied down in an endless series of dependence on others…the individual is not at home even in his immediate environment because it does not appear as his own work; it has been taken from the supply of what was already available, produced by others, and indeed in a most mechanical and therefore formal way, and acquired by him only through a long chain of efforts and needs foreign to himself." He contrasts this with the personal autonomy of the pre-industrial age when, "man has the feeling, in everything he uses and everything he surrounds himself with, that he has produced it from his own resources, and therefore in external things has to do with what is his own and not with alienated objects lying outside his own sphere wherein he is master." G.W.F. Hegel, *Aesthetics: Lectures on Fine Art,* Vol. 1, trans. T.M. Knox, (Oxford: Clarendon Press, 1988) 260–261.

it manifests as a sort of collective akrasia; we do not live according to what our best scientific theories know.[51] Perhaps the most blatant example of this is our refusal to take massive action to correct global ecological damage even as our best climate science tells us we are hurling past a critical tipping point. Yet, our collective akrasia is even more pervasive than this. In most fundamental terms, we act as if we lived in a classical Newtonian universe, while our most advanced theories describe a reality that is far more complex, dimensional, and indiscriminate. Estrangement manifests as the mixture of condescension and rage that we direct toward descriptions of the world that are not linear, particulate, and binary. It is our rejection of shamanic conceptions of nonlinear time as savage or "woo-woo." It is our rejection of those whose gender or sexuality do not conform to heterosexual norms as perverse or confused. We insist that our lived reality should fall into neatly circumscribed, self-serving boxes, while our best understanding tells us that the world does not fit.

An Impartial Stance Values Knowledge in Itself

Within a stance that does not value knowledge as it is actuated and lived in our individual lives, we may feel estrangement as the disconnect between our quest for knowledge and what we need to know to live our own lives. As with the second feature in Sect. 4.9.1.2 above,[52] it may manifest collectively as a confusion of priorities. It is, for instance, the billions of dollars invested in our space programs while so many go homeless and hungry. At an individual level, this confusion manifests as ineptitude. It is not simply the systemic dependence we have in order to care for ourselves, as we saw in the first feature of this section,[53] but the lack of knowhow to care for ourselves. It is not knowing what or how to eat to nourish our bodies well, let alone how to cultivate, harvest, or forage for our food. It is not understanding the time of day, the movement of the seasons, the signs of the climate.

It is not knowing how to find or make shelter on our own. It is not having the strength or knowledge to make means of transportation on our own, let alone the physical fortitude to work and travel with our own bodies as our instrument. We find ourselves not only out of step with Nature, but unequal to Her demands.

Although we have separated the axes for expository purposes, we can see in the overlap of symptoms that they work to manifest estrangement together, and, in fact, they do so in many more ways than discussed here. It might help, nonetheless, to recognize that each axis clusters together certain symptoms. Along the first axis, the

---

[51] This is a practical critique not unrelated to Ladyman and Ross's theoretical critique that our contemporary metaphysics are out of step with what our best scientific theories know. James Ladyman and Don Ross with David Spurrett and John Collier, *Every Thing Must Go: Metaphysics Naturalized* (Oxford and New York: Oxford University Press, 2007). I discuss their work in Chap. 5, esp. Sect. 5.6.

[52] That is, in an impartial stance, knowledge is acquired primarily by observation and reasoning; the subject abstracts knowledge by collecting and analyzing information from the object.

[53] That is, an impartial stance measures knowledge dispersed across society as a whole; society itself is the receptacle of knowledge.

relation between subject and object, the overall feeling of estrangement is that the world that we know is empty. It presents as loss of natural harmony and dis-ease of body and mind. Along the second axis, capturing knowledge, the overall feeling of estrangement is that we do not appear in the world that is known. It presents as loss of reality and dissociative feelings. Along the third axis, calibration of knowledge, the overall feeling of estrangement is that what is known is not for us. It presents as loss of autonomy and of humanity. The busy-ness of bettering the world leaves us behind; it is not clear whether robots will take over the world, or we have rendered ourselves mere automatons.

In estrangement, the first moment of loss, we notice the emptiness or longing associated with features that are not as adequately developed or accounted for in an impartial stance. Yet, it is important to note that we do so from our own standpoint, from our own place of situatedness. Estrangement is not felt from an absolute perspective, or under the guidance of a rigid picture of what it means to live a flourishing life. It is true that some readers might not recognize all – or even *any* – of these losses.[54] Whatever effect the above litany of estrangement symptoms may have, its point is not to demonize an impartial stance. Nor is it to deny that a relational stance comes with its own set of losses.[55] Certainly, as some will be eager to point out, we trade our losses for what we take to be greater gains. We give up the intimacy of an animated world for the detailed knowledge and control that we have over a disenchanted, mechanized one. We give up the intensive knowledge that is stored and valued in ourselves for the extensive knowledge of our society as a whole. We give up the individual knowledge to build our own homes and grow our own food for the diversified knowledge and abilities of the whole. We give up the home education of our children for the range and power of the school system. We give up the self-care of our bodies in exchange for the expertise of highly trained doctors. And so on. The point in recognizing estrangement is not to deny that there are trade-offs; rather, the point lies in the trade-offs themselves. It is to see that there are costs associated with our way of capturing and shaping knowledge of the world, and to recognize that where there are costs, there are lost goods. Our epistemic practice, which is embedded in our way of life, does not capture all of them. We make choices. When we can see this, we can appreciate an alternative practice that relies on a relational stance. It makes different choices for different goods.

4.9.2 The Second Moment: Pull

The first moment of loss, like resonance, helps to bring alternatives to light; we sense something important that lies just beyond our grasp. The second moment, on the other hand, raises not longing or vague familiarity, but difference and

---

[54] I address the reader for whom the dynamic of resonance and loss means nothing below. See Sects. 4.10 and 4.11.

[55] For example, from a stance that takes the world that as minded and animate, like the knowing subject herself, we might experience the world as full of demons and evil that exceeds our control.

incompatibility. Unlike resonance and the first moment of loss, which might not be compelling without a certain experience of another way of life,[56] the second moment is more analytic and available to any sort of reader. What it reveals is that an impartial stance and a relational stance pull in different directions. There is tension between them that cannot be easily resolved. In the language of the paragraph above: the two stances chase different goods in different directions. To the extent that we embrace the one stance, we relinquish the other. But this tension between them is complex. It varies by case and rarely takes the form of perfect opposition.[57] We can describe at least three kinds of irreconcilability, or pull, between the two stances:

Categorical Opposition In some cases, an impartial stance and a relational stance pull in distinctly opposed directions. These make perhaps the easiest cases of irreconcilability. The two stances carve the epistemic domain in different ways, recognizing different types, objects, aims, and formulations of knowledge. If an impartial stance locates knowledge in separation from the object and a relational stance in intimacy with the object, then they will recognize very different experiences as knowledge-giving. This is the difference between the scientist looking through her microscope and the shaman singing to his magic stones. If an impartial stance takes the world as mindless and a relational stance takes it as animate, then they will recognize as meaningful (or, alternately, as nonsensical) claims about very different kinds of objects and agents. This is the difference between the plant teaching the shaman how to use it and the scientist observing its properties. If an impartial stance approaches the object with an attitude of control and a relational stance approaches the object with an attitude of surrender, then they will recognize as useful or legitimate practices that serve very different ends. This is the difference between a weather forecast that predicts the rain and a ritual that asks the sky to rain. If an impartial stance encodes knowledge as subject-invariant and a relational stance encodes it as subject-dependent, then they will recognize very different sorts of formulations as knowledge. This is the difference between the shaman's vision and the beeping of the metal detector. In short, the two stances will disagree on what kinds of experience qualify as knowledge-giving, what properties an object of knowledge can have, what the (specific) aim of knowledge is, and how knowledge should be formulated.

Practical Opposition A second kind of pull between stances may be easier to reconcile at an intellectual level, but still cannot be negotiated easily at a practical level. The two stances conflict in pursuing their specific aims; human finitude prevents them from being easily combined. If an impartial stance measures knowledge by its extension across society as a whole and a relational stance measures knowledge by its intensiveness in an individual life, then we could imagine, hypothetically, an epistemic practice in which both of these measures are maximized. The

---

[56] For more on this point, see Chap. 1 and Sect. 4.11 of the present chapter.

[57] See Chap. 1, Sect. 1.2.4.

individuals of the way of life in which this practice is embedded would have the greatest amount of intimate, relational knowledge of the world, and the society itself would have the greatest amount of extensive, impartial knowledge. We might suppose, moreover, that such a practice could manage to value knowledge in itself as much as it does knowledge as it is lived. The problem with this scenario, however, lies in the finitude of human life and experience. It is already impossible for an individual to master all of our current science. An expert in a given field or sub-field can reach a high degree of intensiveness in her knowledge, but such specialized knowledge is so narrow that her natural human needs must extend far beyond it. So, unless her needs were warped to fit her specialized field, in which case we might hesitate to call hers a truly human life, her knowledge would not obtain the degree of fit between knowledge and life itself for which an intimate, relational stance toward the world strives.

Strong Tension A third, weaker kind of pull is a sort of combination between the first two. Inasmuch as an impartial stance takes the ideal expression of knowledge as literal and a relational stance takes the ideal expression as metaphorical, they might at times agree. After all, the same expression can be both literally and metaphorically true. But this is not always the case, and the stances' occasional agreement belies the fact that, as we have seen, they look for knowledge and count it in very different ways. Similarly, inasmuch as an impartial stance seeks to know its object by test and a relational stance seeks to know by revelation, the two may have some practical overlap or agreement. A scientist, for example, could acquire her ideas by revelation and then test them. The two stances, however, will disagree about which act (impartial or relational) makes the idea true and why it takes priority.

We might notice that the three kinds of pull relate closely to our axes of investigation.[58] Along the first axis (relation between subject and object), as well as the first feature of the second axis (capturing knowledge), the pull is characterized by *categorical opposition*; the two stances recognize different types, objects, aims, and formulations of knowledge. Along the remainder of the second axis, the pull is characterized by *strong tension*; the stances may overlap, but disagree on an ultimate explanation and weighting of factors. Along the third axis (calibration of knowledge), the pull is characterized by *practical opposition*; human finitude prevents the stances from being easily combined. What this variegation shows us is that an impartial stance and a relational stance do not fit neatly together; they take different paths in different directions toward knowing the world. The three kinds of pull that we have identified between them are more complex and less trenchant than absolute opposition. It turns out that the two stances are greatly, but not perfectly irreconcilable; and yet, for this very complexity and imperfection of difference, when we do bring together the two stances, the pull between them does not diminish. Their

---

[58] Again, the reader may wish to consult Table 4.1 below.

entrenched conflict remains like the jagged scar on a skinned knee – the laser cut of the surgeon, much deeper and neater, heals faster and is more likely to disappear.

One way, for example, to bring the two stances together is by context. We could imagine that a single way of life has both a practice that relies deeply on a detached impartial stance and a practice that relies deeply on a connected, relational stance. So, a person who lives in that way of life and participates in these two practices would rely deeply on both stances. Arguably, this is already the case in our own way of life. When a scientist prays in earnest, mediates, or practices yoga, she relies deeply on the attunement of a relational stance. When she is back in her lab behind the microscope, collecting data, she relies deeply again on the detachment of an impartial stance. What we must notice about this case, however, is that the scientist does not rely deeply on both stances at the same time; she alternates between them. This case, then, does not negate or diminish the pull between the two stances. In fact, to point out that the same person has the capacity to rely deeply on both stances in different contexts is really to make at a smaller scale the relativist's point that as humans we have the capacity to rely deeply on an impartial stance and to rely deeply on a relational stance, and that in the contexts of different ways of life, we make different choices between them. The scientist must decide whether to understand the cells under her microscope by singing to them, or by continuing to look through the lens. She must choose. She must make trade-offs. She does not get to rely deeply on both stances in the same context at the same time.

Still, we might imagine bringing the two stances together even more closely in a sort of hybridization. Perhaps a single practice, in different aspects or situations, might rely on both an impartial stance and a relational stance. Arguably, this, too, is already the case in our own science. After all, we have nowhere said that science is limited to an impartial stance, only that this stance dominates science and the rest of our way of life. The difference between our practices, and the ways of life in which they are embedded, lies not in the stark contrast between an impartial stance and a relational stance, but in the different weights in different cases that we give to each. The scientist may pursue an intuition or "hunch" to solve a problem. The mathematician may meditate on the solution to a proof. What is important to note, though, is that they will not give priority to a relational stance; it is merely instrumental to them for what they take to be the higher, more valued work of the impartial stance. So, this is not a case of valuing *both* stances deeply. At a given moment, inasmuch as the scientist occupies the one stance, she removes herself from the other. She cannot sing to her petri dishes and reason disengagedly at the same time. She cannot in the same act seek union with her object and examine it from a distance. At each moment, she must place herself somewhere on the spectrum: at the extreme of one stance or the other, or somewhere in-between. She may even alternate between different stances from moment to moment. But what she cannot at any moment do is to inhabit the entire spectrum between an impartial stance and a relational stance as a whole. Whether by moment, by context, or by degree, she is still forced to make trade-offs between the two.

What remains across all of these different ways of patching the two stances together is their incompatibility, or *pull*: the forced choice of one at the cost of the other. This is how the second moment of loss limits resonance, and, in so doing, distinguishes our picture from a more simply universalist one. The universalist, for example, would want to argue from the fact that we can recognize alternative practices (resonance) to the conclusion that all of our practices engage the world in the same way, and with the same ends, and that we can therefore judge in a neutral way that one is better or more correct than the other. Pull marks a real tension between science and alternative practices. It emphasizes precisely that, though we can make sense of alternative practices, they do not engage the world in quite the same way, with quite the same ends; and it is this difference that prevents there being a simple neutral measure of their conflicting claims against each other.[59]

The other factor that keeps our picture from being a simply universalist one is that resonance[60] is, by nature, a phenomenon rooted in a particular perspective. We craft an understanding of alternative practices from our own experience given the concepts of our own science, rooted in our own way of life. When we piece together different practices and their relationships to each other, it is from our own perspective. We can gain a sense of the whole – of all the different ways humans might engage the world, and of the sort of claims that hold within those practices – but from our own perspective. The result is a sort of relative universal, a perspectival picture of the panhuman: what we know and the terms by which we know it, from our own place within that picture. The distinction between the detachment of an impartial stance and the intimacy of a relational stance, for example, is meaningful given the aims and methods of our science. It might not even figure in a description of the panhuman from the perspective of another way of life. Our picture represents the whole, but it does not transcend to the level of generality, neutrality, and authority of the whole. This means that whatever picture we begin to brush of the panhuman at a descriptive level, it falls apart at the normative level. It breaks down where we attempt to judge practices and their conflicting claims against each other on grounds that we expect to rise above the contingencies of our own way of life. Each practice must make choices among the different ways of engaging the world, but these choices themselves cannot be justified outside a particular engagement with the world. This point should become clearer in the following section.

4.10 Assessment Is Internal to Stance

The dynamic of resonance and loss teaches us that we have reason to take alternative practices seriously. We cannot easily dismiss them as foolishly mistaken about the world. Yet we might grant alternative practices a certain space of reasonableness and still resist the relativist's conclusion that the achievements of science are but a relative success, one dependent on the context of a particular way of life. We might

---

[59] For more on this point, see Sect. 4.10 below and the following chapter.

[60] And the first moment of loss, as well, we might add.

object, for example, that although a relational stance resonates with us, we know to give an impartial stance priority, and it is this choice that has led to the great power and success of our science.

The problem, however, is that the very assessment that our science has greater power and greater success is internal to our way of life. In other words, not only does the specificity of our epistemic stance come from the degree to which we prioritize the impartial stance over a relational stance, but this preference is required in order for us to establish that our science is more successful than other epistemic practices. In Chap. 3, we saw that the success of science depends on an industrialized context where we are constituted as atomistic individuals, Nature is contained, knowledge subsists outside of us, and our basic life functions are sold back to us as commodities. The judgment that the knowledge generated from our science is more powerful and more successful than that from alternative practices depends not only on the context of measurement, but, as we saw in Sects. 4.3–4.9, on the standards by which we measure. It depends on where we measure knowledge: at the level of the individual in action, or at the level of society as a whole. It depends on how we measure knowledge: by its intensiveness in bringing an individual into relation with the world as a whole, or by its extension in uncovering as much as we can find in the world as a whole. It depends on how we recognize knowledge: as that which does not vary from one subject to another, or as that which only has meaning as it is experienced by a particular subject. And it depends on how we characterize the objects that our knowledge is about: as inanimate and mindless, or as having knowledge and purpose of their own.

In short, the very judgment that our science is more powerful and more successful depends on the priority of an impartial stance. Yet there seems to be no way to justify this priority beyond the fact that we inhabit an impartial-dominated stance and it is ours. We find valuable what it marks off as worthwhile and good; we find revealing and important what it defines as knowledge and truth. Though we may feel ambivalence toward the goods and truths of a relational stance, we justify the priority that we give to an impartial stance by arguing that relational thinking – primary process – is infantile and to be subjugated. Only when man reaches the rationality of detached, objective thought does he discover Truth; only when civilization organizes itself by the fruits and demands of an impartial stance does it fulfill the greatness of human potential. This attitude, however, is but a re-assertion of the priority of an impartial stance. It ignores the fact that the infantile modes of engaging the world that we expect a mature adult to leave behind – of narcissism, or of magical thinking, for example – will present many more stages of development in a way of life that deeply values a relational stance. The shaman does not simply act like a child; he relies on a mode of engagement that first arises in childhood. If we identify the shaman's mode of engagement with infantile behavior, it is because our own way of life produces so few examples of it beyond childhood. The very judgment of maturity depends on the weight we attribute to each stance. It should not surprise us, then, that a people like the Chachi, who rely more deeply than on us on a relational stance, complain that our deep reliance on an impartial stance is infantile. From their perspective, we are, at times, so busy reasoning about the world that we cannot make out how to live in it.

But perhaps, the reader might object, knowing how to live in the world does not have much to do with understanding it. That is, there is a question that has been looming in our discussion so far as to what knowledge is in the first place. Though I will not presume to give a comprehensive answer, I will at least fulfill what I take to be the responsibility of helping to orientate us toward one. Knowledge is what we capture of the world. It serves both practical and edifying needs. It helps us to locate and navigate ourselves in the world. We use it to articulate, manipulate, and describe what is. We expect it to have a certain rigor. It should be worked out on our part and reliable on the world's part. But what this amounts to and how we assure ourselves of it is a tremendous question. And if my arguments for relativism have any merit, we should expect the answer to vary greatly from one way of life to another.

For the relativist, the widely used definition of knowledge as "justified true belief" sheds very little light. She is, of course, careful to characterize knowledge broadly. But why should we class what is grasped by standards other than our own as knowledge? Why not define knowledge narrowly enough that alternative practices simply don't count as epistemic? The problem is, I believe, that our own epistemic stance demands a thoroughness of reflection and analysis that renders such a strategy inauthentic.

Here is another way to think of the problem. Imagine that we are struck by the losses incurred by our science,[61] but that we do not want to recognize alternative practices as epistemic. Most of our losses, we might claim, count only in terms of the pursuit of the good life. But science, we might insist, does not pursue the good life; it pursues something very different, which is truth. It aims to tell us what the world is really like. We might then go on to characterize the trade-offs made by alternative practices as mostly incurring losses on the side of truth. So, our practices have very different aims. Science is the epistemic practice par excellence because it tells us what the world is really like. It is the best at giving us truth, although it sometimes does this at the cost of the good life. Alternative practices, on the other hand, aim to give us the good life, but tend to do so at the cost of truth.

I think this argument ignores the degree to which alternative practices using very different concepts and methods can be successful in navigating the material world. I am not sure that it could be made as easily by the observer who has spent time in the company of a highly skilled shaman. More to the point, perhaps, the argument simply reasserts the priority of an impartial stance. It assumes that impartial knowledge is the purest, canonical form of knowledge. It assumes that our concepts are most fundamental, that alternative concepts are impure or inaccurate mixtures of the right set. It denies, for instance, the legitimacy of concepts where our impartial understanding is merged with loving attunement, or, to take the example of the shaman whose knowledge comes also from assuming a particular position of authority within the community, where our impartial understanding is merged with the

---

[61] See Sect. 4.9.

possession of power. It also ignores the possibility that what are distinct concepts in an alternative practice are, in fact, merged in our own way of understanding the world. In short, it denies the insights of deep engagement and the opening that the dynamic of resonance and loss creates for recognizing conflicting epistemic grounds. Certainly, we are constituted as detached individuals by Western capitalism, but what outside our mode of life justifies our predilection for such an impartial variety of truth? We can stick to a narrow definition of knowledge, like ostriches with our heads in the sand, but I think at least we must admit that our epistemic standards are necessarily self-justifying; they have nowhere to stand outside themselves.

4.11   Relativism and the Success of Science: A Shared Space

Table 4.1 summarizes the various moments in the dynamic of resonance and loss. This dynamic is what prevents the success of science from derailing the relativist's view. She can grant the power and success of science as relative achievements, while reserving a space for the relative success of alternatives. As we have discussed before, this need not be any more than a hypothetical space.[62] It need not be a space that the relativist herself fully endorses. But she partitions off within her own experience and representations a space that corresponds to those practices and their legitimacy.[63] She appreciates, for example, the differences between an impartial stance and a relational stance, as well as the choices that we make between them within the context of a particular way of life. The reasonableness that she finds in the Zande stone ritual comes from seeing it in the light of a relational stance.[64] The ritual is not a calculation of when the sun will set. It is more of a plea than a recipe for allowing the agent to arrive at his destination in time. It is made from a perspective in which the agent does not take himself to be entirely separate from the world, and the world, like him, has reasons and purpose of its own. The final determination of whether he makes it to the homestead in time is made not by the position of the Earth and sun, but by the experience of seeing and arriving in that place.

Importantly, we should remember that the relativist makes her calculus of resonance and loss from her own standpoint, using her own concepts and experiences as the only ones available to her, not as absolute standards. The stone ritual does not reduce neatly or ultimately to a plea instead of a recipe for delaying nightfall; this is simply how the relativist comes to appreciate it. And the appreciation that she develops represents much more than a merely methodological stance, a better framework for making sense of other practices and beliefs. She discovers at the same time the

---

[62] See Chap. 2.

[63] For more on the relationship between the relativist and the practices and claims internal to other ways of life, see Chap. 6.

[64] This is the example we discussed in Chap. 3.

Table 4.1 The dynamic of resonance and loss

Axes of evaluation	Impartial stance	Relational stance	Resonance (of relational stance within impartial stance)	(1) Loss – estrangement (within impartial stance)	(2) Loss – pull (across impartial/relational stances)	Disagreement about success
1. Relation between subject and object: detached understanding vs. loving attunement						
Proximity of subject and object	Knowledge is im-part-ial. Subject/object are separated	Knowledge is intimacy. Subject/object are mingled	"…eat you up." "…know by heart." Experiential learning.	Emptiness/ purposelessness of objects (including self).	Categorical opposition: Stances recognize different types, objects, aims, and formulations of knowledge.	Success depends on how we characterize knowledge.
Likeness between subject and object	Object is inanimate. Lacks subjectivity	Object is minded, animate. Possesses subjectivity	Act of mother nature. Car doesn't want to start.	Environmental crisis; disruption of regulatory systems.		
Power between subject and object	Subject aims to control object (power over)	Subject aims to influence object. (power with)	Love. Spiritual practices.	Anxiety over lack of total control.		
2. Capturing knowledge: revealing the object vs. relating to the object						
Process of gathering information	Object-ive, object-focused.	Subject-ive, subject-dependent.	Poetry, music, other fine arts.	Confusion about subjective experience.	Strong tension: Stances may overlap, but disagree on ultimate explanation and weighting of factors.	Success depends on how we recognize knowledge.
Form of information	Literal, concrete.	Metaphorical, figurative.		Inexplicable puzzles, dissociation between mind and world.		
Primary mode of constituting knowledge	Observation, reasoning.	Intuition, revelation.		Incompleteness; meaninglessness of answers.		
3. Calibration of knowledge: in society as a whole vs. in an individual life						

(continued)

Table 4.1 (continued)

Axes of evaluation	Impartial stance	Relational stance	Resonance (of relational stance within impartial stance)	(1) Loss – estrangement (within impartial stance)	(2) Loss – pull (across impartial/relational stances)	Disagreement about success
Measurement	Across society.	In individual life.	Hobbies such as cooking, fishing, sewing, and woodworking.	Alienation from primary life functions.	Practical opposition: Human finitude prevents stances from being easily combined.	Success depends on how we measure knowledge.
Aim	Extensive collection.	Intensive collection.		Inability to synthesize information.		
Value	In itself.	As lived.		Disconnect between knowledge and living life.		

incommensurability of these practices and beliefs with her own – not because she fails to understand them, but because she fails to find any sort of ground on which to champion one set of practices and beliefs over another without presupposing the superiority of the very framework in which they are enacted and held.

While the dynamic of resonance and loss brings to light this sort of incommensurability, it also suggests a relativistic dissolution of the conflict between the claims of different practices. It allows us to think that each claim holds of the world in its own way, but that we have no neutral ground to arbitrate their conflicts. An appreciation of context may tend to lessen conflict because it reveals claims to be in tension with, but not perfectly opposed to each other. Those who are used to defining relativism by conflict or strict opposition may be confused by this effect.[65] Our point has not been to establish different practices and their respective claims as polar opposites. Rather, it has been to show that our science does not achieve an absolute success over alternative practices and cannot, therefore, itself provide a neutral or highest standard for arbitrating conflicts. We may be inclined to say from a relativist perspective that both conflicting claims are right, relative to their own contexts. Such a perspective, however, does not assert itself to be more than a perspective, or to have truths that transcend the conditions of its own understanding.[66] Moreover, we have seen that there is pull, real trade-offs and choices to be made, between the contexts and stances of different ways of life. So, the relativist perspective is not one in which the conflicting claims and their respective practices are neatly united. It does not produce the harmonious, easily judged picture of the universalist.

It is, of course, the relativist's choice whether to grant alternative practices more than the hypothetical space of relative success. Perhaps she will decide to expand or modify her own practices and beliefs based on her analysis of them. Or perhaps she will decide to oppose them vehemently. The reflection, openness, curiosity, and liberality of our own viewpoint open up the possibility of relativism. We can access these other views and recognize the possibility of their legitimacy through the dynamic of resonance and loss. And there seems to be no way to rule that possibility out beyond the brute stipulation that only our way counts.

In some cases, what determines whether we grant alternative practices more than a hypothetical legitimacy will be their depth of divergence from our own science. The greatest difference may strike us viscerally, simply as disgust, for example, and we may not feel the least bit moved to grant them any consideration. However, to return to theme of our opening chapter, the determining factor will often be the presence or absence, on our part, of deep engagement with another way of life. The dynamic of resonance and loss is, in many respects, a specification of the relationship between attributive and reflective symmetry. We can think of the understanding that we are able to construct from resonance and from the first moment of loss as an

---

[65] For more on the relationship between tolerance-based relativism and the form of relativism being defended here, see Chap. 6.

[66] In fact, it does not even assert that its own normative concepts such as "truth" and "right" have exact equivalents, with the same contours and weight in another way of life. For more on relativism as relatively true, see Chap. 2.

instance of attributive symmetry. The registering of loss, similarly, is an example of reflective symmetry. And, to add yet another feature of deep engagement, pull, the second moment of loss, brings to light the complexity of conflict.

What also comes with deep engagement is an appreciation of the context of a conflicting claim and of the alternative practice in which it is embedded. We might come to appreciate, for example, that the Zande claim about a stone delaying sunset involves a subjective concept of time, not our mechanical Copernican concept of time. In this case, the space of possibility for the Zande claim becomes a little bit more palatable because we can imagine that it incentivizes the agent's subjective powers, allowing him to move and to see as well as possible. An appreciation of context might also help us to see that night can fall at different times even in the same region at the same time of year, depending on humidity and precipitation, the type and number of clouds, the exact location of mountains and trees, fires and other unanticipated events, etc.[67] In this case, we warm to the possibility of the Zande claim because a change in the time of nightfall no longer seems quite so impossible. Context might even lead us to the observation that a forest is a microcosm, small and volatile. In a forest, rain is not always a massive storm on our satellite map, but can also be an isolated shower over a hillside. It is not clear that our laws rigidly describe every facet of such a place. Or perhaps some of our theories – the time dilation of relativity, or the observation dependence of quantum theory, for instance – are less in tension with the Zande claim than we assume. However, it is very important to note here that to reason in this way about the claims of an alternative practice is neither to determine their truth absolutely nor to bring them into perfect agreement with our own. It is merely to use our own experience, concepts, and understanding (after all, what other tools do we have?)[68] to engage the possibility of their being legitimate claims, in their own context and way, about a world that we ultimately share.

We have seen repeatedly that the first-person feature of deep engagement can provide the grounds for developing the analogical understanding that lies at the heart of ambivalence. It is also often the motivation for this development. Yet perhaps the greatest motivation for granting a space of legitimacy to alternative practices and their conflicting claims comes from the dangling pieces[69] that we experience in the first person. Evans-Pritchard does not tell us anything about the stone ritual for delaying nightfall, but he does report that when he observed a similar ritual, for shooing away the rain, it appeared to produce results.[70] We must not underestimate the force of dangling pieces. Such dangling pieces are the little anomalies calling out from the edge of our paradigm that alternatives might exist, that they might even

---

[67] This may be most obvious to those who have lived in an area, like the San Francisco Bay Area, that is rich in microclimates, or to those who have spent significant time living outdoors, such as camping or backpacking.

[68] I don't mean to imply that these are always easy, ready or sufficient tools, but rather that there is simply nothing else of which we can avail ourselves.

[69] For more on this feature of deep engagement, see Chap. 1, Sect. 1.2.5.

[70] Evans-Pritchard, *Witchcraft*, 472–473.

have some use and place in this world. And, whereas I have been hesitant to appeal to my own experience in this chapter as much as I did in "Deep Engagement," given that our subject now (science) is the apotheosis of impartial understanding, I must admit that whatever strength my arguments have, they owe to the lure of dangling pieces, the incredible journey of deep engagement through which they dragged me, and the ensuing struggle to make sense of what I found.

Perhaps a full commitment to relativism comes only with the experience of deep engagement. Ultimately, this is not important. Relativism, as we have said many times before, must be relatively true. Deep engagement gives us a better understanding of the kind of experience to which it is relatively true. A sincere relativist should not even aim to convince everyone of her view. But what I do hope my reader recognizes so far are not only the conditions that make relativism plausible, but that the view can be coherent, and that it does not necessarily fly in the face of science. Relativism and the success of science are compatible when we understand success itself as a relative measure. We can appreciate the context dependence of success, the variety of standards, the grounds of their legitimacy, and the fact that standards of assessment for success are internal to a particular way of life. The non-relativist may go on to explain why particular standards are special and should count more than others. But this does not vex the relativist. After all, as the anti-relativist is wont to point out, the relativist must grant that the absolutist is relatively right, too. And the relativist is happy to oblige. She has a sense of the absolutist's space, too; it is where deep engagement is not a possibility, and alternatives fade out of existence.

Chapter 5
The Space Where Relativism and Realism Meet

5.1 The Remaining Objection

In Chaps. 3 and 4 we argued that the success of science does not undermine relativism by constituting either a *neutral* or a *highest* ground on which to arbitrate conflicting claims across different ways of life. When we assumed that science and other epistemic practices were mostly homologous, we found that we could not measure their products or their predictions against each other independently of social, environmental, and conceptual contexts, which varied across different ways of life and led to conflicting results.[1] When we relaxed the homology, granting significant differences in foundational concepts and standards of assessment across competing epistemic practices, we discovered that our very understanding of success itself varies across different ways of life.[2] One might think that if the success of science does not allow us to weigh competing practices against each other in a neutral or highest way, then we have no need to worry about its undermining the very possibility of relativism by constituting an absolute ground for arbitrating conflicting claims across different ways of life. Yet, surprisingly, this possibility, even in light of the arguments of the preceding chapters, retains some force. A realist, for example, could reason along the following lines: Science might not evaluate the world on neutral ground, and we might not be able to establish its superiority in any non-relative way, but perhaps our measures and context just are the ones that latch on most comprehensively to a law-governed, unitary world.[3] Perhaps the contexts and standards of assessment of peoples from other times and/or places just aren't the right ones to evaluate the world as well as we now can. Perhaps the alienation

---

[1] See Chap. 3.

[2] See Chap. 4.

[3] Gellner gives exactly this sort of argument. See Ernest Gellner, "Relativism and Universals," in *Rationality and Relativism*, eds. Martin Hollis and Steven Lukes (Cambridge, Mass.: MIT Press, 1982), 181–200.

© Springer Nature Switzerland AG 2020
A. Luboff, *Facing Relativism*, Synthese Library 425,
https://doi.org/10.1007/978-3-030-43341-3_5

that we experience from our objects of knowledge and the sufficiency we lose over that knowledge just are the high price that must be paid for truth. There may be many ways of understanding the world, but if science comes closest to understanding what really is the case, then the evaluative egalitarianism of relativism is, in fact, wrongheaded; we can arbitrate conflicting claims (at least at the epistemic level) across different ways of life on grounds that, without being perfectly complete or infallible, come close enough.

Now, some readers might find it strange, or simply superfluous, for me to dedicate a chapter in response to this objection. After all, relativism is a view that is often associated (and conflated) with anti-realism. And anti-realism could be very dismissive of this objection simply by claiming that science picks out the most useful theories (for us), not theories that reveal anything about the nature of the world. However, there are two reasons why I take the objection seriously. First of all, I myself court a certain degree of realism throughout this work in at least two respects. The first concerns deep engagement and anthropological experience. In Chap. 1, I introduce the phenomenon of dangling pieces – aspects of human experience that are not in the same way, to the same degree, or perhaps to any degree articulated, recognized, and accounted for in our own way of life, yet that strike the deeply engaged person as very present and real in another way of life. These pieces do not appear as illusions; they interlock with the narratives and experience of many agents and across different aspects of the other way of life as the deeply engaged person comes to know it. In Chap. 4, my discussion of resonance again appeals to a realist aspect of anthropological experience. I argue that a very different practice embedded in another way of life may capture aspects of experience that we can recognize as meaningful and real, despite their lack of emphasis and development in our own way of life. I believe that the anthropological motivations for relativism are at the same time motivations to take another way of life seriously. The deeply engaged person is, in general, motivated to account not for the fantasy and error – or even just the mere contingency – of another way of life, but for both the alacrity and difference with which it navigates the world. In this respect, I am not sure that the deflationary account of cross-cultural difference that anti-realism might provide is quite enough.[4]

My work also courts a certain degree of realism in its defense of the coherence of relativism. In Chap. 2, my introduction of the concepts of "resistance" and "responsiveness" makes reference to a reality that in important respects transcends our experience. I argue that relativism does not necessarily collapse into an "anything goes" view because even within the contingencies of a relativistic framework we can recognize a world that constrains our claims, a world in relation to which our claims develop responsively. We can recognize this degree of transcendence without implying that our means themselves of capturing or calibrating the world transcend the contingencies of our way of life. I suggest that such a conditioned transcendence

---

[4]For more on this point see, Richard Shweder, "Post-Nietzschean Anthropology: The Idea of Multiple Objective Worlds," in *Relativism: Interpretation and Confrontation,* edited by Michael Krausz (Notre Dame, IN: Notre Dame Press, 1989).

is what distinguishes relativism from arbitrariness, and gives content to concepts like "relative truth" and "relative rightness." Ultimately, I believe the ability to incorporate such a degree of realism is a virtue of my version of relativism.[5]

The second reason why I am not more dismissive of the realist's objection is that the intuitions behind scientific realism lend themselves rather easily to a critique of relativism. And they are, I believe, so natural in our thought that many who do not consider themselves scientific realists fall in easily, often unwittingly, with this line of argument. It behooves any relativist, then, not to simply dismiss the realist's intuitions about the comprehensiveness of science, but to take great care with them. Either she should explain why they are mistaken, or find some way to accommodate them within her own view. My route will be to do a little bit of both.

5.2   The Realist Argument Against Relativism

Hilary Putnam once famously claimed, "The positive argument for realism is that it is the only philosophy that doesn't make the success of science a miracle."[6] The assumption that scientific success and ontological acuity go hand-in-hand has proven, nevertheless, rather difficult to cash out. Perhaps the best-known attack on scientific realism is what has come to be known as Laudan's "pessimistic meta-induction."[7] In short, if the central terms of what science recognizes as successful theories – that is, theories that are good at explaining, predicting, and unifying phenomena – are proven, time and again, by their successor theories not to refer to real entities, what makes us believe that those of any successful theory every will? If all central terms of what we recognize at a given time as successful theories are destined, ultimately, to go the way of "phlogiston" and "ether," why do we cherish in them hopes for uncovering the nature of the "Really Real"? Why assume that success has any metaphysical import at all?

Despite the, by now, rather well-known anti-realist attacks on scientific realism, I believe that Putnam's claim retains a certain intuitive appeal for many of us. After all, science is our tool for articulating, describing, and manipulating our world. When it gives us accurate predictions, comprehensive explanations, and new inventions, we'd like to think that this is because it provides us with a very close grasp of what there is. If the concepts and terms of science were largely mistaken or imaginary, then how could we, time and again, be so successful? Even if we point to the contingent social facts about how science is constituted and practiced, these alone

---

[5] For more on this point, see Chap. 6.

[6] Hilary Putnam, *Mathematics, Matter and Method* (Cambridge: Cambridge University Press, 1975), 73.

[7] Larry Laudan, "A Confutation of Convergent Realism," *Philosophy of Science*, Vol. 48, No. 1, (Mar. 1981), 19–49. In referring to this name, I mean only to avail myself of what has become popular shorthand for the argument; I do not mean to take a stand on the debate as to whether the argument deserves to be called a, "meta-induction."

do not seem to explain the success of science without the additional assumption that our theories latch on, deeply and quite accurately, to the structure of an independent world.

Putnam's quote may not get us all the way to a robust realism, but it does warm the way, so to speak, toward a form of scientific realism, toward believing that, in some fashion, the objects and mechanisms of scientific theories correspond to entities and processes in the world itself. Yet, it is, in fact, only a small jump from such sympathies toward scientific realism to a full argument against relativism. The only missing piece is an additional assumption that the real comes together as a single, determinate, largely knowable world. This assumption, of course, traditionally goes along with scientific realism, and is supposed to be encouraged, again, by the success of science itself. It is taken that not only are the entities and processes described by science real, but that they nearly exhaust all of the content of the real. In other words, science is so comprehensive that it does not just describe a part or aspect of experience, but, potentially,[8] everything there is, as it is, without omission.

Now, the problem for relativism lies in that this assumption (that the real comes together as a single, determinate, largely knowable world) apparently does not leave as much room for alternative epistemic practices as a robust relativism would require. If all epistemic practices have as their object the same, determinate and knowable world, then it appears that there can only be three, mutually combinable, sources of variation between them:

(1) *Incompleteness* – One or more of the practices capture only *some* (but not all) of the features of the world.
(2) *Hidden equivalence* – The differences between practices are merely apparent.
(3) *Error* – One or more of the practices does not grasp the world well; it fails at articulating, describing, and/or successfully manipulating the world.

What the assumption of one, determinate world no longer allows is the claim that different practices carve out radically different worlds; they must just carve out pieces of the same world, with their own style, and varying degrees of accuracy.

Once we reduce the field to these three possibilities, it takes only a further assumption of the success and comprehensiveness of science to turn any apparent variety and conflict between practices into an innocuous epiphenomenon. Let us consider, first of all, the case of variation caused by incompleteness. If different epistemic practices, A and B, are sensitive only to certain features of the world, such as those at a particular scale and from a given perspective, then we could imagine that, inasmuch as they do not articulate, describe, and manipulate the same aspects of the world, they may differ greatly from each other. This could, at times, produce a sort of relativistic effect, whereby the two practices appear to make conflicting claims that cannot be evaluated by any absolute, neutral, or highest standards. However, if the world is single, determinate, and largely knowable, then we may also reasonably expect that there could exist a practice, X, at a greater level of

---

[8] That is, allowing for science to resolve any remaining mysteries as it progresses.

abstraction, which encompasses the scales and perspectives relevant to both A and B, and tracks all the features of the world to which they are sensitive.[9] Such a practice X would provide us with common grounds for reconciling any conflicting claims between A and B.

As it turns out, when we grant the success and comprehensiveness of science, we take it to be precisely such a practice X. In fact, we endorse the success and comprehensiveness of science so far that it not only satisfies the possibility of an X existing, but becomes a sort of maximal X, with the potential to track quite accurately all the real features of the world. We take science to be the ultimate enquiry of everything there is in the world, exactly what it is, and how it works. And so in science we have not only common, but highest grounds on which to evaluate the conflicting claims of different epistemic practices. It turns out, moreover, that these practices are different only inasmuch as they fail to track the features of the real as completely as science does. The success and comprehensiveness of science dissolves the variety of relativism into simple instances of inadequacy. Different epistemic practices do not capture different truths; they simply fail to capture the same truths completely.

In the case where A and B track the same features of the world, at the same scale, and from similar perspectives, the belief in an objective, determinate, and knowable world leads us to the two remaining sources of variation mentioned above: either what appear to be different, sometimes conflicting claims about what the world is and how it works are, in fact, equivalent and just need to go through some process of translation; or, at least one of the epistemic practices under consideration is simply mistaken at some point in its descriptions, articulations, and manipulations of the world. If there is one world that is just one way, and is conducive to one complete description, then there is not room for more than one right answer; there are only equivalent variations of the right answer, and wrong answers. When we grant the success and comprehensiveness of science, we take that it is well on its way to compiling this one complete description of the world. It offers us a sort of highest grounds on which to evaluate the conflicting claims of different epistemic practices, and what we discover is that not only can we evaluate claims beyond relativistic constraints, but the substantial differences that relativism was supposed to account for in the first place do not really exist. If claims are right, they must agree with those of established science, and this relation of agreement becomes a means of translating between the different practices. But if we can move so easily between different epistemic practices, then there cannot be much substantive difference to account for in the first place. On the other hand, if the claims of an epistemic practice are wrong, then the variation they produce is not an interesting epistemic phenomenon, though it may be perhaps an interesting historical or developmental

---

[9] In a limiting case, where either A (or B) encompasses the scale and perspective relevant to B (or A, respectively) and tracks all the features of the world to which the other practice is sensitive, then A (or B, respectively) is simply identical to X, and the argument proceeds without further disruption. (Note that the "or" here must be exclusive. In a case where the inclusive "or" is realized, we must appeal to additional arguments for equivalence and/or error, which are both considered below.)

phenomenon. All we have found is a mere lack of knowledge, not a substantial alternate knowledge for which we must account.

5.3   A Thought Experiment

According to the argument from scientific realism against relativism, the success of science not only establishes a very tight link between the entities, properties, processes, etc. posited by scientific theories and the real world, but also significantly reduces the possibility of substantive alternate epistemic practices. In other words, science tells the story of what the world is like and how it works so well that there is no room for competing epistemologies (though some may be left for imitators and false pretenders). In sketching this argument, I have been careful to draw out the role played by two assumptions, which otherwise are often left quite tacit:

- The real comes together as a single, determinate, largely knowable world.
- Science is comprehensive and highly successful in its account of the world.

These assumptions help transform what might be a merely local or relative success of science into a stunning ontological coup d'état. Although we already saw in Chap. 4 some reasons to be suspicious of claims about the unqualified success of science, I would like here to press the set of metaphysical assumptions that this success is often taken to support. My target, roughly, will be the claim that science provides us with a comprehensive account of a largely knowable world. What I hope to show is that even the realist's understanding of a largely "knowable world" leaves more room for alternate epistemologies than we might imagine at first blush (or when we are so forcefully under the spell of the "great success of science"). We can locate a depth of incompleteness in all forms of knowledge, which can help give a rich sense to the claim that different epistemic practices carve out different worlds, even when we conceive of the real as ultimately a single whole.

As I have discussed in Chaps. 1 and 4, the space in which we recognize alternatives is not one that we fully inhabit as our own; we reach it through constructive experience and through exercises of analogy and imagination. In Chap. 1, we explored this space at a practical level through the anthropological exercise of deep engagement. In Chap. 4, we explored it at an epistemological level through the dynamic of resonance and loss. I would now like to invite the reader to explore this space at the metaphysical level through what I will simply call, "a thought experiment."

Consider, for a moment, our perception. We hear sound only within a certain range of frequency, at a certain distance from us, and with a certain degree of precision. We hear the voice of the little girl who taps us on the shoulder, the call of the robin on the branch just across the way, and the loud zoom of the jet that flashes overhead. We do not hear the very high sounds or the very low sounds that screech and rumble even right next to us. We do not hear the conversation of our friends a block away, let alone in the next town or county over. Nor do we notice the fine variations in what otherwise sound to us like sounds of the same shape and pitch. Yet, what sense of hearing would we have if all of these limitations were lifted? If in experience we were presented with every sound of the real, at every range and distance, with every possible degree of precision, what would it be like? Could we have any perception at all? Or would it strike us as a vast cacophony and silence booming at once?

Likewise, we are sensitive only to certain wavelengths of light and see only at a certain scale, with certain grains of resolution, within a certain distance. We see our fingertips, squirrels, and mountaintops. We notice on them details like sheaths of flesh, pieces of fur, and caps of snow, respectively. And they are available to us at specific distances: the fingertips before us, the squirrel within a few dozen feet, and the mountaintop tens of miles away. We do not see the infrared or the ultraviolet even as they hit our own bodies. Unaided, we have no sense of the cells and molecules in our fingertips, or of the mountain range, planet, and galaxy of which the mountaintop is just a small part. Yet what would it be like to see everything, in the fullest spectrum, at every grain of resolution, within all distances, from a Planck length[10] to a gigaparsec?[11] Could we even fathom what it would be like to see everything just in the space bounded by our two fingertips? Is it not vastly full? What could a presentation be like of so many patterns and so much information? Would there be anything for us to discern? Or would it strike us as a vast oneness of everything and nothing at once?

Our sense of time, similarly, is limited to intervals of a certain scale. We perceive in half-seconds, minutes, hours, and years, but not in yoctoseconds[12] or millennia. Our sense of time is also primarily linear and monodirectional. Yet, to consider the importance of our particular kind of perception in time, we need not even consider the possibility of other trajectories in time. We need only ask ourselves what it would be like if our awareness captured just this very moment, right now, at every scale. Although we have little sense of phenomena that are super fast, this is no reason to think that they are insignificant or scarce. The real may present organized structure, with characteristics we have perhaps never fathomed, at smaller and smaller intervals of time. This second may hold more information than we could ever process in our lifetimes. It may even be infinitely full. But what would it be like if our awareness captured every moment that exists in this now? Could we perceive anything at all? And yet, somehow, we pass, in a moment of Zeno's magic, from one second to the next. We pick out phenomena only at a given level, at a particular scale, and the yoctoseconds are as meaningless to us as our lifetimes must be to a creature perceiving in moments as dilated as the life of our universe.

---

[10] A Planck length is $1.616199(97) \times 10^{-35}$ of a meter.

[11] A gigaparsec is a distance of about 3.26 billion light-years.

[12] A yoctosecond is 10^{-24} of a second.

5.4   Incompleteness and the Metaphysical Space for a Genuine Variety of Epistemic Practices

What I believe this thought experiment shows us is that if our perception is of the real, it is essentially an awareness of only certain features of the real: of audible sound, of visible light, of ordinary time, and so on. There may be features of the real that not only our senses, but our words, even our imaginations, fail to capture. More importantly, our perception is rooted in a particular scale; we perceive these features within a certain range and with a particular degree of acuity. Yet while our perceptions are in this way limited, we have no reason to believe that the real also is. It must have structure with respect to these other features and scales. At least, all of our investigations of the world beyond our immediate senses have so far shown this to be the case. And what I believe this suggests is that what we refer to as, "the real" – the counterpart to our thought, that which is the ultimate ground of our experience – may be richly, if not infinitely, complex. Yet we can grasp the extent of this complexity only by extrapolation and metaphor. It is nothing that we can perceive directly. There is nothing for us to grasp in the perception of sound or light or time at every scale.

What I also believe this experiment suggests is that our finite perception is essentially both a taking in and a blocking out. It involves not only the positive achievement of being sensitive to certain features of the real, but, critically, the negative achievement of failing to sense everything else. In fact, we may think of a perspective as determined not only positively by the features of the real that it brings to light, but negatively by the features that it screens off. My perspective is as much defined by the fact that I perceive in intervals of time such as seconds and days as by the fact that I cannot perceive in intervals as small as yoctoseconds or as large as millennia.

Because a finite perception must be of something and not everything, our awareness depends on incompleteness. What allows us to experience the real is as much a sensitivity to certain features as an insensitivity to others. A world and objects come into view for us because we both take in and screen out the real. Yet if the real possesses an indefinitely rich complexity, then we must screen out vastly more than we take in. The condition of possibility of our finite perception must be the ineffability of the remainder of the real.

Now, it is true that science explores far beyond what we can perceive. My point, however, is not about so much the particular limits of our perception as what it takes for a world and objects to come into view. I assume that the presentation of a world in experience, however it occurs, and whatever it consists of, is the very foundation of our knowledge; without it, there is nothing for us to know. And I claim that such a manifestation of finite givenness is necessarily incomplete. It is both a taking in and a screening off. The fact of our knowing anything at all depends on the impossibility of our knowing indefinitely more. Of course, this is not to say that our knowledge of the real could not or does not in some sense deepen with further investigation. But it does mean that there must always be an impenetrable horizon.

And more importantly, it means that our knowledge sits on this horizon; our knowledge comes into being only because of this horizon, and it can never fully be excised. Any system that we develop for describing, articulating, and manipulating our world is, vis-à-vis the real, necessarily incomplete. Indefinitely more of the real lies impenetrably beyond its scope.

In this sense, it becomes very confusing to say that one epistemic practice, such as Western science, is superior to another practice, such as Chachi shamanism. To claim that one comes closer to the real in any absolute sense is like trying to argue that the number 3891 is closer to infinity than the number 976. We have no way of organizing the indefinitely rich complexity of the remainder of the real to make this comparison meaningful. We can, however, easily compare the two numbers the other way around. That is, 3891 is clearly farther from zero than 976, and in this sense the former is certainly greater than the latter. Once we limit our consideration to a determinate range of well-ordered objects, we can make all sorts of comparisons. For instance, on a number line of integers from 0 to 4000, the number 3800 is much greater than 976, but still less than 3891.

If the real is indefinitely complex, it cannot provide us with a background for making such comparisons. But in our finite perceptions, and in our further endeavors to articulate, describe, and manipulate the world that is presented to us in experience, we do seem to impose exactly the kinds of limits of scale and range and type that make these comparisons possible. We might think that the relevant limits range from more general a priori constraints, related to the kind of perceiving creatures that we are, all the way to very particular historical, contextual, and personal constraints involving geography, language, culture, class, gender, family, and so on. It might help, then, to make a distinction between the real as a whole, on the one hand, and our world – the piece of the real that we experience concretely, on the other. For the relativist, there is no harm in the claim that relative to a particular carving of the real, that is, relative to a particular way of life, a particular epistemic practice is more successful in grasping the world than another. Relative to a particular relationship with the real, as manifested in a particular way of life, concepts like truth/falsity, right/wrong, accuracy/error, progress/regress can become invested with rich meaning. It is outside such a system of filtering the real – of taking in and screening out – that comparison becomes meaningless.

This distinction, between a world, which is a piece of the real presented in finite experience, and the real as a whole, helps make room within the realist's picture for the relativist's claim that different perspectives carve out different worlds. The relativist can accede that, ultimately, the real is one whole, and all experience is part of it. But because of its indefinitely rich complexity, it can be carved into any number of worlds of finite experience. There is no reason to think that there is just one possible carving, or that different carvings may be brought into relation with each other by a simple transformation. In some cases, the only common ground between two carvings may be the real itself, in all of its complexity. In other cases, different carvings may possess degrees of greater and lesser overlap across any number of domains.

Although ultimately all creatures and everything that they perceive must be part of the real so defined, it may not always make sense to group all perceivers and all things[13] into the same world. We may say that we share our world with other creatures only inasmuch as their world overlaps with our own and we can detect the part of the real that they are. If another kind of creature carves a world of finite experience so radically different from our own, we may not detect that it is the subject of any experience at all. That is, we may assume that it has no form of consciousness simply because we fail to grasp the terms of its engagement with the real. We may not comprehend that it, too, takes in and filters out the real, placing itself in a world of finite experience. For example, we (in our way of life) know the earth only as an object, not as a subject. Although we do not detect in the earth any form of consciousness, this does not rule out that it is a subject of experience in some way that we cannot, or can only with difficulty, fathom. There may be a set of perceptive abilities, restricted to a certain scale and range, which places the earth in a world of finite experience and establishes it as a conscious agent. If our scale and concerns are so different than the earth's, then our failure to acknowledge its consciousness must be quite understandable. To the earth, we must be something like the flora in our gut is to us. We interact with each other, we depend on each other, but we do not inhabit the same conscious world.

Not only may we fail to detect a piece of the real as a subject, but we may fail to detect it as existing at all. This could easily happen if it is a piece of the real for which we have no corresponding perceptive abilities. In this case, we may only imagine or infer that it exists. By definition, the most extreme examples of failures of detection cannot even be given. However, it is easy to come up with examples of pieces of the real that we detect only with extreme difficulty, such as subatomic particles. What we identify as the Higgs boson is a piece of the real that lies at the very edge of the range of our perceptive and conceptual abilities. Perhaps what other ways of life identify as spirits, demons, and angels are also pieces of the real that humans detect only with extreme difficulty, and for which we Westerners, especially, lack a very rich characterization.

5.5   Reacting to Rich Realism

5.5.1   Uneasiness About Other Worlds

Indeed, the possibility of radically different perspectives on an indefinitely complex real invites all sorts of flights of fancy. However, I think it is important to acknowledge that there is something about such speculation that tends to strike us as too sexy, too racy, perhaps even trashy. It is a picture for us that at once attracts and repulses. A part of us wants to believe that the real is much greater than the world

---

[13] I leave it open at this point whether all things can be, in some way, understood as perceivers.

we know, that it is full of other things, other beings, and other powers. As very young children, we seem to have a sense, from at least the womb and the first few months of mothering, of infinite oneness, of being a piece of an infinitely greater whole.[14] This is not a sense, however, that we typically go on to nurture and develop in our way of life. Yet it does seem to be what (sometimes for us, and much more often for those of certain other ways of life) serves as a foundation for developing strong spiritual, imaginative, and intuitive powers. And these, I propose, are precisely the powers that we need to engage the possibility of knowledge and being existing outside our own sphere. Part of our difficulty, then, in accepting the idea of many worlds within a richly complex real lies in our tendency to correct and repress this spiritual sense. What we learn to recognize is oneness re-directed onto the self (not extended outwards), a world that matches our horizons (not outstrips them), and knowledge founded in what we grasp (not what lies beyond). Our world is too full, too complete and self-sufficient, to acknowledge any others. Yet, being the kind of conscious creatures that we are, we cannot banish our spiritual sense entirely. We do not fit neatly into the atomistic world that we ourselves circumscribe. We still have something like a vestigial spiritual sense, a vague longing for an enchanted world.[15] And it is, I believe, to this repressed, forgotten sense that an idea like multiple worlds within a richly complex real appeals. In the language of the previous chapter: at an inner, often buried level, it resonates with us.

At the same time, however, such a romantic idea lies in strong tension with the scientific world of testing, matter, and proof to which we are very heavily acculturated. It threatens the power of our scientific world. It shrinks the status of our world from being the whole world to being but one world among many. It surrounds our singular set of truths with alternate sets that lie outside its grasp. It throws our highest procedures and norms into competition with others. And this is why, I believe, rich realism repulses as much as it attracts, because in the very act of satisfying a sort of primitive desire, it unwinds our most sophisticated picture of what our world is and who we are.

5.5.2   The Burden of the Argument

It can be tricky to put forward a view that inspires such deep ambivalence. To be clear and, perhaps, to put certain readers at ease, let me state directly: I am not arguing for the absolute truth of such a rich realism. Indeed, as a sincere relativist, I have no idea how to go about offering such a proof. I only know how to argue that,

---

[14] Pierre Hadot, following Romain Rolland, calls this, "the oceanic feeling." Pierre Hadot, *The Present Alone is Our Happiness: Conversations with Jeannie Carlier and Arnold I. Davidson,* translated by Marc Djaballah and Michael Chase (Stanford, CA: Stanford University Press, 2007), 5.

[15] For a very provoking discussion of disenchantment and the possibility of re-enchantment, see Morris Berman, *The Reenchantment of the World* (Ithaca, NY: Cornell University Press, 1981).

relative to a context that I hope my reader will recognize as her own, or as close to her own, or at least as meaningful or interesting vis-à-vis her own, a particular view possesses certain virtues – it is coherent, well-suited, fruitful, and so on. I do not pretend to have an absolute view at any level, least of all, at the metaphysical. My point is that, for those who are inclined toward realism – by the great feats of science, by the dangling pieces of deep engagement, or by some other means – rich realism could be a provocative alternative to the more constrained scientific realism.

Ultimately, a satisfactory exposition of rich realism would call for a more detailed analysis of the terms, and of their relations, that I have been using here, such as: experience, perspective, perceptive abilities, consciousness; real/world, subject/object, finite/indefinite, and so on. It might involve forays into the history of philosophy to examine the work of those who have presented kindred visions, such as Leibniz, Spinoza, or possibly the ancients of Elea.[16] As exciting as I find the prospect of such a journey, it would carry us far afield; and, more importantly, it far exceeds what we need to argue here. My point is that a realist perspective coupled with an acknowledgment of the feats of science does not necessarily lead to the conclusion that science provides us with a comprehensive account of a single, largely knowable world. If the real is of an indefinitely rich complexity and all claims to knowledge essentially involve the filtering out of vastly more than they take in, then the success of science is much more modest than the scientific realist takes it to be. The feats of science entail only that science gives us a relatively effective grasp of a world that is but one rendering of the real. They do not exclude the existence of other worlds that are pieces of the real grasped in other ways. They do not give science a monopoly on success. And they do not provide us with close to absolute grounds for evaluating the success of other epistemic practices. The feats of science, under a rich conception of the real, leave open the possibility that other epistemic practices, embedded in other ways of life, also manipulate, articulate, and describe a piece of the real with relative success. In other words, rich realism is consistent with the variety of relativism defined by entrenched conflict that I have been defending throughout this work.

While I do not mean to argue for the absolute *truth* of rich realism, I do believe that its very *possibility* shifts the burden of the argument back onto the scientific realist. I have shown that a certain metaphysical picture, of a singular world comprehensively described by science, enters as an important premise in the scientific realist's argument against relativism. And I have argued that there is another possible conception of the real, which is motivated by reflection on the nature and limitations of our finite experience. This alternate conception acknowledges the success of science while allowing a space for relativism. It helps show how we can claim, on the one hand, that science effectively articulates, manipulates, and describes a

---

[16] Certainly, there are many other possible ways of grounding the view as well. Michael Krausz, for example, uses teachings from the Hindu and Buddhist traditions to elaborate a metaphysical view which seems fairly close to rich realism and is meant to support of a form of global relativism. Michael Krausz, *Dialogues on Relativism, Absolutism and Beyond: Four Days in India* (Lanham, MD: Rowman & Littlefield Publishers, 2011).

piece of the real, and allow, on the other, that different epistemic practices, embedded in other ways of life, may also effectively articulate, manipulate, and describe a piece of the real. Moreover, it begins to give us a sense of why we may not, in any neutral way, be able to weigh these claims of effectiveness against each other. It is now up to the scientific realist, I believe, to explain why we must accept his restricted conception of the real in such a strong way. That is, why we must grant not only that it is a possible and well-motivated version of realism (which is as much as I have asked in the case of rich realism), but why anyone who acknowledges the realist's basic intuition about a world that transcends our experience must grant its truth (since it enters as a premise in the argument against relativism).[17]

5.6 The Anti-relativist's Response

5.6.1 The Broad Claim to Comprehensiveness

At this point, we might consider two general lines of response that are available to the scientific realist. We will deal with them singly, although they may, with some creativity, be combined. First of all, the scientific realist could argue that there simply is not anything left out of the scientific world for the remainder of the real to be. This does not mean that science already gives us a complete account of the real, but that it will eventually provide us with a very good account of just about everything there is. Given the exceptional rate of progress over the past couple of hundred years, the time of a nearly complete science does not even seem very far away. So, whatever structure the real might have relative to other perspectives and scales, it cannot be anything that lies far outside our grasp. We are safe in our assumption, then, that the scientific world extends to all of the real. It is, in effect, the one and only world.

Now, typically, such a claim about the comprehensiveness of science relies on a deterministic and atomistic picture of the real. We are to imagine that ultimately there exists some kind of fundamental micro-particles, whose causal interactions will be described by our most complete physical theory. Once we understand the workings of these micro-particles, we will be able to build our explanation up to the less fundamental sciences, level by level, from physics to chemistry to biology to psychology to economics…until science gives us a complete, determinate picture of everything there is and how it works. We must notice, however, that there is something very funny about this picture of how science is supposed to be completed. A

---

[17] Remember, not all relativists share this intuition; I am only arguing here on behalf of those who do. Those who do not would be much more dismissive of the realist's arguments in the first place. As I explained in Sects. 5.1 and 5.2 above, however, I believe that the relativist who is motivated by deep engagement, who wants to distinguish her view from an "anything goes" view, and who acknowledges the success of science (albeit relativistically), as I do, needs to engage the realist and his arguments much more carefully.

significant group of philosophers of physics, including James Ladyman and Don Ross, has argued that it is, in fact, out of step with our best science. It fails, they claim, to take into account the most successful developments in recent fundamental physics, such as Relativity Theory and Quantum Theory.[18] If they are right, a realism that relies on a picture of fundamental particles and their causal interactions would be best described as "antiquated," not "scientific."

What I believe is as striking as the thrust of this argument is the fact that most well-educated people, like me, are so poorly qualified to evaluate it. However, we can at least acknowledge the unfairness of basing our metaphysics on science that we so little understand. We can, at the same time, do our best to grapple with it at least in very general terms.[19] Relativity Theory dissolves absolute simultaneity; there is no way to establish that Event A happened before Event B outside a given reference frame in spacetime. Quantum Theory leaves open the possibility of time symmetry; it is expected that a successor theory may not respect the arrow of time as we know it. What can we make of causality without a sense of absolute succession in time? These two results cannot leave our folk notion of causality, of what it means for Event A to cause Event B, unchanged. We must also consider that in Quantum Theory the states of objects are entangled; there is no way to isolate distinct individuals independently of the act of observation. In effect, there are no observer-independent individuals at the quantum level. Given these results, what exactly do we mean when we suppose that science will give us a comprehensive account of all there is by building up from the causal interactions of fundamental micro-particles?[20] In what way are the interactions causal? In what sense are the micro-particles individuals?[21]

Ladyman and Ross, in fact, are prepared to answer these questions. They believe that our folk notions of causality and objecthood are simply too parochial to describe the real at a fundamental level. Instead, they propose a metaphysics inspired by and consistent with the results of contemporary physics. They suggest that we think of the real not in terms of the causal interactions of fundamental micro-particles, but in terms of structure. Their motto is, "structure all the way down." What the real is at the most basic level, and at every level, is not the "micro-bangings" of particles, but relations of information. We can always describe this structure using the language of mathematics. However, it is only at particular levels of scale that features such as

---

[18] James Ladyman and Don Ross with David Spurrett and John Collier, *Every Thing Must Go: Metaphysics Naturalized* (Oxford and New York: Oxford University Press, 2007).

[19] Of course, philosophers of physics do this with much more sophistication. Still, it remains remarkable how little impact their work has outside their area of specialty. In no way do I pretend to do their job here. I only mean to echo Ladyman and Ross's plea that anyone who considers himself a scientific realist should take our most fundamental science seriously.

[20] We might also ask how comprehensive the world described by science could be when physicists now estimate that, given the existence of dark matter and dark energy, the kind of matter familiar to us makes up less than 5% of the universe! In other words, according to our most fundamental science, we know next to nothing about the overwhelming majority of what there is. See, for example, http://science.nasa.gov/astrophysics/focus-areas/what-is-dark-energy/

[21] Ladyman and Ross, *op. cit.*

objects, forces, causal relations, and natural kinds emerge as successful tracking devices of real structure. For example, at the macroscopic scale, and in sciences such as biology that pertain to it, objects and something a bit closer to our folk notion of causality work as very successful tracking devices. We can use them productively to capture all sorts of relations of information, for instance, about ecosystems, organisms, and species change. But this does not mean that objects and causality are as fundamental as, or reducible to, structure itself. At the quantum scale, for instance, they clearly break down. We can no longer track sub-atomic particles in terms of individual objects or quantum relations in terms of classical causal relations. While we can understand the real at every scale in terms of mathematics and relations of information, more specific devices for articulating structure pertain only to certain scales.[22]

In effect, Ladyman and Ross argue that an important lesson of fundamental physics is the relativity of scale. We can fit all of the sciences together not by building them up from each other, level by level, in the sort of reductive scheme that I sketched above, but by taking each of them to describe structure at real yet irreducible levels of abstraction or scale. So, biology, chemistry, and economics all capture the structure of the real, but they have different means, appropriate only to their level of abstraction or scale, of grasping information. Ladyman and Ross call this view, which affirms the cohesiveness yet separateness of all the sciences, "rainforest realism."[23] We may think of it as a form of non-reductive realism about science. Because of the emphasis on scale and on reality grasped by different, irreducible perspectives, we might also think that there is, in Ladyman and Ross's own parlay, a certain "consilience" between their views and the rich realism that I described above. After all, if we acknowledge that different branches of science articulate the real in effective but irreducible ways, because they, in effect, grasp different pieces of the real, then why should we not go all the way and acknowledge this space of effectiveness not just for different branches of science, but for different epistemic practices as well?

Here, Ladyman and Ross are clear that they are not willing to make the jump, which leads to a very sharp difference between rainforest realism and rich realism. They consider themselves defenders of "a radically naturalistic metaphysics";[24] only science (and, specifically, only science that is compatible with fundamental physics) informs us about the real.[25] In this sense, Ladyman and Ross are extreme

---

[22] *Ibid.*

[23] *Ibid.*

[24] *Ibid.*, p. 1.

[25] They define these limits by what they call the *Principle of Naturalistic Closure* (PNC): "(1) Any new metaphysical claim that is to be taken seriously at time *t* should be motivated by, and only by, the service it would perform, if true, in showing how two or more specific scientific hypotheses, at least one of which is drawn from fundamental physics, jointly explain more than the sum of what is explained by the two hypotheses taken separately, where this is interpreted by reference to the following terminological stipulations: (2) Stipulation: A 'scientific hypothesis' is understood as an hypothesis that is taken seriously by institutionally bona fide science at *t*. (3) Stipulation: A 'spe-

scientific realists. In fact, one way that they explain their structural realism is that it is a more sophisticated form of scientific realism, capable of overcoming the common anti-realist critiques. If we want to know what it is that is uncovered by science but remains constant across the paradigm shifts of scientific revolutions, the answer is: structure. For example, they believe that we can trace the same core relations of information from Classical to Relativistic physics in the language of mathematics without mystery. In Maxwell's original equations, it is not the ether that is real, but the structure grasped by the equations themselves.[26]

For our purposes, however, what is most important about this part of Ladyman and Ross's argument is that, like the simpler version of scientific realism that we considered above, it takes the success of science to imply the comprehensiveness of science. We can safely assume that science alone reveals the structure of the real because we see how effective science is at articulating, manipulating, and describing this structure. In other words, what justifies Ladyman and Ross's radically naturalistic metaphysics is an appeal to the overwhelming success of science. The difference between the rich realism that I sketched above and their more restricted rainforest realism hinges on this judgment of success. We are to accept that only a variety of sciences, and not a variety of epistemic practices more generally, grasps the real effectively from different yet irreducible perspectives because we can see that science as a whole already does such a good job of telling us everything there is to know.

Or does it? At this point, I believe that we can no longer keep the considerations from Chap. 4 on hold. If success itself is a relative measure, then how can appealing to it help the scientific realist eliminate the possibility of rich realism? He will either have to explain how the causal picture of fundamental "micro-bangings" is, in fact, in touch with contemporary science and so leaves no room for other epistemic practices; or, he will have to explain how an alternate view like structural realism, which takes itself to be deeply motivated by current science, can eliminate alternative epistemic practices by any way other than a culturally relative constraint. If we can recognize the grounds of their legitimacy and success through a dynamic of resonance and loss, then we can also recognize the possibility that the real may be articulated through different epistemic practices using different levels and scales in ways that are irreducible to and incommensurable with the terms of any science.

---

cific scientific hypothesis' is one that has been directly investigated and confirmed by institutionally *bona fide* scientific activity prior to *t* or is one that might be investigated at or after, *t*, in the absence of constraints resulting from engineering, physiological, or economic restrictions or their combination, as the primary object of attempted verification, falsification, or quantitative refinement, where this activity is part of an objective research project fundable by a *bona fide* scientific research funding body. (4) Stipulation: An 'objective research project' has the primary purpose of establishing objective facts about nature that would, if accepted on the basis of the project, be expected to continue to be accepted by inquirers aiming to maximize their stock of true beliefs, notwithstanding shifts in the inquirers' practical, commercial, or ideological preferences," *ibid.*, pp. 37–38.

[26] *Ibid.*

5.6.2   *The More Limited Claim to Comprehensiveness*

The scientific realist, however, still has another available line of response to the possibility of rich realism. He may object that the matter is really much simpler than I have portrayed it. The claim about the success of science was never a claim about the real in itself, he might say. It is and always has been a claim about the success of science in manipulating, articulating, and describing the *world*, and as far as the objects of science are concerned, we all live in the same world. There is no need here to slip in the distinction of "different ways of life" and to suggest that they, in effect, carve out of the real something like "different worlds." There is no significant difference across cultures between our faculties of perception. We all perceive light and sound in about the same range and with the same acuity. Likewise, we sense in space and in time in just about the same ways, and at the same intervals. Being humans, we are all presented, ipso facto, with more or less the same world of experience; and, more importantly, it is at this world, with such a level of generality, that science is directed. To introduce finer levels of variation is to take the discussion beyond the level with which science is concerned. Here, any inherent incompleteness in our knowledge is irrelevant, because we all experience the same piece of the real and, ultimately, we all have the same analytic and perceptual capacities for manipulating, articulating, and describing it.

To make such an anti-relativist argument is, again, to make certain tacit assumptions about the nature of our experience, its relation to the real, and the possibility of substantively different ways of human life. The argument allows that the real, that which stands in relation to our experience, may be, as rich realism proposes, indefinitely complex. However, it assumes that the portion of the real that we engage concretely, that which we experience as the world, has certain special properties. Importantly, it assumes that such a world of experience is self-standing. In other words, our experience screens out the remainder of the real so well that the complexity of the latter, and perhaps even its existence, need not be taken into account. Our science is best at articulating, manipulating, and describing our world of experience, which, at such a level of generality, we share with all ways of human life – end of story. Any insurmountable incompleteness in our knowledge, any further complexity in the real to which our science fails to respond, simply does not matter.

The problem with this assumption, however, is that it seems to get the part-whole relation inside out. Only a whole can be self-standing, foundational, absolutely given, unconditioned. Parts, on the other hand, must always be understood in relation to other parts, or in relation to the whole itself. They are necessarily conditioned, incapable of serving as absolute foundations. To assume that our finite experience can be self-standing, that it somehow screens out the complexity of the real such that it can be fully or best explained without reference to that remainder, is to attribute, mistakenly, I believe, the properties of a whole to its parts. Our finite experience, like the knowledge that we build in it, is of parts. We understand in space and in time, at a certain scale, with a certain degree of acuity, relative to certain analytic tools and certain perceptive abilities. In one sense, we can overcome these limitations. We (in our way of life)[27] use mathematics, science, and engineering to understand in space and in time at different scales, with greater degrees of acuity and generality, relative to more powerful analytic tools and keener, broader perceptive abilities. In a deeper sense, however, we can never transcend these limitations. Our knowledge must always depend on some kind of ordering system, with respect to some scale, with some degree of acuity, elaborated using some kind of analytic tools and some form of perceptive abilities. Yet beyond that ordering system will always lie the possibility of one with greater generality, at further scales, with greater acuity, using more powerful analytic tools and keener, broader perceptive abilities. At no point does our knowledge pass from being finite to being infinite, from being knowledge of parts, related and dependent upon each other, to being knowledge of a whole, given completely and independently of anything else.

It may help to think of these limitations in terms of our causal understanding in time.[28] For example, physicists trace the origins of our universe back to the Big Bang. Specifically, they believe that they may be able to trace the events that led to our universe as we know it as far back as 10^{-44} seconds after the Big Bang.[29] But what happened 10^{-45} seconds after the Big Bang? What happened 10^{-46} and 10^{-47} seconds after? What happened 10^{-3000} seconds after the Big Bang? And what happened before the Big Bang? We can always ask a further unanswered question. No piece of knowledge that we acquire is unconditioned, perfectly complete. There appears to be no natural end to our explanations. We finally stop not on absolute or self-supported ground, but simply where we peter out, where, as Wittgenstein says, our spade turns.[30]

The horizon of our knowledge, it seems, must always be drawn by unanswered questions. There is no ultimate stopping place, no ultimate explanation to ground our knowledge. In this sense, our claims to knowledge cannot help but make at least tacit reference to the remainder of the real. They do not hold themselves up alone; at their edges they must always dig into the depths of the yet un-grasped, unfathomed, and unknown.

---

[27] I leave open here the possibility that other ways of life may have different tools for expanding knowledge.

[28] By using this example, I do not mean to imply that there is something privileged or ultimate about our causal understanding in time. I agree with Ladyman and Ross that this seems only to be an effective mode of understanding relative to certain features of the real at a certain scale. My point is that we can expect any mode of understanding, any successful "tracking device," in Ladyman and Ross's terms, to run into an analogous difficulty. We can never in finite experience, or in the understanding that we build in it, come across unconditioned knowledge. This point, and the spirit of my argument here in general, I take from Kant's *Critique of Pure Reason,* translated by Norman Kemp Smith (New York: St. Martin's Press, 1965).

[29] Hildegard Meyer-Ortmanns, "Introduction," in *Principles of Evolution from the Planck Epoch to Multicellular Life*, edited by Hildegard Meyer-Ortmanns and Stefan Thurner (Berlin, Heidelberg and New York: Springer, 2011).

[30] Ludwig Wittgenstein, *Philosophical Investigations,* translated by G. E. M. Anscombe (Oxford: Blackwell Publishing, 1953), § 217.

This dependence on the remainder of the real leads us to question another assumption about the comprehensiveness of science. If our knowledge claims must at least tacitly refer to a remainder beyond their grasp, and if the real itself is indefinitely complex, then we should not be so quick to assume that the world of our experience is susceptible to a best ordering. The scientific realist seems to believe that while other epistemic practices may grasp something of the structure of the real, science grasps this structure most thoroughly; it gives us the best way to identify everything there is in the world and how it works. The possibility he ignores is that not all epistemic practices may be grounded in the very same aspects of the remainder of the real. It may be that they exploit somewhat different areas of complexity. In every epistemic practice, at some point, our spade must turn; but we may not all be digging in quite the same direction. After all, if we are reaching toward a richly complex remainder, there may be any number of ways of grasping at it. In this case, the Chachi shaman and the Western scientist could both have knowledge of the real, but it would be rooted differently. The aspects of the real lying just beyond the scientist's knowledge of the Big Bang would not be the same as those lying just beyond the shaman's knowledge of spirits. While both epistemic practices would have the same ultimate foundation – the real as a whole – they would not belong to the same chain of understanding, ordering, and reasoning about the real. In this sense, we could say that they have different *effective* foundations, different places in different topographies where their spades turn. Across such different effective foundations we could expect to find no immediate grounds for arbitrating any conflicting claims that could be considered neutral, highest, or absolute.

Of course, to grant that different aspects of the real may support our knowledge claims is not to deny that the latter are constrained by the real.[31] Certainly, within the context of a given epistemic practice, we can determine that some claims hold while others fail. Moreover, to acknowledge that the claims of different practices may be grounded differently is not to deny that there could be a kind of overlap between practices concerning what are reliable claims. But admitting this possibility does not at all imply the existence or even the possibility of common standards for resolving conflicting claims. Some kind of overlap is what we need for there to be disagreement in the first place, for us to realize that we are to some extent talking about the same thing. But overlap against a background of rich realism does not provide different practices with a common foundation. It does not promise reconciliation at any simple or convenient level. Nor does it imply that the knowledge of different practices will fit neatly together like pieces of a giant puzzle. Rather, overlap in the context of rich realism suggests a picture of human experience and understanding that may be irreducibly plural.

This picture throws into question another assumption, one of the most blatant, in the argument for the comprehensiveness of science. We are to believe that, for all intents and purposes, every human epistemic practice carves the same world of

---

[31] For more on this point, please see my discussion of *responsiveness* in Chap. 2.

experience. This, I believe, is simply to ignore the evidence of dangling pieces.[32] It is to assume that when we reduce other practices and their claims to the terms of science, nothing significant is lost. What survives the reduction we call, "proto-science," and the rest we attribute to some mixture of fantasy and luck. The problem with such a reduction, however, is that it places a very heavy burden on these latter categories. When the Chachi shaman cures a venomous snakebite using medicinal plants, we may be able to call it proto-science, but the elaborate rituals that he uses to communicate with spirits, must be for us all fantasy. Science rejects the major premise of the shaman's practice, that revelation is a reliable source of knowledge. It does not, moreover, recognize the objects and forces in terms of which the shaman's knowledge is constituted. For science, there are no immaterial beings, and they certainly cannot perform actions on the physical world. This means that we must attribute to sheer luck everything the shaman achieves through such means that we might be inclined to regard as a success. When he uses his rituals to discover the correct location of a missing object and it is found there, when he makes predictions about the future and they come true, when he treats his patients' illnesses and they get better, we have recourse only to deflationary explanations. We are to believe that the bulk of the shaman's practice proceeds by the force of contingency, coincidence, and confusion.

We may agree with Putnam that the success of science inclines us toward realism, but such a limited space for other epistemic practices forces us to believe in a different sort of miracle: that peoples for thousands of years, across nearly all times and places, have, like the Chachi, lived in gross deception. In fact, even anthropologists and other outsiders who have had the opportunity to live with some of them are prone to fall into the same folly. And yet, somehow, these peoples have not only managed to feed and clothe themselves, to build shelter and cure the sick without Western science, but they have sailed the seas, constructed giant pyramids, and followed the intricate movements of heavenly bodies. This suggests that the no-miracles argument for realism may be more general than Putnam thought. It inclines us to believe that not only science, but potentially all long-standing epistemic practices provide us with a close grasp of the real. If different epistemic practices articulate, manipulate, and describe pieces of the real that are only somewhat overlapping, not the same, and if they do so using a different balance of tools that are grounded at points in different areas of complexity of the real, then we should expect that different epistemic practices grasp the real with relative effectiveness. It would also be the case that we have no highest, best, or neutral grounds for arbitrating their conflicting claims.

_____

[32] See Chap. 1.

5.7   Fitting Realism and Relativism Together

I have argued that even on a realist interpretation of our science, there is room for competing epistemic practices and the evaluative egalitarianism of relativism. In Chap. 4, we saw that what prevents us from reducing alternative practices *merely* to the terms of Western science is *loss*. Competing practices make incommensurable trade-offs between, for instance, an impartial stance and a relational stance. They pull in different directions; their different modes of engaging the world and the different content that they capture do not fit neatly together with each other like pieces of a puzzle. At the metaphysical level, the correlate is the possibility that different practices may rely on different fundamental ontologies, which exploit overlapping, yet different aspects of the real, to different degrees and employing incommensurable terms. This helps us to understand how the underlying metaphysical picture that makes relativism and realism compatible is not simply a complex scientific realism. It also helps us to articulate the many and the one of relativism, to see how there can be one reality grasped in many overlapping, yet conflicting ways.

Chapter 6
Broad, Compelling, and Coherent Relativism

6.1 Entrenched Conflict

It is a commonplace for philosophy instructors to complain that nearly all of their first-year students are relativists. If they can accomplish nothing else in an introductory philosophy class, they say, at least they can disabuse their students of this naïve view. There is no reason to take the prevalence of naïve relativism, however, as an indication of the naïveté of all forms of the view. In general, the fact that a particular view is held naïvely signals a need for greater reflection, not the need ultimately to abandon the view itself. We might just as well see the prevalence of relativism as a sign of its relevance for our times. My goal throughout this work has been to develop and defend a robust relativism, one that answers to our relativistic impulses without succumbing to the logical and practical pitfalls of more naïvely formulated versions of the view. In this final chapter, I will review some of the major features of my view and begin to describe what it is like to embrace it.

If there had been a subtitle to my work, perhaps it could have been, "What Ruth Benedict Should Have Said."[1] In my discussions of deep engagement and of the dynamic of resonance and loss, I have tried to elaborate what I take to be the vision of many a social scientist in a way that is satisfying to the philosopher. The result is something akin to cultural relativism, a version of relativism that is rather broad, both in the content that it declares to be relative, and in the factors to which such content is supposed to be relative. These latter factors include the historical, social, linguistic, and geographical contingencies to which human life is subject. In the case of the Chachi, for instance, they involve having migrated to the southernmost portion of the Chocó bioregion, living in an expanse of tropical rainforest bordered by Andean highlands to the East and the Pacific Ocean to the West, having survived the Incan and then the Spanish Conquest, having been subject to Catholic and later Protestant evangelization, speaking a Chibchan language belonging to the South

---

[1] Or, at least what she should have said to appease the philosopher.

© Springer Nature Switzerland AG 2020
A. Luboff, *Facing Relativism*, Synthese Library 425,
https://doi.org/10.1007/978-3-030-43341-3_6

Barbacoan family, now mixed with Spanish, living as multigenerational family units in raised huts along the shore of navigable rivers, and so on. I have often referred to these factors, as a form of shorthand, by what is their net effect: (the construction of) a particular way of life.

It can be helpful to think, after Benedict, of each way of life as its own unique pattern that brings into play different features of human possibility.[2] Relativism at a broad scale strives to capture the idea that life can be constructed and organized in ways that are entirely other – ways that are effective, autonomous, and irreducible to our own. In a sense, this means that everything – the way groups articulate, order, manipulate, and value their world – is relative to a way of life. Relativism, however, is typically characterized not so much by the inner shape of a way of life, as by the outer effects of such articulations, orderings, manipulations, and valuations. In this case, the content that is relative to a way of life becomes the claims, both explicit and implicit, that a group makes about what is true, what is actual, what is causally effective, what is good, what is beautiful, what is proper, what is noble, and so on. When the Chachi do not offer assistance to a person who is troubled and crying, at stake are their (implicit and explicit) claims that this is a right action, that a good person must control his displays of emotion, that there is nothing another can do to assist in an affair so utterly private, and so on. Similarly, when a Chachi shaman calls upon his magic stones to identify the source of illness in his patient and to effect a cure, at issue are his (implicit and explicit) claims about the nature and cause of the illness, the veracity of his understanding, and the actuality of the concepts and mechanisms that he employs.

By focusing on implicit and explicit claims, we may sharpen the relative content of our view, but we do little to limit its scope. And it is this latter aspect that perhaps most unnerves the traditional analytic philosopher, who is by training anxious to pin down ideas and to avoid sweeping generalizations. A way of life encompasses and interweaves the narrower domains in which we often consider more specific forms of relativism, such as moral, linguistic, or epistemic relativism. I am happy at least to concede that it can be useful to think through relativism in terms of concrete cases, and that narrower labels may help, to a certain extent, to focus our dialogue. Nevertheless, our discussion of deep engagement, and of the *complexity of conflict,* in particular, has given us reason to be weary of the impulse to confine relativism to narrower domains. Frequently, our arguments in a given domain depend on claims in other domains. As we saw with the example of offering assistance to an adult who is crying,[3] what makes this a right or wrong action depends not only on claims about morality, but on claims about human development, emotions, and social space. We find this same interdependence of domains even in examples strictly within Western life, such as in the debate about abortion. The standard arguments about whether or not it is acceptable to abort a fetus depend not only on moral claims, but on claims about the nature of life, cognition, and feeling. Or, to turn again to a cross-cultural

---

[2] Ruth Benedict, *Patterns of Culture* (Boston: Houghton Mifflin, 1934).
[3] See Chap. 1.

example, as the anthropologist Richard Shweder has observed, whether or not we approve of a practice such as sati, the live cremation of a widow on her husband's funeral pyre, depends not only on moral claims, but on claims about the reality of reincarnation and the nature of the soul.[4] Even whether or not we find hideous a son's eating fish and cutting his hair after the death of his father depends on extra-moral claims about spiritual purity and pollution.[5] In fact, these last two examples stress yet another complexity of conflict, which is that different ways of life do not always agree about the nature, boundaries, interactions, or even the existence of certain domains. When we consider relativism only in narrowly circumscribed domains, then, we assume the primacy of our own concepts and distinctions. We end up overlooking large areas of difference and begging a very important part of the question against relativism. In this respect, I am quite unabashed in my defense of a relativism that is very broad and might answer to the name of "cultural relativism."

While such a view encompasses many interwoven levels, it does become particularly pressing in two domains. The first is the practical domain of prescription, action, and judgment, often referred to as "moral relativism." The second is the theoretical domain of description, prediction, and explanation, associated with cognitive and epistemic relativism. When two or more divergent ways of life encounter each other, the political questions of whose interests will prevail, whose will be subjugated, whose will, as a result, be transformed, play out in these moral and theoretical dimensions. They become questions of who knows the right way to act and must show (by conversion, by forced indoctrination, by absolute coercion…) the other. Who best understands the way the world works and must enlighten the other. Who best organizes life and must meld his structures onto the society of the other…Because of their strategic importance, I have let our exploration of relativism gravitate toward these two dimensions. From our discussion above it should be clear, however, that considering the epistemic and moral dimensions of broad (cultural) relativism is a distinct pursuit from considering epistemic and moral relativism in turn.

Perhaps a different subtitle to this work could have been, "What Isaiah Berlin Did Say."[6] The view that we have developed here stresses that there are multiple ways of solving the human puzzle, and that these do not fit neatly together. They are built in different social and environmental contexts, using different foundational concepts and standards of assessment. The space of reasons and the space of actions are laid out differently in different ways of life. The claims made in different ways

---

[4] Richard A. Shweder, *Thinking Through Cultures: Expeditions in Cultural Psychology* (Cambridge: Cambridge University Press, 1991), 15–17.

[5] Richard A. Shweder, "Relativism and Universalism," in *A Companion to Moral Anthropology*, ed. Didier Fassin (Chichester, West Sussex, U.K. and Malden, MA: Wiley-Blackwell, 2012), 85–102.

[6] John Gray, *Isaiah Berlin* (Princeton, NJ: Princeton University Press, 1996). Berlin considered himself a pluralist, not a relativist. Berlin, perhaps, would have liked that my version of relativism supports a certain degree of realism (see Chap. 5) and grants what I think was a very important insight to him: that conflict is real and, to a certain extent, inescapable.

of life about what that world is like and how it should be often overlap enough to engage each other, often even enough to conflict with each other, but not always enough to resolve such conflicts. Different ways make different choices in favor of different goods – different values, different species of truth, different relations to the surrounding world. These goods are in conflict with each other; they cannot all be held to the same degree in a single way of life. Even our methods of capturing and assessing these goods are often in tension with each other.[7]

In our investigations, we have found some truth to the relativist slogan that, "people of different cultures live in different worlds," though it is, admittedly, rather hackneyed and a bit misleading. Distinct peoples often are aware of each other, can interact with each other, and can experience the same physical event together. Even when separated by space or time, they leave traces – in writing, artifacts, structures, legends, etc. – that can be picked up and, at least to some extent, deciphered by others. We are rarely as insulated from each other as the metaphor suggests. In the final analysis, it seems that there must be just one world, which would be the container for any alleged different worlds. Yet, however hyperbolic the imagery of inhabiting different worlds may be, we have at least seen in our discussions of deep engagement and of the dynamic of resonance and loss[8] that the world can take on significantly different shapes for different groups. In our exploration of the *complexity of conflict,* we learned that different groups may divide lived and conceptual spaces in very different ways. Not only may they separate domains, such as the personal and the communal, in very different places, but the way in which they draw these distinctions may also vary greatly, such as by ritual, by physical markers, by inner act, and so on. We saw this complexity again between an impartial stance, which conceives of the world as a collection of inanimate objects distanced from the subject, and a relational stance, which conceives of the world as animate objects forming a collective whole, of which the subject herself forms a vital part. In our exploration of *dangling pieces,* we saw that different ways of inhabiting the world do not reduce neatly to each other. Different groups may elaborate different facets of experience to greater or lesser degrees. There is an unaccounted remainder when we move from one way of judging, organizing, and interacting with the world to another. We found these pieces again in the modes of attuned understanding, like revelation and intuition, which an impartial stance dismisses as mere silliness. In our exploration of the *first person,* we learned that it is possible and unparadoxical to gain an understanding of a very different way of life. Lived experiences, relationships with others, and a return to a childlike state help us to grow into an understanding of very different practices and beliefs. We learned again in our discussion of *resonance* that we can build an understanding of a contrasting stance by starting with smaller pieces in our own way of knowing the world that resonate with it. In our exploration of *attributive symmetry,* we saw that other ways of accounting for and negotiating the world can

---

[7] For more detail, see Chap. 4 of the present work.

[8] Chapters 2 and 4, respectively. All of the examples in this paragraph refer back to the arguments of these chapters.

have their share of coherence and functionality, just like our own. And still, as we learned in our exploration of *reflective symmetry,* all ways have their share of incoherence and disfunction, including our own. We revisited this back and forth movement, reinforcing both the validity and the difference of other ways of life, in our analysis of the *dynamic of resonance and loss.* In particular, the two moments of loss, *estrangement* and *pull,* turned the reflective gaze back on our own way of life, emphasizing the trade-offs and costs involved in our own systems of understanding. Together what these investigations suggest is that different groups carve the world in different ways. We saw in our discussion of realism how these different accounts could capture what is ultimately the same world in ways that are nevertheless incommensurable.[9] While it is a bit inaccurate to say that, "people of different cultures live in different worlds," a more appropriate formulation of the relativist slogan might be, "people of different cultures live in distinct, sometimes incompatible renderings of the world."

In the end, our explorations have led us to a broad relativism that incorporates the insights of cultural relativism and is defined by *entrenched conflict:*

> Our normative claims, as much in the theoretical as in the practical (and other) domains, about what is real, what is true, what is good, what is right, and so on, are inextricably tied to a particular way of life such that when they conflict with each other across different ways of life, we have no absolute, neutral, or highest ground on which to arbitrate their conflict.

In the following section, we will specify the terms of this definition and some of the ways in which it differs from the more common strawman versions of relativism.

6.2 Distinctiveness of Entrenched Conflict

6.2.1 Not Defined by Polar Opposition of Claims

Many common characterizations of relativism define the view in terms of diametrically opposed pairs of claims.[10] In the moral domain, this might amount to something like, "For the Chachi, it is right not to offer assistance to an adult who is crying. To US Americans, it is right to offer assistance to an adult who is crying. In this way, the concept of 'right' is relative to a given way of life." A similar line in the epistemic domain might run, "For the Chachi, demons are real and can bite

---

[9] Chapter 5.

[10] Bernard Williams formulates and criticizes such a version of moral relativism in "An Inconsistent Form of Relativism," in *Relativism: Cognitive and Moral,* eds. Michael Krausz and Jack W. Meiland (Notre Dame: University of Notre Dame Press, 1982), 171–174. Reprinted from *Morality: An Introduction to Ethics* (New York: Harper & Row, 1972), 22–26. Harvey Siegel formulates and criticizes a similarly paradoxical version of epistemic relativism in "Relativism, Truth and Incoherence," *Synthese* 68 (1986): 225–259. Reprinted as "The Incoherence Argument and the Notion of Relative Truth" in *Relativism Refuted* (Boston: D. Reidel Publishing Company, 1987), 3–31.

people during the night while they sleep. For US Americans, demons are not real and cannot bite people during the night while they sleep. In this way, the concept of a real entity is relative to a given way of life." Of course, in each case it would take more examples and more detail to convince us that the conclusion might be justified. The greater problem with these sorts of characterizations of relativism, however, is that they veer too far toward the paradoxical. While the relativist, in a weak moment, might relish their sensationalism, they are simply misleading. The juxtaposition of P and not-P leads the anti-relativist to wonder how a view that apparently entails both P and not-P could ever be coherent.[11] Meanwhile, the simple description of the conflict leads the universalist, after discovering a little more background to the opposition between P and not-P, to conclude that there is no significant difference between the claims of different ways of life in the first place; we would all agree if we just had the right facts and reasoned correctly.[12]

While the relativist has responses to such opponents, and providing them has formed a large part of the work of this book, I believe that relativism is both more palatable and more accurate when characterized differently. In fact, the *complexity of conflict* teaches us that it is rarely the case that two different ways of life conflict with diametrical opposition. What first appears to be a conflict between P, grounded in one way of life, and not-P, grounded in another way of life, turns out, on closer examination, to be a conflict between P and not-P′, claims which are grounded in different ways of life and are in tension with each other, but are not diametrically opposed. In the case of offering assistance to an adult who is crying, we saw that the Chachi and US Americans do not have the same ideas of what identifies a mature adult, of the sort of act that crying constitutes, or of the social space in which such an event transpires. They do not even agree about what acts could count as assistance.[13] In at least these ways, "It is right to offer assistance to an adult who is crying," is not the same claim for the two groups, and we may more accurately refer to the type of opposition here as between P and not-P′. Yet, in many such cases, P and P′ do pick out overlapping events, so that both groups point roughly at the same agents and actions, one with approval and the other with disapproval. This is what we mean by entrenched conflict between claims that are in tension with each other without being diametrically opposed.[14]

The case of the biting demon is in some ways analogous to that of the crying adult. Not only do we find differences between their base claims, as in the case of P and P′, but their corresponding concepts are of very different thicknesses. The Chachi know that the demons are real. If they doubted whether they had identified one, they could ask others for corroborating details – or call in a shaman, or perhaps various shamans. They have ways of interacting with the demons that help them feel

---

[11] We addressed this criticism in Chap. 2.

[12] We addressed this line of reasoning in Chaps. 1, 3, and 4.

[13] Chapter 1.

[14] The astute reader might recall here that, in Chap. 4, we described this conflict as between P and א, emphasizing the difference between each way of life's respective claims. In order to see the equivalence between these two definitions, let "א" be defined as, "not-P′."

better and make the bites go away. Most US Americans, on the other hand, do not have any sort of robust concept that corresponds to the demons. We typically can only account for the intersubjectivity and effectiveness of the Chachi's dealings with the demons in a way that is reductive and pejorative, attributing the success of the dealings to some combination of proto-science, confusion, and illusion.

What also skews P and P′ is that the two claims must be formulated in two languages of very distinct linguistic families, whose lexical and grammatical resources and constraints do not neatly match up. The Chachi language, for instance, has only one adjective, "ura," and its negation, "urajtu," to describe what is good/bad, right/wrong, real/fake, or true/false. "Ura" is also a word used to thank people.[15] It recognizes what is well-ordered, appropriate and, by virtue of this fact, pleasing. In this order, goodness, rightness, reality, and truth are not distinct. Belonging to it, being "ura," describes an immanent quality, not something that can be reified or that can stand apart from the object and its relations to other objects or to the speakers themselves. So, without context, there is no difference between a bad demon and a fake one; both are, "urajtu diabulu." A translator could go on to explain to a Chachi that demons are not real for his US American interlocutor. He could say something like, "Uyalalaa diabulunu keenguetyu deeve." Yet the verb, "keenguenu,"[16] which is negated here to explain that, "the demon is not real for the stranger," captures not only what is real for a person, but what a person believes and knows. So, this explanation would not distinguish between what are in English at least three different claims: that demons aren't real for the stranger, that the stranger doesn't know about demons, and that the stranger doesn't believe in demons.

Similarly, if we wanted to explain that there is no truth to the claim that there are demons (let alone that they bite people at night while they sleep and that there are methods that cure this affliction), the closest translation that we could get to "truth" in the Chachi language would be, "ura palaa." "Palaa" is a cognate borrowed from the Spanish "palabra," or "word." So, we could translate "truth" as something like, "well-ordered word." But "palaa" is a relatively new term for the Chachi. They call their language "Cha'palaa," which means something like, "people-word." Interestingly, the indigenous group that is most closely related to the Chachi,[17] from whom they appear to have separated around the time of the Spanish and Incan invasions, call their language, "Tsafiki." "Tsa" is the same root as "cha," meaning, "people," and "fiki" refers to "mouth" (fi) and "action" (ki). Their language, then, means something like, "people-sound-making." In the way that the Chachi use it, "palaa,"

---

[15] It has even been adapted to greet people; for instance, "ura kepenene," means, "good morning." The Chachi, however, did not have a custom of greeting each other with salutations before their interactions with the Spanish. A Chachi who went to live in the city liked to explain this using the following scenario: *A Chachi man is sitting near the riverbank working. His neighbor rows by along the opposite shore. Each sees the other out of the corner of his eye. They have greeted.* We might say that the Chachi mode of quiet understanding (see Chap. 1 for more discussion) precludes the need for greetings.

[16] Or its variant, "keerenguenu."

[17] The Tsáchila, or Colorados, who live near Santo Domingo, Ecuador.

though borrowed from Spanish, retains this reference more to the act of speaking than just to a word in itself. So, even "ura palaa," this rough correlate of truth that we could cobble together in the Chachi language, is not a species of truth that separates from the speaker, or from the very act of its being said.

There is much more that could be argued here both about language and about conceptual differences.[18] However, at the moment I am after a much simpler point, which should be clear enough. What we can see from these linguistic differences is that the Chachi and the stranger's claims are in conflict with each other without being negations of exactly the same claim. Their conflict is created by lines that are jagged and barbed, not neatly cut. And it is this complexity that distinguishes our version of relativism defined by entrenched conflict from versions of the view defined paradoxically as the conjunction of a claim and its exact negation (albeit in different cultural contexts).[19]

6.2.2   Not Dependent on a Reified Concept of Culture

A common criticism of strawman relativisms is that they rely on a reified concept of culture, as if in our interactions we arrived at a line drawn on the ground with a sign that says, "A new culture starts here."[20] Though our version of relativism distinguishes different contexts by reference to different cultures or ways of life, it does not imply that cultures themselves are reified, unchanging entities. In fact, as we have seen in our discussion of *reflective symmetry*[21] and will explore in greater detail

---

[18] While I have not addressed the former, for reasons discussed in Sect. 6.2.3 below, I have dealt with the latter especially in Chaps. 1 and 4.

[19] For more on relativism and overcoming paradox, see Chap. 2.

[20] Martha Nussbaum has criticized relativism along these lines. See, for example, Martha C. Nussbaum, *Women and Human Development: The Capabilities Approach* (Cambridge and New York: Cambridge University Press, 2000), 48–49, and Martha C. Nussbaum and Amartya Sen, "Internal Criticism and Indian Rationalist Traditions," in *Relativism: Interpretation and Confrontation,* ed. Michael Krausz (Notre Dame, IN: University of Notre Dame Press, 1989), 299–325. Interestingly, it also seems to be a common postcolonial criticism of relativism. See, for example, S. Charusheela, "Social Analysis and the Capabilities Approach: A Limit to Martha Nussbaum's Universalist Ethics," *Cambridge Journal of Economics* (2009) 33:1135–1152, S. Charusheela, "Women's Choices and the Ethnocentrism/Relativism Dilemma," in *Postmodernism, Economics and Knowledge,* eds. S. Cullenberg, J. Amariglio and D. Ruccio (New York: Routledge, 2001), and S. Charusheela, "Postcolonial Thought, Postmodernism, and Economics: Questions of Ontology and Ethics," *Postcolonialism Meets Economics,* eds. E. Zein-Elabdin and S. Charusheela (London: Routledge, 2004). Critics who often lump postcolonialism and relativism together might be surprised by the former's rejection of the latter. My sense is that the most significant difference between the relativism that I have developed here and quite a bit of postcolonial work is not a reliance on cultural essentialism (which I disavow), but my insistence that a coherent relativism must be defended in a way that is self-consciously relativistic (a move which, not incidentally, might go quite a ways in silencing such critics).

[21] See Chap. 1.

below,[22] a robust relativism, by encouraging us to encounter other ways of life and to gaze into their practices and beliefs, often leads us to reflect back on our own claims and the conditions of our own way of life. It thus does not preclude, but often foments cultural fluidity and change.

It does, nonetheless, rely on our ability to distinguish different groups. I take it that these groups should have some kind of natural coherence; their members should at some level identify with each other. Yet, we can divide them in different ways and for different purposes. Such divisions are idealizations, neither perfect nor absolute. Certain divisions, though, will make relativism a more interesting thesis than others. Relativism becomes most pressing when the groups that we are considering contain more than one or a handful of members each, when their respective ways of life diverge significantly, and when they are, as Bernard Williams would say, in real conflict[23] with each other. Otherwise, the problem is not that relativism is untenable, but trivial.

6.2.3   Not Defined by Complete Untranslatability or Incomprehensibility

Relativism is sometimes characterized by a failure of translation across different languages.[24] I have refrained from associating different ways of life with different languages because very distinct groups may speak the same or related languages.[25] Nevertheless, where we find no lack of vocabulary to capture meaning across different groups, we may still identify a lack of equivalent expressions, ideas, or organizing concepts. So, at a general conceptual level, the failure of translation is important not only for linguistic relativism, narrowly conceived, but also for the broad relativism that we have developed here. Yet, it is important to understand that the failure that we have described is *partial*. The conceptual differences that we have found across different ways of life are neither crystalline nor perfectly opaque. In the latter

---

[22] See Sect. 6.3.2.

[23] Bernard Williams, *Ethics and the Limits of Philosophy* (Cambridge, MA: Harvard University Press, 1985). Note that Williams uses this distinction to urge the opposite point: that in cases of real conflict, our commitment to our own practices and beliefs is simply too strong for us to be relativists. He believes that we can only endorse relativism at a distance, in cases where the conflict between ourselves and radically different others is mediated by a large gap of space and/or time. Williams here seems to conflate relativism with what is sometimes, but not necessarily, its consequence: tolerance. I discuss this conflation further in Sects. 6.2.5, 6.3, and 6.3.1 below.

[24] This is the version of relativism famously criticized by Donald Davidson in "On the Very Idea of a Conceptual Scheme" in *Relativism: Cognitive and Moral,* eds. Michael Krausz and Jack W. Meiland (Notre Dame, IN: University of Notre Dame Press, 1982), 66–80. Reprinted from *Proceedings of the American Philosophical Association* 47 (1973–74): 5–20.

[25] Think of the Amish in rural Ohio and of the urbanites in NYC, or of the Afro-Ecuadorians in the Chocó rainforest and the Spanish of middle-class Madrid.

case, relativism would be inconceivable.[26] There would be nothing for anthropologists to report about other ways of life if they could not in some way and to some extent grasp the concepts at play in another way of life. *Attributive symmetry*, let alone the other features of deep engagement that we have discussed and the phenomenon of resonance, would be impossible.[27] On the other hand, the relativist cannot claim that the anthropologist, or another similarly situated cultural interloper, steps completely outside of herself to capture a radically different conceptual scheme. This would imply that the anthropologist transcends relative constraints and occupies a neutral perspective. In both cases, relativism unravels.

In Chap. 2, we saw how a partial failure of translation allows the relativist to represent difference without violating relativistic constraints or succumbing to incoherence.[28] She relies on analogical thought, the exercise of imagination, extrapolation, and inference to represent another conceptual scheme within her own. Her grasp of difference always remains tethered back to her own place of situatedness, to her own concepts and experience. In our discussions of deep engagement and of the dynamic of resonance and loss, we developed, moreover, two rather detailed pictures of how this process can work. In the case of deep engagement,[29] the relativist begins to make sense of another way of life through the back and forth of attributive and reflective symmetry. The deepest failures of equivalence strike her as dangling pieces. She reaches them by building new bridge concepts in the first person, through direct experience, relationships with others, and a return to a childlike state. From her own experience and conceptual material, she builds a model of another way of life. Yet its irreducibility to her own remains marked by the complexity of conflict. Perhaps she, and even her subjects, changes or grows in the process. Perhaps they all find more common ground than existed before this coming to know each other, but they never reach fully outside their own perspectives or hit what would be for all ways of life neutral ground.

The dynamic of resonance and loss describes this same analogical process at the level more of the "armchair" anthropologist than of the participant observer immersed in another way of life.[30] Yet, it defines a similar space in which we recognize a different perspective without abandoning our own. Resonance identifies small seeds of similarity between our knowing stance toward the world and that of another way of life. These serve as analogical building blocks for modeling a stance that emphasizes and develops different features than our own. The emptiness of the first moment of loss invests these features with meaning and importance for us. The complex tensions of the second moment of loss, meanwhile, cement the difference and irreconcilability of our stance and another.

---

[26] See Davidson, "On the Very Idea."

[27] See Chaps. 1 and 4.

[28] Specifically, the relativist's response to the charges of conceptual incoherence, Chap. 2, Sect. 2.5.

[29] For more detail, see Chap. 1.

[30] For more detail, see Chap. 4.

While we cannot revisit the full arguments from the previous chapters here, the difference between our version of relativism defined by entrenched conflict and the more strawman formulations of the view should be clear. The latter invariably evoke an air of paradox, as they tend to be defined in terms of complete untranslatability and incomprehensibility.[31] The former, on the other hand, not only evokes, but *relies on* a deep sense of ambivalence, which it uses to articulate a partial failure of translation and understanding.

6.2.4 Not an "Anything Goes" View

Relativism is often understood as synonymous with arbitrariness: If truth is relative, then anything can be true; and everything is as true as it is false. The same follows for rightness, goodness, and the rest of our normative concepts.[32] I believe that such a grasp of relativism can be as frightening for those who are inclined to hold it as it is frustrating for those who try to engage them.[33] The version of relativism that we have developed here, however, does not collapse into nihilism. We have seen that to grant a role to contingency in our practices and beliefs – even to incorrigible, inextricable contingency – is not to declare them *merely* contingent.[34] Whether the world alone, or some shared human aspect of it, can arbitrate conflicting normative claims on non-relative grounds is a very different matter than whether the world alone, or some shared human aspect of it, makes an essential contribution to our normative claims. And it is only the latter that is upheld by our version of relativism. Deep engagement both encourages and is consistent with the realist observation that the world constrains our thought and gives it content. In this sense, it allows for a kind of relative transcendence: the inference, itself tied to a particular perspective (a perspective that happens already to acknowledge a plurality of perspectives), that our claims are responsive to and expressive of a transcendent reality. Yet this relation does not raise our claims themselves above the contingent contexts in which they are formulated, hold meaning, and inhere. They point to a transcendent reality without becoming transcendent themselves. This degree of realism is what distinguishes the atheistic claim that all of us are bound up in shades of illusion from the polytheistic claim[35] of entrenched conflict: that all ways of life capture pieces of the world in incommensurable ways.

---

[31] I am not sure that any relativist actually defends this view, but Davidson defines and ridicules it in his famous article, cited above.

[32] For the full development of this line of objections and the relativist's response to them, see Chap. 2.

[33] Such as the instructors of first-year philosophy students, mentioned above.

[34] See Chaps. 2 and 5.

[35] For more on the atheistic/polytheistic contrast of anthropological engagement, see Richard A. Shweder, "Post-Nietzschian Anthropology: The Idea of Multiple Objective Worlds," in *Relativism: Interpretation and Confrontation,* ed. Michael Krausz (Notre Dame, IN: University of

Our version of relativism contains a further limit to arbitrariness in that it only concerns what appear to be robust claims upheld in the context of a given way of life. It does not address random claims or ad hoc practices and systems of belief. Of course, we may disagree about what it means for a certain context to count as a "way of life" and for a claim in such a context to be "robust." This complicates relativistic evaluation, but it does not in any way compromise the view, which, after all, acknowledges and expects disagreement.

6.2.5   *Not Defined by Tolerance*

Relativism is a view so closely associated with tolerance that in some of its more strawman versions it is actually formulated in terms of tolerance.[36] The relationship between the robust relativism that we have developed here and tolerance is much more complex. It generally *inclines* us toward tolerance because it reserves a space for the legitimacy of other practices and beliefs. It creates this space by suggesting that even normative claims that are in conflict with our own may be judged reasonable and well-supported in their native context. However, it certainly does not entail or require us to be tolerant. In cases of extreme conflict, this space for tolerance will easily be exhausted. What will weigh most strongly with us is not the potential relative coherence of the claims with which our own are in conflict, but the judgment that, given our most careful understanding of what the world is like and how we should act in it, such claims cannot possibly be right. And on these relative grounds, we can oppose the claims of another way of life and their associated practices and beliefs. We will discuss the possibility of such criticism in more detail in Sect. 6.3 below.

6.2.6   *Not an Absolute Claim*

Our version of relativism is very careful to explain that the view itself is held on relative grounds. In this way, it avoids the many paradoxes that come from asserting relativism absolutely.[37] Moreover, it brings to light the experiences and context relative to which relativism is true. Relativism is relative to the experience of deep engagement with what we come to recognize as a different way of life.[38] It is relative to the ability to contextualize the successes of our science, including their trade-offs

---

Notre Dame Press, 1989), 99–139. Reprinted in Richard A. Shweder, *Thinking Through Cultures* (Cambridge, MA and London: Harvard University Press, 1991), 27–72.

[36] We addressed the incoherence of such formulations, and how to overcome it, in Chap. 2.

[37] See especially Chap. 2.

[38] See Chap. 1.

and costs.[39] We might also note that relativism is relative to the social and political context that generates a conversation about absolutes in the first place. In particular, it is relative to a historical, European self-conception as world conquerors and leaders of a new, better way. Moreover, it is relative to an epistemic tradition that gives particular emphasis to the binary distinctions that we draw between such pairs as self/other, universal/particular, and true/false.[40]

When we acknowledge that relativism is relatively true, we must also acknowledge the sense in which relativism is relatively false.[41] For relativism to acknowledge the legitimacy of a view that judges relativism itself to be false, that view must be held coherently within its own context, or way of life. Relativism does not endorse the validity of random, ad hoc views that do not meet their own internal standards of coherence. But it seems reasonable that an anti-relativist could formulate absolutism coherently, and that, in such a context, the relativist must recognize that relativism is relatively false. Because the relativist denies that any standards of assessment have transcendent normative authority, she does not grant that relativism is absolutely false.[42] Moreover, she specifies that, for relativism to be relatively false, a way of life must not only formulate absolutism coherently in its theoretical language, but produce the social conditions that make deep engagement impossible. Interestingly, these are precisely the conditions that fascism aims to produce.

6.3 A Space for Criticism

We should notice that relativism, especially the version developed in this work, does not entail that different ways of life will always be in conflict with each other. We have, of course, points in common with all forms of life, and even more with all human ways of life. To address relativism within a particular domain or with regard to our claims about a specific phenomenon is already to assume much shared experience and common background. The relativist recognizes that there are areas where

---

[39] See the end of Chap. 4 for more on this sense.

[40] On this distinction, see Simone de Beauvoir, "Introduction," in *Le deuxième sexe I: Les faits et les mythes* (Paris: Éditions Gallimard, Collection Folio/Essais, 1949 and 1976), 11–32. This tradition is not merely epistemic, as we may quickly note in the charge to pairs such as: white/black, man/woman, and citizen/slave. I regret that there is not space in this work to discuss the relationship between relativism and feminism or other theories of oppression/liberation, yet I cannot resist at least the quick comment.

[41] For more on this line of argument, see Chap. 2, esp. Sects. 2.2.2 and 2.2.3. For more on the sense in which the relativist acknowledges that relativism is false for the absolutist, see also the end of Chap. 4.

[42] On this point, she and the anti-relativist will continue to disagree. In other words, for the relativist, it is relatively true that, for the anti-relativist, relativism is absolutely false. This does not, however, entail that relativism is absolutely false for everyone, or even that relativism is relatively false for the relativist, since she constructs this understanding of the anti-relativist's claims in an analogical space, not a normatively transcendent space. (See Chaps. 2 and 4.)

we already agree, and still more where we can construct agreement, whether by good will or by force. What she disputes is that our conflicts can be resolved non-relativistically, that is, by appealing to some sort of neutral, highest, or absolute standards. For her, even the way that we evoke a common world and track common elements across all ways of life is itself dependent on the social and environmental context, foundational concepts, standards of assessment, and modes of reasoning that inhere in a particular way of life. Moreover, these very features themselves do not often match up neatly across one way of life to another. So, whereas the relativist recognizes that all humans are human and that we ultimately inhabit one world, she insists that we disagree in important and incommensurable ways about what it means to be human, what our one world is like, and what such understanding entails.[43]

For the relativist, our entrenched conflicts have no highest, absolute, or neutral arbiter. She can certainly grant, however, that we affirm and deny claims relative to our own way of life, either from an internal or an external perspective. For example, from an internal perspective: The Chachi affirm that the cause of the shaman's death was the jealousy and scheming of his younger apprentice. Or, from an external perspective: the Western doctors who hear the Chachi's story of the shaman's illness and subsequent death determine that he died of pure physical causes and that the Chachi's beliefs about the evil spells conjured by his younger apprentice are mere superstition. It is true that, to a certain extent, from the perspective of relativism itself the conflict between these two sets of claims dissolves. For example: the (relativist) anthropologist determines that the Chachi's beliefs and the Western doctor's beliefs are, in their own contexts, both effective ways of addressing overlapping phenomena (corresponding, roughly, to the death of the shaman). However, there are two very important points to notice about this sort of dissolution of conflict. First of all, it does not violate the constraints of relativism by arbitrating the conflict on highest, absolute, or neutral grounds. It arbitrates the conflict from the perspective of relativism itself, a perspective that, as I have argued throughout this work, is itself relative. It depends on a particular awareness and analysis of the diversity of practices and beliefs that we find across the historical and anthropological record, which, I hope, the reader will find relevant and compelling, but certainly do not stand as obvious and unchanging across all perspectives and times.

Secondly, we should notice that this dissolution of conflict happens at the periphery of the relativist's perspective, in an analogical space. It does not lead the relativist immediately to believe that everyone everywhere is right. Or that being right is rather meaningless and cheap, since it can be attributed to just about anyone, anywhere, and in many conflicting ways. As we have seen, the relativist reaches this space through analogy, extrapolation, and constructive experience.[44] It is a space that she infers more than she inhabits. Of course, the relativist could make the

---

[43] For more on the relativity of universals, see Chap. 4, esp. Sect. 4.9.2. See also Chap. 1, esp. Sect. 1.2.4.

[44] See Chaps. 1, 2, and 4, in particular, for more detail.

decision to give that space more importance, to use it more to judge the world around her and to guide her actions. But there would be something confused about identifying it as her primary space, that is, to attempt to use it as her only means of judging the world around her and of guiding her actions. After all, we can only reach that analogical space by extrapolating from our own experiences, practices, and beliefs. To cease to identify with a particular way of life and to try to identify with all ways of life, or with none at all, would be to undermine the very construction of the space in which relativism exists.[45] It would also be to forget our own agency and creative powers. While it does not seem quite possible to own the analogical space of relativism solely, we can, hopefully, use our experiences within it to reflect back on, to inform, and to change our more primary space of judgment and action. I will discuss this possibility further in Sect. 6.3.2 below.

6.3.1 Criticism of Others

How does the relativist respond to foreign practices, such as those of the Kwakiutl cannibal society, that violate her deepest moral convictions? While her first reaction may be repulsion and disgust, her second will be an attempt to contextualize the practices, to understand how they fit into the web of beliefs and practices of Kwakiutl society. Her awareness of the variability of practices and beliefs and of the relativity of concepts like rightness demand at least this much. But at the end of such reflection, the relativist is free to continue to believe that the practices are abhorrent. She may even decide to take action to prevent or change them. Such action is not in tension with her endorsement of relativism as long as she is clear that she opposes cannibalism from her own sense of right, which is relative to her own way of life. She may say, "Eating human flesh offends my deepest sense of what is right, of what it means to respect the humanity in others." Such a statement would only violate her relativism if she made the further claim that her beliefs are grounded in universal or absolute truths, which all people either already adhere to, at least implicitly, or would adhere to if they went through an adequate process of reflection. This inconsistent claim for the relativist would be something like, "Eating human flesh offends our deepest sense of what must be right for all people, in all places and times; it is a failure to respect in others what we must all recognize as an essential part of our humanity."

Reflection is not unique to relativism as a moral view, but because the process of contextualization is so central to the view, the relativist may be more likely than others to revise her initial reactions and to refrain from moral critique. In other words, the relativist may be more tolerant than others. Yet it is important for her to reserve this possibility of moral critique. It is true that conflict is more nuanced, more complex for her. The world is not divided into good and evil, but shaded by

---

[45] This does seem to be, nonetheless, the move that causes relativism to slide into nihilism.

many rights, many wrongs, and many contexts that ground them. The relativist
needs the possibility of moral critique not only to respond to the anti-relativist who
holds that atrocities like the Holocaust demonstrate the incoherence of her view, but
to respond to her own sense of justice. She may believe that what is right and what
is wrong varies from one way of life to another, that there is no absolute way to
characterize such concepts, and that different ways may be valid in their own context, yet deeply in tension with each other. And still she may hold, as we saw in
Chap. 2 in the case of truth, that her relative sense of right is more than merely
subjective and arbitrary, that it responds to something beyond, something greater,
something in the world that is independent of her.

How does the relativist respond to theoretical beliefs belonging to other ways of
life that seem blatantly false in contrast with her own? As in the moral case, she will
work to place those beliefs in the context of the foreign way of life. Upon reflection,
she may decide that the beliefs conflict too deeply with her understanding of the
world for her to accept them. Or, she may simply declare that she has failed to grasp
how those beliefs cohere within the other way of life itself. But she is also free to
endorse those foreign beliefs, not quite as her own, but as judgments about the
world that capture and respond to it in some determinate way. They are beliefs that,
in their own way, quite different from her own, succeed in describing, ordering, and
manipulating the world. Because truth for the relativist is neither unique nor ranked,
but contextualized and world-determined, she can accept that when the Chachi shaman sings to his stones, he communicates with spirits who answer questions and
perform acts. They can tell him that when Don Esteban was visiting he lost his
watch bathing in front of Franco's house, and that it is now hidden in the water,
beside a rock. They can help him manage Franco's wife's health condition, which
the Western doctors will call "diabetes." They can give him the knowledge that one
day a white woman will come to the village and marry his favorite grandson. And
she, the relativist, can accept that these foreign beliefs somehow capture the world,
as do her own beliefs about science and matter, without insisting that at the end of
the day the world must reduce to the one set of beliefs or the other.

In this same way, the relativist allows moral beliefs that are in tension with her
own. She could not take out a lash and whip her children's bare skin to teach them
a lesson. She could not be silent with her children and refrain from explanation in
the expectation that they would learn by quietly observing at her side. She could not
ignore an adult who was crying, and such an event would certainly not inspire in her
disgust. Yet she can see the different roles and dimensions that elements like lash-
ing, silence, and crying have in Chachi culture, and she can accept that these practices, in a very different way than her own, capture and respond to the moral world.

For her moral beliefs, just like her theoretical beliefs, respond to the world, are
capable of being infirmed, and are open to revision. The relativist's beliefs are frag-
ile, fallible, yet real. She may decide at times that, despite their limitations, they
warrant strong action. It is true that, because the relativist is inclined to situate foreign practices and beliefs within their native context and to consider them very
carefully, her threshold for intolerance is generally rather high. Yet she certainly
can, when sufficiently provoked, stand against other ways of life. She can declare

that she believes their practices and beliefs to be wrong. She can try to dissuade people from adhering to them. She can even, if roused enough, actively intervene in another way of life by force. Yet she must oppose foreign practices and beliefs from her own perspective, her own understanding of what is good and right, what is acceptable and what is intolerable. She can urge, for example: *I have considered practice X, what it means to such-and-such people, how it fits into their way of life, and the sort of trade-offs between incommensurable goods that it involves. Nevertheless, it violates so deeply my sense of what is right and worthwhile that no analogical exercise significantly alters my assessment, and I am compelled to oppose it.* What is unavailable to the relativist is a universal justification. She cannot say: *I have discovered that X is wrong for all people in all ways of life, and therefore I must oppose it.*[46]

We might think, then, that the relativist's grounds for intolerance are weaker than the universalist's. And in a sense they are. The relativist only has grounds for relative critique. She cannot expect that everyone will agree with her. She cannot assume that everyone who reasons well will reach her same conclusions. She can never hope for her arguments to acquire a godlike authority. Yet in another sense, the very relativity of her claims may make them stronger. They are unpretentious. The relativist expects disagreement and seeks to understand it. She does not confuse "enlightenment" with conversion and coercion. She knows that in cases of true disagreement, common ground is not discovered, but constructed.[47] Because the relativist acknowledges complexity, she is perhaps better positioned to work through entrenched conflict. She can look across a terrain of complex disagreement and identify the patches and routes that might work to forge broader understanding. And she expects herself to grow as much in this process as she hopes that those on the other side of the conflict will as well.

There is much more to say about what sort of resources the relativist might furnish for addressing conflict.[48] In these rapidly globalizing, postcolonial times, however, I cannot help but think that her tools must be more realistic and agile than the universalist's. They seem more appropriate to a way of life whose authority on the global stage is no longer incontrovertible. And they seem more capable of capturing the important nuances of our confrontations.

---

[46] Which also seems to suggest that: *You should oppose this, too.* And: *If only such-and-such people reasoned correctly, they would recognize their errors as well.* Of course, the relativist is equally opposed to these claims as well.

[47] See Chap. 3.

[48] A project I hope to take up in the future.

6.3.2 Criticism/Construction of Ourselves

The funny thing about our rapidly globalizing world, though, is that it tends to dissolve differences in the very moment of bringing them to our attention. The same
channels that allow us to confront each other are, at the same time, making us much
more like each other. Some might wonder whether the homogenization of different
peoples and the disappearance of other ways of life fomented by global capitalism
render the entire exercise of developing a robust relativism moot. I would like to
urge, on the contrary, that the increasing loss of cultural diversity makes relativism
all the more relevant and important. Recognizing that different ways of life capture
different goods, ones that do not quite correspond to our own, but nourish the human
spirit in important ways, and at varying costs, is critical not only for making decisions about how and whether to encourage the globalization of others,[49] but also for
making decisions about the form and direction of our own way of life – one that,
regardless of its goodness, we are coming more and more to share.

The possibility of intolerance for the relativist points to something else that we
touched upon above: the need to grasp the world in some way. If normative concepts
such as truth and right are relative to a way of life, this does not mean that they are
merely determined by a way of life, but that we need a way of life in order to grasp
and determine them. And yet the elevation of alternatives that comes with relativism
places us in a position where we cannot blindly endorse our own way of life.
Relativism opens up a space for criticism not only of others, but of ourselves. We
see our own practices and beliefs up against all of the alternatives that we have
encountered or that we can imagine. We take stock of the trade-offs involved in
holding on to our fundamental concepts and distinctions, our standards of assessment, our modes of engagement. And we find ourselves immersed in the process of
critically evaluating our own way of life. Through this process of critical evaluation,
we begin to see not only the grounds of legitimacy of other practices and beliefs, but
the possibility of changing our own. We begin to see the possibility of actively constructing and recreating our own practices and beliefs. Their loss of hegemony is our
gain in a certain kind of freedom, of autonomy and self-creation. It opens up the
possibility of moving ourselves toward what is better, not in any absolute sense, but
in a context that we ourselves help to shape. In this respect, what is most ethical for
the relativist becomes perhaps not a particular set of principles, virtues, or actions,
but a set for which she actively takes responsibility.

For instance, the understanding that a relativist develops through the dynamic of
resonance and loss of what I've called an "impartial stance"[50] might lead her to see
that prioritizing an understanding of the world as a collection of disenchanted
objects has, on the one hand, led our science and technology to flourish, but has, on
the other, alienated us from our own work and agency, from each other, and from

---

[49] A process in which we participate actively and consciously as much as passively and
inadvertently.
[50] See Chap. 4.

Nature. And she might at some point decide that the cost of these trade-offs is too high – that she would be happier and our world healthier if we moved toward a more relational stance. Of course, it is not an option for us to run back to the enchantment of a romanticized past, but we can use an appreciation of how more traditional communities build connection with their environment as a sort of guide. We can recognize what modes of engagement capture the goods that we would like to regain, and we can use them to embark on the self-conscious project of re-enchantment, of constructing new practices, concepts, and systems that bring us back into a more balanced relation with our environment. This is not to say that we will recover quite the same goods as we admired in another way of life, or that we will have them in the same degree, but that a deep appreciation of alternative ways of life might be just the sort of compass that we need for finding the direction that leads us out of our most pressing contemporary problems.[51]

6.4   Conclusion

Throughout this work, I have defended relativism not from an absolute perspective, but in a mode that recognizes itself as historically and culturally situated. To argue that relativism is relatively true is to allow that it will not be true for all groups and for all ways of life, but that it may in some important way be true for us. There are clearly ways of life in which relativism is false, or in which it cannot even be formulated – perhaps, we might say, in which it does not need to be formulated. What I have worked to show is that relativism is a coherent and fruitful view that responds to the complexities of not only a multicultural world, but of deep intercultural engagement. We could, of course, refuse the experience of deep intercultural engagement or erase the multicultural signs of our world. There seems to me to be a willful ignorance about this first possibility; we do not truly eliminate the need for relativism by simply corralling ourselves in a provincial life. The second possibility, I fear, is rapidly threatening to become a tragic reality by virtue of forces that are not willful – that is, reflective and human – enough. Our rapidly globalizing world not only brings different ways of life into conflict with each other, but quickly melds them into what is becoming a single sort of generic way of life characterized primarily by capitalist consumerism. I do not see that we have adequately taken into account the great losses of this homogenization, or that we have taken ahold of the process itself as reflective, compassionate, human agents. I fear, rather, that we are mere instruments of an unthinking, material process that we ourselves unwittingly unleashed quite a ways back in history. It is, perhaps, not absolutism generally, but the absolutism of this totalizing process that is relativism's most critical target. I hope that relativism can be an instrument for recovering the cultural goods that are

---

[51] See also, Alyssa Luboff, "Relativism, Realism, and the Roots of the Ecological Crisis," in *Ecocultural Ethics,* ed. Rayson K. Alex et al. (Lanham, Boulder, New York and London: Lexington Books, 2017), 65–75.

being lost in this process, and, most importantly, for recovering our own agency, our ability to direct the course of the process itself.

More so than truth, or relative truth, I hope to have earned relativism a space of possibility. It need not be the strawman, the view rejected as soon as it comes up, the negative contrast against which only an opposing positive view can be drawn. It is a view that, given our awareness of both contingency and diversity, we cannot help but consider. It holds together in the face of the logical challenges of the anti-relativist. It does not unwind in the light of the manifest success of science. It leaves a space for us to affirm our own practices and beliefs. It provides new tools for navigating the challenges of our rapidly globalizing world. A relativist cannot hope for much more than this. For her, it is as much as *any* theory could claim: to be a coherent, productive, and appropriate view for our times.

Admittedly, this space of possibility for relativism is not exclusive. We certainly cannot say that it is the only view for our times. It does, however, make us question those who are so quick to dismiss relativism as a view that cannot be for any time. Perhaps they have just failed to think it through, to provide it with a careful elaboration and considered defense. Perhaps they have experienced no motivation (such as deep intercultural engagement) to do so. Yet there seems something more pernicious than mere ignorance behind this failure. What concerns me most is not the case where the possibility of relativism is simply missed, but where it so vehemently denied. I believe this is not so much a reaction to relativism as to the alternative ways of life that it brings into view. It is a denial of their shared legitimacy, their shared power.

Relativism, in effect, redistributes power among conflicting ways of life. In particular, it throws into question the authority of superior values and knowledge that is often used by one way of life to subjugate another. One might ask, then, whether the real motivation for relativism is not sociological, epistemological, or moral, but political. For the relativist, however, the stronger truth runs perhaps the other way around: it is the sociological, the epistemological, and the moral that are, without the insights of relativism, clandestinely political. Yet the relativist would not assert even this truth on absolute grounds. It is a claim that, like her theory as a whole, she finds appropriate and meaningful for our times. The careful relativist knows that at the point of any absolute reduction of truth, her truth unwinds. She must be content to have done her part to level the playing field, to have shown that we have compelling reasons to believe that we all stand, at the end of the day, on the ground.

Bibliography

Benedict, R. (1934). *Patterns of culture*. Boston: Houghton Mifflin.

Berman, M. (1981). *The reenchantment of the world*. Ithaca: Cornell University Press.

Boas, F. (1887a). Museums of ethnology and their classification. *Science, 9*(228), 587–589.

Boas, F. (1887b). The occurrence of similar inventions in areas widely apart. *Science, 9*(224), 485–486.

Boas, F. (1887c). Response to John W. Powell. *Science, 9*(229), 612–614.

Boas, F. (1889). On alternating sounds. *American Anthropologist, 2*(1), 47–51.

Boas, F. (1922). *The mind of primitive man*. New York: The Macmillan Company.

Boas, F. (1940). *Race, language, and culture*. Chicago: University of Chicago Press.

Boghossian, P. (2006). *Fear of knowledge: Against relativism and constructivism*. Oxford/New York: Clarendon Press/Oxford University Press.

Charusheela, S. (2001). Women's choices and the ethnocentrism/relativism dilemma. In S. Cullenberg, J. Amariglio, & D. Ruccio (Eds.), *Postmodernism, economics and knowledge*. New York: Routledge.

Charusheela, S. (2004). Postcolonial thought, postmodernism, and economics: Questions of ontology and ethics. In E. Zein-Elabdin & S. Charusheela (Eds.), *Postcolonialism meets economics*. London: Routledge.

Charusheela, S. (2009). Social analysis and the capabilities approach: A limit to Martha Nussbaum's universalist ethics. *Cambridge Journal of Economics, 33*, 1135–1152.

Cook, J. W. (1999). *Morality and cultural differences*. New York: Oxford University Press.

Davidson, D. (1982). On the very idea of a conceptual scheme. In M. Krausz & J. W. Meiland (Eds.), *Relativism: cognitive and moral* (pp. 66–80). Notre Dame: University of Notre Dame Press. Reprinted from *Proceedings of the American Philosophical Association* 47 (1973–74): 5–20.

de Beauvoir, S. (1949 and 1976). Introduction. In *Le deuxième sexe I: Les faits et les mythes* (pp. 11–32). Paris: Éditions Gallimard, Collection Folio/Essais.

Diamond, J. (1999). *Guns, germs, and steel: The fates of human societies*. New York/London: W.W. Norton & Company.

Duhem, P. M. M. (1906). *La théorie physique: son objet et sa structure*. Paris: Chevalier & Rivière.

Evans-Pritchard, E. E. (1937). *Witchcraft, oracles and magic among the Azande*. Oxford: The Clarendon Press.

Forster, M. (1998, June). On the very idea of denying the existence of radically different conceptual schemes. *Inquiry, 41*(2), 133–185.

Foucault, M. (2009). Le gouvernement de soi et des autres. In F. Gros (Ed.), *II, Le courage de la vérité: cours au collège de France, 1983–1984*. Under the direction of François Ewald and Alessandro Fontana. Paris: Gallimard/Seuil.

© Springer Nature Switzerland AG 2020
A. Luboff, *Facing Relativism*, Synthese Library 425,
https://doi.org/10.1007/978-3-030-43341-3

Geertz, C. (2000). Thinking as a moral act: Ethical dimensions of anthropological fieldwork in the new states. In *Available light: Anthropological reflections on philosophical topics*. Princeton: Princeton University Press.

Gellner, E. (1970). Concepts and society. In B. R. Wilson (Ed.), *Rationality* (pp. 18–49). Oxford: Blackwell.

Gellner, E. (1982). Relativism and universals. In M. Hollis & S. Lukes (Eds.), *Rationality and relativism* (pp. 181–200). Cambridge, MA: MIT Press.

Goodman, N. (1978). *Ways of worldmaking*. Indianapolis: Hackett Publishing Company.

Gowans, C. (2010). Moral relativism. *The Stanford encyclopedia of philosophy* (Fall 2010 Edition, E. N. Zalta, Ed.). http://plato.stanford.edu/archives/fall2010/entries/moral-relativism/

Gray, J. (1996). *Isaiah Berlin*. Princeton: Princeton University Press.

Hadot, P. (2002). *Exercices spirituels et philosophie antique*. Paris: Éditions Albin Michel/ Bibliothèque de «L'Évolution de l'Humanité».

Hadot, P. (2007). *The present alone is our happiness: Conversations with Jeannie Carlier and Arnold I. Davidson* (M. Djaballah & M. Chase, Trans.). Stanford: Stanford University Press.

Hegel, G. W. F. (1988). *Aesthetics: Lectures on fine art* (Vol. 1, T. M. Knox, Trans.). Oxford: Clarendon Press.

Hollis, M., & Lukes, S. (Eds.). (1982). *Rationality and relativism*. Oxford: Basil Blackwell.

Horton, R., & Finnegan, R. (Eds.). (1973). *Modes of thought*. London: Faber & Faber.

Kant, I. (1965). *Critique of pure reason* (N. K. Smith, Trans.). New York: St. Martin's Press.

Krausz, M. (2011). *Dialogues on relativism, absolutism and beyond: Four days in India*. Lanham: Rowman & Littlefield Publishers.

Krausz, M., & Meiland, J. W. (1982a). Introduction to 'The fabrication of facts'. In M. Krausz & J. W. Meiland (Eds.), *Relativism cognitive and moral* (pp. 13–17). Notre Dame: University of Notre Dame Press.

Krausz, M., & Meiland, J. W. (1982b). Introduction to 'Subjective, objective and conceptual relativisms'. In M. Krausz & J. W. Meiland (Eds.), *Relativism cognitive and moral* (pp. 30–33). Notre Dame: University of Notre Dame Press.

Krausz, M., & Meiland, J. W. (1982c). Introduction. In M. Krausz & J. W. Meiland (Eds.), *Relativism cognitive and moral* (pp. 1–9). Notre Dame: University of Notre Dame Press.

Kuhn, T. S. (1970). *The structure of scientific revolutions* (Enlarged 2nd Edition). Chicago/London: The University of Chicago Press.

Ladyman, J., & Ross, D., with David Spurrett and John Collier. (2007). *Everything must go: Metaphysics naturalized*. Oxford/New York: Oxford University Press.

Laudan, L. (1981). A confutation of convergent realism. *Philosophy of Science, 48*(1), 19–49.

Laudan, L. (1997). Explaining the success of science: Beyond epistemic realism and relativism. In A. I. Tauber (Ed.), *Science and the quest for reality*. New York: New York University Press.

Lévy-Bruhl, L. (1922). *La Mentalité Primitive*. Paris: Librairie Félix Alcan.

Luboff, A. (2017). Relativism, realism, and the roots of the ecological crisis. In R. K. Alex et al. (Eds.), *Ecocultural ethics* (pp. 65–75). Lanham/Boulder/New York/: Lexington Books.

Lyons, D. (1982). Ethical relativism and the problem of incoherence. In M. Krausz & J. W. Meiland (Eds.), *Relativism cognitive and moral* (pp. 209–225). Notre Dame: University of Notre Dame Press. Reprinted from *Ethics* 86 (1976): 107–21.

Malinowski, B. (1922). *Argonauts of the Western Pacific: An account of native enterprise and adventure in the archipelagoes of Melanesian New Guinea*. New York: Dutton.

Malinowski, B. (1932). *The sexual life of savages in North-Western Melanesia: An ethnographic account of courtship, marriage, and family life among the natives of the Trobriand Islands, British New Guinea*. London: Routledge.

Mandelbaum, M. (1982). Subjective, objective, and conceptual relativisms. In M. Krausz & J. W. Meiland (Eds.), *Relativism cognitive and moral* (pp. 34–61). Notre Dame: University of Notre Dame Press. Reprinted from *The Monist, 62*, 4 (1979): 403–23.

Marx, K. (1978). Estranged labour (Economic and philosophic manuscripts of 1844). In R. C. Tucker (Ed.), *The Karl Marx reader* (2nd ed., pp. 70–81). New York/London: W.W. Norton & Company.

Meiland, J. W. (1977). Concepts of relative truth. *The Monist, 60*(4), 568–582.

Meiland, J. W. (1980, April). On the paradox of cognitive relativism. *Metaphilosophy, 11*(2), 115–126.

Meyer-Ortmanns, H. (2011). Introduction. In H. Meyer-Ortmanns & S. Thurner (Eds.), *Principles of evolution from the Planck Epoch to multicellular life*. Berlin/Heidelberg/New York: Springer.

National Aeronautics and Space Administration. *What is dark energy, dark matter*. NASA Science: Astrophysics. http://science.nasa.gov/astrophysics/focus-areas/what-is-dark-energy/

Norris, C. (1997). *Against relativism: Philosophy of science, deconstruction and critical theory*. Oxford/Malden: Blackwell Publishers.

Nussbaum, M. C. (2000). *Women and human development: The capabilities approach*. Cambridge/New York: Cambridge University Press.

Nussbaum, M. C., & Sen, A. (1989). Internal criticism and Indian rationalist traditions. In M. Krausz (Ed.), *Relativism: Interpretation and confrontation* (pp. 299–325). Notre Dame: University of Notre Dame Press.

Plato. (1997). Theaetetus. In J. M. Cooper (Ed.), *Plato complete works* (pp. 157–234, M. J. Levett, Trans., Revised by M. Burnyeat). Indianapolis: Hackett Publishing Company.

Popper, K. (2001). Facts, standards, and truth: A further criticism of relativism. In P. K. Moser & T. L. Carson (Eds.), *Moral relativism: A reader* (pp. 32–52). New York: Oxford University Press.

Priest, G. (2006). *In contradiction: A study of the transconsistent*. Oxford: Clarendon Press.

Prinz, J. J. (2007). *The emotional construction of morals*. Oxford/New York: Oxford University Press.

Putnam, H. (1975). *Mathematics, matter and method*. Cambridge: Cambridge University Press.

Putnam, H. (2005). *Ethics without ontology*. Cambridge: Harvard University Press.

Quine, W. V. O. (1953). Two dogmas of empiricism. Reprinted in *From a logical point of view: 9 logico-philosophical essays*. Cambridge, MA: Harvard University Press.

Rovane, C. (2009). Did Williams find the truth in relativism? In D. Callcut (Ed.), *Reading Bernard Williams* (pp. 43–69). New York: Routledge Taylor & Francis Group.

Rovane, C. (2010). Why scientific realism may invite relativism. In M. de Caro & D. Macarthur (Eds.), *Naturalism and normativity* (pp. 100–120). New York: Columbia University Press.

Ruse, M. (1999). *The Darwinian revolution: Science red in tooth and claw* (2nd ed.). Chicago/London: The University of Chicago Press.

Shweder, R. A. (1989). Post-Nietzschean anthropology: The idea of multiple objective worlds. In M. Krausz (Ed.), *Relativism: Interpretation and confrontation*. Notre Dame: Notre Dame University Press. Reprinted in Shweder, R. A. (1991). *Thinking through cultures* (pp. 27–72). Cambridge, MA/London: Harvard University Press.

Shweder, R. A. (1991). *Thinking through cultures: Expeditions in cultural psychology*. Cambridge: Cambridge University Press.

Shweder, R. A. (2006, March). John Searle on a Witch Hunt: A commentary on John R. Searle's essay 'Social ontology: Some basic principles'. *Anthropological Theory, 6*(1), 106–108.

Shweder, R. A. (2012). Relativism and universalism. In D. Fassin (Ed.), *A companion to moral anthropology* (pp. 85–102). Chichester/Malden: Wiley-Blackwell.

Siegel, H. (1986). Relativism, truth and incoherence. *Synthese, 68*, 225–259. Reprinted as "The incoherence argument and the notion of relative truth." In *Relativism refuted* (pp. 3–31). Boston: D. Reidel Publishing Company, 1987.

Swoyer, C. (2014). Relativism. *The Stanford encyclopedia of philosophy* (Spring 2014 Edition, E. N. Zalta, Ed.). http://plato.stanford.edu/archives/spr2014/entries/relativism/

Taylor, C. (1982). Rationality. In M. Hollis & S. Lukes (Eds.), *Rationality and relativism* (pp. 87–105). Oxford: Basil Blackwell Publisher Limited.

Tylor, E. B. (1881). *Anthropology: An introduction to the study of man and civilization*. London: Macmillan.

Warren, K. (1990). The power and promise of ecological feminism. *Environmental Ethics, 12*, 125–146.

Westermarck, E. (1932). *Ethical relativity*. New York: Harcourt, Brace and Company.

White, L., Jr. (1967). The historical roots of our ecological crisis. *Science, 155*, 1203–1207.

Williams, B. (1982). An inconsistent form of relativism. In M. Krausz & J. W. Meiland (Eds.), *Relativism cognitive and moral* (pp. 171–174). Notre Dame: University of Notre Dame Press. Reprinted from *Morality: An introduction to ethics* (pp. 22–26). New York: Harper & Row, 1972.

Williams, B. (1985). *Ethics and the limits of philosophy*. Cambridge: Harvard University Press.

Wilson, B. R. (Ed.). (1970, 1974, 1977). *Rationality*. Oxford: Basil Blackwell.

Wittgenstein, L. (1953). *Philosophical investigations* (Anscombe, G. E. M., Trans.). Oxford: Blackwell Publishing.

Wong, D. B. (1989). Three kinds of incommensurability. In M. Krausz (Ed.), *Relativism, interpretation and confrontation* (pp. 140–158). Notre Dame: University of Notre Dame Press.

Wong, D. B. (2006). *Natural moralities: A defense of pluralistic relativism*. Oxford/New York: Oxford University Press.

Index

© Springer Nature Switzerland AG 2020
A. Luboff, *Facing Relativism*, Synthese Library 425,
https://doi.org/10.1007/978-3-030-43341-3

169